RECORD

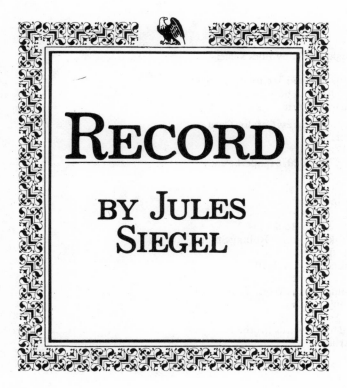

RECORD

BY JULES SIEGEL

The Book Division of Rolling Stone

Library of Congress Catalog Card
Number:
77/181711
SBN 0/87932/020/6 (paperbound)

First printing

Straight Arrow Books
The Book Division of Rolling Stone
625 Third Street
San Francisco, CA 94107

Distributed by the World Publishing
Company

Printed by: Edwards Brothers,
Ann Arbor.

RECORD

BY JULES SIEGEL

For Chrissie

13   FAMILY SECRETS

34   IN THE LAND OF MORNING CALM, DEJA VU

48   ANOTHER DAWN

63   THE BIG BEAT

72   BOB DYLAN

82   THE SUBCONTRACTOR

88   GOODBYE SURFING, HELLO GOD!

105   THE MAN WHO BELIEVED IN CHRISTMAS TREES

118   CONVERSATIONS WITH EMINENT AMERICANS

        THE SMOTHERS BROTHERS
        JACK NEWFIELD & PAUL GORMAN
        JOHN SINCLAIR
        ABBIE HOFFMAN

142   THE BLACK PANTHERS

153   ANGER

164   WEST OF EDEN

186   THE EVERGREEN HOME

204   MIDNIGHT IN BABYLON

222   THE REFUGEES

233   THE REPLACEMENT

Jules Siegel in the role
of Recording Angel reads
the Holy Scripture, consults
the oracle

51. Chen
The Arousing
(Shock, Thunder)

and, finding the omens
propitious, invokes the
muse "Oh Spirit, that
dost prefer before all
Temples th'upright
heart and pure, instruct
me," he prays, using
the language of the blind
poet, and, in his own

voice, "Hail and welcome imperial presence. Guide my progress, strike my chains, lift my sight out of darkness, and join my trembling word scribble directly to the pounding power of the Great Source: speak rushing rapids of the Original Voice into my art and spill my visions out on the scatter stream of Life.

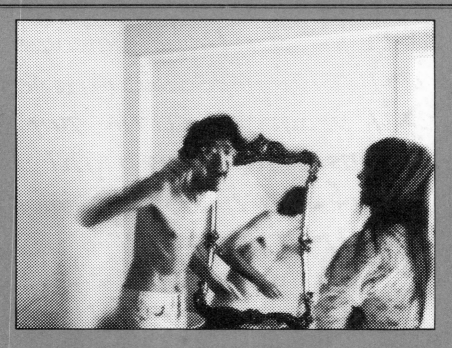

You have begun a journey into the mind of a being who, like you, is trapped in a prison of flesh. To while away the time he composes these messages to an outside which may or may not exist.

Family Secrets

My father was not without faults. A warm, decent, soft-spoken man who had once done eight years for armed robbery in Dannemora, a maximum-security prison for incorrigibles, he had been a street-fighter, a tough-guy who associated with famous murderers and other important criminals, a stickup man, a bootlegger, a confidence man, a loan shark. He was a compulsive gambler and, for a time, an alcoholic. In his youth, he smoked opium, which was what gangsters did to relax in those days. They called it kicking the gong around.

Little of this bothered me very much. When I was very young I accepted completely the family story that Daddy was a button manufacturer, or, later, a theater-ticket broker. As I grew older and learned more by careful eavesdropping, I became proud of his romantic past. In later years, all that I can remember disliking about him was that he did not know how to eat ice cream neatly and refused to learn. I have since come to understand that you learn how to eat ice cream when you are a child or not at all.

My father did not have a childhood in which he could have learned many such middle-class niceties. He was born in White Russia, perhaps in November of 1901, but he had no birthday, no records having been maintained of so insignificant an event as the appearance of an Elias Siegelovitch in the village of Horod, in Minsk Province, near Vilna. When the family came to America, the name was to become Siegel, a compromise arrived at by my grandfather, who thought that it ought to be changed to something completely American, such as Slater, and his children, who considered anything less than Siegelovitch cultural treason.

Although my father's brothers and sisters may not have know it, Siegel comes closer than Siegelovitch to the ancient form of the name. The "ovitch" simply means son of. Siegel is the phonetic representation of the Hebrew letters Sin, Gimel, Lamed, the abbreviation for Sagon Levi. Sagon means priest. Levi is one of the tribes of Israel. There are two kinds of Levites—the ordinary kind and the Cohens.

In the temple of Solomon, the Cohens officiated at the sacred service and the Levites supplied the music, poetry and other incidental effects. To this day only Cohens may be ordained as priests. Moses, was of Levi. His brother Aaron merely translated for him, for the stutter with which the Bible says Moses was afflicted is thought by scholars to have been really an Egyptian accent. What are priests but translators, anyway?

Like most genealogical disputes, this argument between the Levys and the Cohens is certainly of little interest to outsiders. It is also insignificant. Any man may trace his ancestry back to Adam, if he likes, but that doesn't give him exclusive inheritance rights in the Garden of Eden. In fact, if we scrape several layers of myth from the Bible, it appears that all the tribes of Israel at one time considered themselves to have been descendants of the pig, their sacred totem animal. Anthropological opinion now seems to be unanimous that this, not fear of trichinosis, is the reason beneath the taboo against pork. If one is civilized, one does not eat one's ancestors any more than one eats human flesh.

We ought not, perhaps, trust such faint historical memories, but this might be a compelling addition to the theory of evolution. Perhaps the unknown common ancestor from whom man and the ape descended was a pre-primate pig. Even today, all men share many traits with pigs, including, occasionally, devouring our young. At Bikini and Eniwetok, shaved pigs were used as experimental victims to test the likely effect on human skin of nuclear radiation.

Humans and pigs taste alike. Cannibals call human flesh "long pork." A butcher in Germany who killed several people during a World War I meat shortage sold their flesh as pork. One of the men who was tried in mid-19th century Massachusetts for eating less lucky companions while lost at sea testified to the similarity.

Whatever the case might be in modern times for accepting the relationship between man and pig, it was gospel throughout the Middle East in antiquity. A swine god totem was the slayer of Adonis in the springtime fertility rituals upon which Easter is based. Today neither Arab nor Israeli will eat pork. Neither will they eat human flesh. Yet at one time, before they were civilized, they undoubtedly did, if only on ritual occasions, when a piece of the sacrificial pig or a piece of the sacrificial human victim, standing as a surrogate for a god, assured to those who at it the qualities and special essences of the god.

As religious scholars have pointed out, the Christian ritual of the Eucharist is a symbolic survival of cannibalism. Thus, at the bottom, all of us, Christian, Jew, Moslem, are descendants of men who ate each other. Existence is cannibalism. This is the way in which all beings are ultimately related to each other: we living are fed upon those who died. In this sense none of us have anything to be proud of.

Nonetheless, my father and his brothers and sisters were proud of their name, proud of their tribe; for they came out of individual anonymity so blank that their names, maintained generation after generation, were much their only possessions. But even the commonest noun in any language has at least as much etymological history in it as the name Siegel, if you know where to look. My father's struggle was to ascend from this darkness by whatever means came quickest to hand. That he chose wrongly is no great shame. Had he been less good, he would have succeeded.

His problem was that he had a great deal of Cossack in him, but not enough. A Cossack, you understand, is someone who wants freedom enough to kill for it. A martyr, which is the exact opposite, is someone who wants freedom badly enough to die for it. In between are the people who want to be left alone to make love. My father, one of the lovers, was too squeamish to kill and too smart to get killed. He wanted freedom only enough to steal for it. Had he stayed in Russia he might have, like Stalin, robbed banks for a great cause. It was his fate to come to America, where he stole in a lesser cause: himself. Still, it was all in the name of freedom, and in my history of how the world got to be the way it is, my father is a greater hero (and a greater criminal) than Stalin, a man he admired almost as much as he admired Franklin Delano Roosevelt.

*E*arly in the new century, my grandfather came to America alone, then sent cabin-class tickets for the rest of the family. In 1906, my grandmother and her children followed Barnet Siegel to America. Before leaving Minsk, they had a portrait taken by a photographer. In it, my father's round-cheeked face, topped by white hair which darkened to a deep brown as he grew older, frowned. His brother

Sam, a couple of years younger, held a balloon the photographer had given him. My father wanted that balloon and never got it; in most of the pictures taken of him in later years there is the same frown.

That picture is lost, remaining vividly in family memory only because everyone remembered the balloon and his frown. Like the picture, the old world is lost now except for certain pieces torn out of the newspaper of the mind. I see them in brown and tan and black, pictures very much like those that appear in books and magazines about the way it was going West.

The first is the interior of a peasant kitchen. The room is almost filled with a great stove made of stone, waist-high, with a wide, thick, smooth top upon which straw has been piled. Snuggled in featherbeds, the entire family has bedded down upon the warm stove for a deep winter's night in the custom of the country.

Another picture is not quite even a photograph, little more than a sketch in a quick, coarse hand—a horse-drawn sled driven by a bearded man across an empty page of snow. This is my grandfather, traveling from their village into the city. It almost moves.

Now comes a slowly flickering piece of movie film panning through a birch forest, across an open meadow, to a little farm. In a boy's hand, held against a mouth (my own, entering the scene from sixty years away), is an egg. This is my father sucking eggs that he has stolen from the chicken coop on his uncle's farm and punctured with a needle. He will return the blown shells to the hen's nests, creating a mystery of empty eggs for the family.

Here is a dark painting in the style of Alfred Ryder, a running figure silhouetted against a gaint moon. It is early autumn. My father, seeing the harvest moon fill the center of the sky out in the country night, has mistaken it for something only he can ever tell you about, and is running to get aboard.

The motion picture camera starts again. The boy, exhausted and trembling, lies full against the soil of his birth, already prepared for death.

J wish that I could publish these visions the way I see them. I have made them out of conversations I remem-
ber, the oral tradition of the family. These people were not important enough to the world at large to merit permanent attention in any great collection, but I have a private museum in my head, where their shadows are projected occasionally for the amusement of the curator when he is in a mood for movies.

As we come closer to the present, the blurred nostalgia of the oldest stories I heard my father and his family tell gives way to the increasing bitterness that began with that long-ago frown.

They left Russia from a port city, where they visited briefly with cousins named Kaganovitch, distant relatives of the Lazar Kaganovitch who became President of the Soviet Union.

The cousins offered them no food, letting them eat the herring my grandmother brought with them from Minsk. For nearly fifty years following that insult, the Siegels did not speak to the Kagans. When all of those originally involved were either old or dead, my mother induced the survivors to give up the feud. A cousins club was then formed. Its monthly meetings, at which enormous quantities of food were served, gave them all great satisfaction for a number of years.

On shipboard, my grandmother presented her cabin-class tickets to the purser, who took them away and sent the family down to steerage with the other emigrants. Protest was no use. During the voyage, the first-class passengers sent bananas down to the poor people in steerage. My father ate a banana and got sick. As far as I know, he never willingly ate another. It does not appear to have occurred to him that he may have been seasick.

My grandfather met them on the other side. A blacksmith in the old country, he had applied here for a job as an ironworker and was given a broom. He went to work in the garment industry. He had a relative who had been pressed into labor on a bridge being built over an icy river by Russian Army engineers. For hours, the man stood waist-deep in water that was moving too swiftly to freeze. When he was brought out, his legs were permanently paralyzed. The soldiers gave him a glass of whiskey and sent him home in a wheelbarrow. What good was it to complain?

No one ever heard my grandfather raise his voice. His wife was the disciplinarian.

mistakes don't count...

Lesson I: "How to be a writer"

technical notes:
(learning how to
use a lettering brush
this pen is a Rapidograph ooo
Osmiroid 75
B4 nib
Artone ink
Pelikan ink in
Rapidograph)

Do you
appreciate
all this,
dear reader?

in the long run. but the reason I'm afraid to write is that I'm afraid to make mistakes. Every Friday night my mother used to pray in front of the candles on the kitchen table that I wouldn't make mistakes. I have always hated her for that. And still do. For the absolutists in the audience — the candles, not my mother were on the table. If we believed in censorship, we would delete the "and still do" as repetitious. A mistake! Change it? Censor it!

She seems to have been a cold woman. On his first day on New York's Lower East Side some bigger boys put an egg in my father's pocket and slapped it. When he started to cry, they offered him a cherry. He swallowed it in a gulp and gagged. There was fire in his mouth, his throat, his stomach. They had given him a cherry pepper. He ran home to his mother, who gave him bread to eat, but no other comfort. Some fifty years later, after minor surgery, he was placed in a hospital room with an old man whose skin was turning blue. Just so, in 1917, had my father's mother died. When he came home from the hospital, he told me that he never remembered her ever kissing him.

His parents may not have been much on kissing, but they were respectable people who had an apartment on Madison Street with an inside bathroom when plenty of immigrants were satisfied with a toilet in the hall. They did the best they could for their children, most of whom turned out all right. Only my father was a disgrace. "Shame and sorrow for the family," goes the refrain of an old song. He stole sugar from the sugar bowl and swindled pennies from the baker who charged a small fee for cooking weekend roasts overnight in his slow ovens. Discovered in crime, he escaped to the rooftops and spent nights at his aunt's apartment on Henry Street. She had so many children and so many troubles that another made no difference.

"Tante Ida could always feed another mouth," he told me. "She could make soup out of water and salt and a penny's worth of greens. In the morning there was coffee and hot rolls. Everyone grabbed but there was always enough. She was a sad woman. She followed funeral processions through the streets and wept—not for the dead, who were only neighbors or even strangers, but for herself. Where else could she cry without making her children and husband sad? She waited for funerals."

The Siegels did not believe in public tears or other open emotional displays. Their family functions were dignified affairs at which the men drank whiskey and, if it was a wedding, confirmation, or other happy occasion, old women with hair on their lips danced Cossack steps. At funerals, the main thing was to be on time. There was always someone who arrived an hour early, winning the privilege of arbitrating promptness disputes. A wet face was a sign of weakness worse than being late. Especially at the funeral of Barnet Siegel they insisted on perfect decorum, but it was broken by a shrieking man.

"Uncle Barney! You're gone now, Uncle Barney!" sobbed Tante Ida's son Nathan. My father's brothers and sisters looked away from each other in shame. Someone hushed Nathan, but the funeral was clearly ruined, even though everyone had been on time.

*T*hroughout his life my father was no embarrassment to his family in his ordinary social contacts with them, but he was an angry, impatient man whose slow, quiet speech masked a cruel temper. As a young man, he was strong and liked to fight with his fists. At the beginning of World War I in America, he was already evidently a serious enough delinquent for Lillian Wald, a founder of the Henry Street Settlement, to take a personal interest in his salvation.

She got him a job running the game and entertainment center at a defense plant in Virginia. For security reasons, the workers lived in a guarded compound which they were not permitted to leave. They were hungry for entertainment. My father gave them the kind they liked best: gambling. He came back home at the end of the war, he told me, with several thousand dollars.

He bought a new car for a few hundred dollars. The salesman taught him how to shift the gears and he drove home to show off. The first passenger was his youngest sister, who wanted to go uptown. After a choppy start, the car got moving smoothly enough, but they soon came to an obstacle: a streetcar. My father was unable to deal with the complexities of passing the trolley. They continued uptown behind it, stopping when it stopped, starting when it started.

He was not much better at dealing with money. "Grandpa pleaded with me to put the rest of the money in a bank," he told me. "I was too smart for that. I had friends who knew what to do about money. They took me to Wall Street and showed me a car they called the Riviera. I was just in time to get the last piece of stock in the company. I gave them the money and that was the last I heard of it, or of them, or of the Riviera."

Smart money — that was what he was always interested in. For the most part it eluded him, although there were times when he was right in the middle of it.

"I'm with the Combination," he told my mother. It was after the Crash. Prohibition was still the law of the land and the Depression had only just begun to reach the bottom. The Combination was where the smart money was. There was open gambling in a big nightclub on the opposite bank of the Hudson River, a lavish place perched on the Palisades. My father wore a tuxedo and put the bank to bed every night, securing the casino's cash. He had just come home from those eight years in prison and met my mother. She was separated from her first husband and had a little boy.

"Your mother was the most beautiful girl in Harlem," an admirer of hers told me. Harlem was a white community then, a lot better than the Lower East Side, but still rough. Downtown, the criminals tended toward murder. It was a shooting gallery operated by Murder, Inc., the Combination's enforcement agency. Uptown, the main attraction was bootlegging and gambling. When my mother was 12 years old, she and her girlfriends delivered bottles of bathtub gin for her father, a baker who was an organizer of the bakers' union as well as a part-time manufacturer of alcoholic beverages. One of her brothers was a cantor; the other was a partner in a speakeasy elegantly decorated with many small lamps shaded in translucent red.

In such speakeasies, the hat-checking and cigarette concession brought in good money. In order to insure an honest tally, her brother's friend had his girlfriend in the job in his own club. One week, the girl was ill. A replacement was needed.

"How about little Evelyn?" the friend asked her brother.

"Over my dead body," was the reply.

No one quite trustworthy enough being found, my mother, then 14, wound up with the job after all. A tough-guy named Pussy picked her up every evening and drove her to the place, sat behind her in the checkroom to make sure that no one bothered her, and drove her home at night. He habitually carried a pistol and took the job of protecting her virtue very seriously.

Into the speakeasy came Billy Leeds, the tin-plate heir. He wanted my mother to sit at his table and drink champagne with him.

Pussy moved forward. The tin-plate heir explained that he meant nothing out of order, just that she sit with him. He was willing to pay a hundred dollars for the privilege. The gangsters conferred and issued their decision. Soon, my mother was sitting at the tin-plate heir's table drinking champagne, but next to her, pistol displayed, was Pussy.

"I couldn't have been safer in a convent," she told me.

At 17 she left high school to marry a local smart-money man. He was a good provider, but that was all. He was never home. In the morning on the night table there would be piles of money.

"I was only a young girl, but I knew that a child has to have a father," she says. "I went back to live with my sister. It was a terrible time. When your father came, he was like a knight in shining armor. His friends called him Jimmy."

"What's your real name?" she asked.

"Eli."

"I like Jimmy a lot better," she told him. He was always Jimmy to her and her family and his friends, and always Eli to his family. One of the great wonders is the way in which my mother would slip into calling him Eli among his relatives. She never made a mistake.

She brought him back together with his family and took him away from the gangsters. His career in the Combination was finished. Many years later, he was asked to come to work in Las Vegas, but he refused.

"Las Vegas is no place to bring up children," he said. He had two children, he told his friend from Las Vegas. The older one was pre-med and the younger was going to be a writer. The older one was my mother's son by her first marriage. My father legally adopted him. I was a grown man before I found out that my brother was really my half-brother. By that time, it made no difference to me.

Our parents had a great love affair, one that lasted and filled our home. As a child, I once accidentally walked in on them in the act of love. My father's movements were slow and gentle and the two of them were so lost in each other that they never saw me watch a moment, then step back out of the bedroom and close the door as quietly as I could. When they were in their 50s, they would kiss in the doorway like teenagers.

"I was in love with your mother, you know," a friend of the family once told me. "We all were. You couldn't count the number of men who were killed over her. When she started going out with your father we knew we were out of the running. He was a big-time gangster from the Lower East Side. The first time I saw him he was all dressed in gray; he was wearing a gray coat and pearl-gray suede gloves, gray spats and a gray fedora hat turned down in back like Mayor Walker. He was driving a big Franklin motor car, which was better than a Cadillac in those days. Why, it was like a Rolls Royce. He was really big time."

It is pleasant to think of him as big time, and he may well have been, but in my memories he has always been someone who tried very hard to earn a living after running out of the smart money. He was ill-equipped for the job, simple arithmetic being about the extent of his business tools. He could have been a strong-arm man, but he had educated himself too well to be very good at breaking heads except in anger.

"Jimmy was a big reader, you know," an old friend of his told me. "He always had his nose in a book." This friend was not famous for brightness. He was arrested on a Sullivan law violation for possession of a pistol without a permit. Before the trial, someone paid someone to substitute an old, rusty, broken-down revolver missing a firing pin. Possession of this was no crime under any law, and the man ought to have gotten off. Unfortunately, nobody bothered to tell him about the deal.

"That's not my gun!" he blurted angrily when the Civil War relic was introduced as evidence at the trial. Thus does justice triumph.

My father's favorite author was Dostoyevsky. One of his favorite books was *The House of the Dead,* which is about Dostoyevsky's experiences in Siberian prison camps.

"This is exactly the way it was," he said after he finished it. "Nothing changes. All these people were in prison with me." This was one of the few times he ever admitted directly that he had done time. Not much of a talker, he spoke little about his past and less about what he did for a living. I was almost 20 years old before he revealed anything important by design.

The secrecy was part of an obsession with propriety. My father wanted his children to have normal lives, no matter what his life might be. He came close to succeeding, but he was a gambler who lost too heavily to maintain a middle-class household very long. Going broke was a pattern. It happened every three years or so. First he would be late with mother's allowance. Then he would disappear for a couple of days in which we were held in terror that he might be dead. Finally, he would telephone. My mother would take her savings out of the bank, borrow money from friends, and bankroll him again. For a long time we would be almost poor.

Despite this, we were usually as comfortably middle-class a family as any. Under any circumstances, we went to the country for the summer. My brother and I had better clothing than most of our friends and went out-of-town to college. In the winter, there was Lakewood, New Jersey, and Miami Beach, Florida. The food on the table was ample and good. The house was filled with books and records and we got a television about the same time everyone else did. We ate in restaurants and had catered affairs. We lived in good neighborhoods. When my brother and I were little my mother had a fulltime, live-in maid.

When my mother and father first married they lived in a big apartment house on Ocean Avenue, Brooklyn, a borough my father liked for its suburban atmosphere. In 1939, because my mother's friends were living in the Bronx, we moved to 1478 Walton Avenue, where we stayed for 21 years while my brother and I grew up.

It is customary today to want to forget that one lived in the Bronx, but I remember it with increasing affection. Although my father was earning his living as a loan shark while most of the other fathers drove trucks, sold curtains, built restaurants, manufactured dresses, we fitted comfortably into a community structure there that supported us and protected us and liked us— an extended family based on shared lives.

A personification of this extended family was Alfred Roeder, superintendent of 1478 Walton Avenue and its sister building, 1454. An Austrian veteran of World War I who spoke with an accent and walked with a limp, he was not merely the superintendent, he was *Mr. Roeder.* To every boy and girl— and there were many children among the hundred and fifty or so young families—he was a representative of law and order, the first in a line of substitute fathers mothers could invoke, if necessary, when husbands were not at home. A child in boiling hysterics could usually be shut down by the threat, "I'm going to call Mr. Roeder." If not, and this was rare, he could be called on the telephone and he would actually come. There is no known case of his failing to calm any child under ten years of age.

As we grew older, we knew it was Mr. Roeder we had to watch out for when carving our initials in the hallway plaster. Once caught in the act of destroying the premises, there was higher authority to account to—the landlord, Mr. Fish, who might bill your parents for the damages. Whether or not this happened depended upon which Mr. Fish you got. As there are many judges sitting in a courthouse, so there were a number of Fishes, half of them fat, half of them thin. There was medium-sized Mr. Fish, the father, an elderly man who had built these apartment houses and several others besides, but he never bothered with the crimes of children. There were his thin sons, Irving and Abe, and his two fat sons, Bennie and Ruby. They all repaired plumbing and did other complicated maintenance work.

The Fishes and their wives and children lived in apartments in their father's buildings, which the old man had named after his grandchildren. Each building's name was incised on the lintel over its entrance. Since Mr. Fish had more grandchildren than buildings, he had to double up on 1478 and 1454, which were called the Robert-Alan and the Ronald-Alan. Across the street at 1475 was the Sondra, the newest of the three Fish apartment houses on our block, separated from the others not only by its *moderne* architectural style, but also by higher rents and an unfriendly superintendent named Mr. Olson who was an expert electrician. His son, Henry, a blond boy with glasses, could make a radio out of a bed spring and undoubtedly had something to do with the invention of color television.

There was a fourth building but it was not owned by the Fishes. The four apartment houses on the block made up a village of three hundred or more families, most of them young householders with children. There were a few elderly people, including one patriarch with a white, biblical beard. Two doctors and a dentist lived there. So did a couple of bookmakers. In a basement apartment in 1454 there was a schoolroom for lessons in Hebrew and Yiddish language and history taught by Mr. Weissberg, a learned man who might have been an atheist, so archaeological and anthropological was his presentation of the Bible.

For every miracle, Mr. Weissberg had a rational explanation. A red alga turned the Nile to blood. The algae drove the frogs out of the river. The frogs died and attracted lice and flies. These vermin spread disease which killed cattle and afflicted the Egyptians. The Red Sea was crossed during an especially low tide. The only thing he never bothered to explain was how Moses was able to predict all of this was going to occur.

We children who attended Mr. Weissberg's school have grown up believing there is some kind of natural and understandable force operating beneath even the most inexplicable events. We lived, after all, in a highly predictable world rarely penetrated by outside horrors. We had large, clean apartments rising above enormous, high-ceilinged lobbies richly furnished with carpets, marble tables, carved chairs. Designed in a grand old *ersatz* that owed a lot to the public rooms of Italian palaces, they had baroque plaster ceilings and imitation travertine walls. Between twin false fireplaces in each building were the polished brass doors of elevators operated by kindly black men who booked policy on the side. In the summer, striped awnings were unfurled from each window and the entire street was blazoned with color.

We were "comfortable," our parents told us if we asked how much money we had. The rich people, who we knew were not very much richer than we, lived two blocks up a steep hill on the Grand Concourse, the Park Avenue of the Bronx, a great boulevard stretching the entire length of the borough. Laid out in the French style, the Grand Concourse is so wide that elderly people seldom attempt to cross it in bad weather. Following faithfully the design principles created by Baron Haussman in the aftermath of the Paris Commune of 1848, it is too wide for barricades and perfect for the deployment of troops and artillery.

The Grand Concourse was prophetically built in the concept of the city as a battlefield, but when I lived in the Bronx the plan was meaningless to us. We knew

Wudja say?

Do you remember those
movies in which the hero
(usually John Garfield),
fleeing from the police,
would wind up in a
50¢ a night furnished
room lying awake wor-
rying while a neon sign
blinked EAT or BAR

all night outside?

Chrissy and I have the same
room = only it's $32 a day
and the sign says MONY
9:45/33°
MUTUAL OF NEW YORK

Now that is
inflation!

nothing about the Draft Riots of 1863. I have visited there recently, however, and found that this translation of Baron Haussman's ideas now begins to make sense.

Mr. Roeder retired many years ago and the Ronald-Alan and the Robert-Alan and the Sondra have been sold to a corporation. Old Mr. Fish is dead and so is his thin son Irving. Ruby and Bennie have moved away. Even my mother, who has lived in California for the past eight years, returned to her old friends in the Bronx and saw, finally, that she no longer belonged there. Old people fill the streets. At night, the Grand Concourse, where she and my father would walk miles on a warm night, is empty. The dry cleaner at 174th Street has a buzzer lock on his door so that he can screen out dangerous people. The poor are moving in.

Much of the deterioration is only the working of time, but, perhaps equally important, it is the result of neglect. Everything man-made must be tended or it will die. Life itself is an effort even for us who are born to it. The arteries corrode, the glands dry up, the cells begin to die. "Who owns this property?" the inspector general asks on one of his rare visits to a forgotten place. No one knows who owns it. The inhabitants pay their rent by mail. The checks are entered as symbols on a piece of electronic tape. Someone on a distant planet is able to buy another pleasure. The abandoned tenants howl for service and end by burning down the neighborhood.

Walton Avenue between 171st Street and 172nd Street is not yet a slum, but the death of the street is only a few years away. It is a death that could not have happened while the Fishes lived there and owned the buildings — not because they were saints or altruists or even very competent, but because each day they had to face their tenants. They were accountable directly for every faucet that dripped, for the toilet that wouldn't work, for the brick and stone itself. They were part of the structure.

More than that, they were good landlords, compassionate people, friends to their tenants — even when it came to collecting rent. The only time I remember a Fish coming up to our apartment for the rent instead of waiting until it was brought down to their office on the ground floor was on a winter day when they were short for a fuel bill. As sweating black men unloaded coal, Abe, Irving, Bennie and Ruby went

from apartment to apartment apologetically explaining why they needed the overdue money.

During World War II, a man who lived with his wife and small children on the sixth floor of 1478 was horribly burned in a defense plant accident. He was in a hospital for months and disabled for more than a year. Not once during this time did the Fishes ask for the rent or any part of it.

The burned man, who eventually paid his entire back rent, told the story to his friends, who told the story to their friends. We children heard it at the dinner table and never knew that we were witness to a miracle. It was something we accepted as nice, but only right. In the same way, we knew that America would win the war, that bombs would not fall on Walton Avenue, that the soldiers would come home and we would be given new bicycles with fat rubber tires.

About the only thing we were really afraid of was the dark, but it was no great shame to leave the light in the hallway on and to open the bedroom door. Protected by a 40-watt bulb, and Mr. Roeder, we slept easily behind a guard of fathers and mothers and older brothers and sisters, snug in fortifications built by Mr. Fish and his sons, screened by armadas of soldiers, sailors, pilots, rifles, howitzers, jeeps, tanks, destroyers, cruisers, battleships, and Flying Fortresses.

*n*one of it was strong enough to keep reality out. Even when my father was working at Todd Shipyards, Hoboken, N.J., there was danger. He had taken a job as a plumber's helper after barely getting out of some kind of mess just after Pearl Harbor. There is no way of knowing now exactly what it was, but it was serious enough for the cops to order him to keep out of their way.

At the shipyard, he turned out to be an adept mechanic. They were modernizing old destroyers, installing distilling units that could convert sea water to fresh. He learned silver soldering and soon had a master pipefitter's ticket from the union. Whether or not he earned this on skill alone is hard to know, He liked to exaggerate his ability to do a little bit better for himself than he thought he really deserved.

"I was an apple boy," he told me. "You

There are no crimes against humanity— only crimes against one's Self.

polish apples and things go a lot easier."

He ran a modest coffee racket, selling the other workers hot coffee that he made with government beans and government equipment. He also had some kind of gambling pool going. And when they handed out overtime, he was not overlooked, often going out to sea on the two- or three-day shake-down cruises during which the men from the shipyard earned double and triple time for each hour spent on board.

His hands were calloused and hard. His rough work clothes were dirty when he came home. His tools were worn and chipped and greasy. He had one suit, a gray sharkskin my mother called "the uniform." Their total entertainment schedule consisted of a weekly movie. He woke at four every workday morning, went to bed early at night, and paid his income tax for the first time in his life. Every month he gave a pint of blood to the Red Cross.

One night two cops came to our door to pick him up for questioning in a grand larceny matter. My mother's older sister, Jenny, was visiting with us when they arrived.

"You can't take this man in," she told the policemen. "This man is straight. As God is my witness, he is strictly legitimate. Just this minute he came home from working in the Todd Shipyards." She showed them his tools, his workclothes, his hands, his pay envelopes. She brought my brother and me out and made us show the officers our homework books. It was an incredible performance. They went away and never came back.

All his life he had moaned, "If I only had a trade." Now he was learning one. Yet he couldn't really see himself as a plumber. After some three years in the shipyard, he took the savings and went back to Eighth Avenue to make loans at six dollars for

five. In the long run, he probably would have made more money as a plumber than he did as a Shylock. Shylocking is a business for men who are quick at figures, cold as bankers, and willing to use force or the threat of it to insure prompt payment. From what I saw, my father ran his business as a kind of social club. He had no real office, just sitting and telephone rights in a little hand laundry on Fifty-first Street near Eighth Avenue, not far from Madison Square Garden. Later he operated out of the lobby of the Garden Hotel, which was replaced a few years ago by a Howard Johnson Inn. Most of his day was spent walking from place to place in the theater district, seeing his customers, picking up payments, making new loans, exchanging gossip. All year round his face was a ruddy tan from the sun and his body was lithe and compact from the exercise.

He could be a brilliant judge of character, but he too often allowed his cunning to be overruled by his desire to play God. He made loans to people he knew were no good. Sometimes they were large loans, much larger than his bankroll could stand. When they went sour, he would yell and threaten, but something kept him from going further. Some of it had to do with fear of scandal that would come back to Walton Avenue. None of it had anything to do with physical cowardice or any personal distaste for violence. He was not especially afraid of getting hurt or even killed. He was afraid of being embarrassed.

Once, while walking through the little-used underpass that connected one side of the 50th Street Eighth Avenue IND station with the other, he felt a man put something that felt like a pistol against his back.

"Give me your money. I have a gun," the man said.

My father's entire bankroll was in his pocket. "Gedaddahere, creep," he answered.

"I'm warning you, I'm a desperate man."

"If you're so desperate, go ahead and shoot." The hold-up man ran away. My father explained the incident to me. "I knew who he was. It made me angry that a crumb like that thought he could knock me over that easy. Did he think I was so soft all he had to do was put a gun in my back and I would hand over my bankroll? He wasn't going to get it that easy. He was going to have to kill me for it."

*I*n a summer of terrible disappointment for all of us, my father made me understand much of what he was. I was in the Army at the time, in basic training at Fort Dix. I had entered Cornell University on a scholarship, failed to be pledged to a fraternity, broken my foot in gym early in the term and spent the rest of the year not attending classes. I would drink at night and read during the day, sitting back in the library stacks pulling books almost at random from the shelves.

When I ran out of money, I wrote papers for other students — five dollars for a short composition, $25 for a term paper. Through this work I found out something interesting: teachers always gave the papers a grade that was just about the same as the student's class average. One composition, for which I had gotten an A from my English teacher, received a D from another when submitted as the work of a D student.

I received a letter a month from the Dean of Students asking me to come in and explain why I wasn't attending classes. I answered none of them. At last, a graduate student was sent over to bring me in. The dean tried his best to offer me an alternative to Dismissal for Academic Reasons. I told him to do whatever he pleased. I had already volunteered for the Army. In June, I came home, passed my physical, and began to find out what it was really like to have no freedom of choice.

My brother, incurably infected with medical-school fever, had been refused admission to each school in the United States, victim of a higher educational system swollen to bursting with veterans studying on the GI Bill. He had gone to France to be a medical student at the University of Paris, where he realized after a year that he would never understand enough French to become the kind of physician he wanted to be.

While he was visiting in England he met a couple with a fancy name who told him that for a thousand dollars they could get him into a school in Great Britain. On the trans-Atlantic telephone, my father told him that he would wire the money as soon as he needed it. But how could they be sure, he asked, that these people would deliver what they promised?

My brother, as innocent and straight a boy as ever was blinded by overpowering want, was full of trust. My father, who knew that the perfect mark in any con game is the honest man willing for the first time in his life to do something shady, was not so trusting. The following day, after he made inquiries through old friends with private international connections, he dictated a letter which I typed and mailed to London.

"Dearest Son," it began. "You know how hard it is for me to write a letter. I am not an educated man and I do not know how to express myself in words. So you will have to forgive me if I make mistakes. The only thing I have learned in life is that in a family love is more important than grammar.

"Your mother and I love you. When you ask for something we get the chance to show you how much we love you. I wish that I were a better father so that I would be able to fulfill all your desires. If the money you ask for will get you what you want you will have it immediately.

"Tell your friends to go and see Mr. John Cotton. [I have changed the name here in order to avoid embarrassing the real person.] He is a good friend and experienced in handling deals like this. He is a well-known sportsman in England who is highly respected for integrity. He will personally guarantee that your friends will be paid as soon as they come through with their end.

"Son, I am sure that your friends truly want to do you a favor. But the people they are dealing with on the other side could be unreliable. Once the money is handed over there is no way of getting it back.

"If your friends are sincere they will be happy to have a man like Mr. Cotton be a go-between as is customary in this kind of matter. He will certainly make an arrangement with them that will protect everyone and avoid unpleasant misunderstandings.

"We will be waiting anxiously to hear from you. Your mother says to tell you that she is praying for things to come out the way you want. Whatever happens, we are behind you one thousand percent. Your loving father, Daddy Jim."

"That's the last he'll ever hear from them," my father predicted. He was right. "What people there are in the world," my father said. "They live off human misery."

"Always remember this," he told me. "You become a sucker the minute you get involved in larceny with professionals. You

today we are in Lagunitas, California. It is 7:40 pm; my name is Jules Siegel. I am pissed off at Wayne Ceballos because he will not come out here to the Chinese House to talk to me. He has heard there are bullet holes in the walls. There are. But maybe soon there will be bullet holes in the walls of the buildings of San Francisco. The battleground has no special limits of time or space. For myself, I would rather be terrified... than bored.

haven't got a chance of winning. They've got you figured a thousand different ways before you even open your mouth. They know who you are and where you come from. They've already counted the money in your pocket and they can smell the balance in your bank account. Cheating is their religion. When you come into their church you pay for everything they let you think you're stealing."

My brother returned home and got a job at an employment agency placing technical and scientific help. He searched everywhere for the magic connection to medical school. His health failed. An abscess fulminated in his foot.

I went with him to our family doctor, who decided to try a therapy of his own devising. He would aspirate some of the pus from the abcess and replace it with penicillin. He inserted the needle and my brother howled in terrible agony, the truest scream of pain I ever heard. Years later he found out that the treatment was useless.

In the summer, he came down with fever and nausea. The doctor who came to the house to see him diagnosed the condition as a touch of flu, but even I guessed what the yellow in my brother's eyes meant. Another doctor realized that he had hepatitis. A hearty eater, my brother now lived on boiled chicken, which he hated. It was about the only thing he was allowed to eat.

In the wake of the hepatitis came the emotional depression frequently associated with viral infections. One by one, the rejection letters arrived from medical schools. The last hope was a mystery man in Chicago who would do anything for my mother and had connections all over the country. The mystery man wrote letters, made long-distance calls, asked for a reference a priest. My father produced a monsignor who testified on church stationery that this boy had a holy vocation for healing arts evident to all who knew him. He recommended him without reservation for his intelligence, honesty, and spiritual sensitivity.

"It sounds as if you have a wonderful son," the monsignor told my father as he handed over the document. "I'd like to meet him some day."

"Thank you, Father, I appreciate everything you've done."

"It's nothing," said the churchman. "What else are we here for but to help one another? Good luck to you and your boy. Tell him not to despair. What is difficult for man is easy for God."

On a Friday, in the middle of a New York City heat wave that boiled the pavements, my brother, still recovering shakily from hepatitis, went down to the schoolyard to watch the kids play basketball. When he came home, the cleaning lady told him that the man from Chicago had called and would call back. My brother lay on his bed and waited for hours.

The doorbell rang. It was a friend of his, home from medical school. As a pre-medical student he had achieved a straight-A average but was nonetheless rejected by 23 medical schools. The case was brought to the attention of a congressman, who threatened an investigation of the ethnic quota system in American medical schools. One of the schools was induced to reconsider his application and a place was found for him. "You'll make it; I know it," he said. "You were born to be a doctor."

"God bless you for coming," my mother told the boy when he was leaving. "You don't know what you did for him."

At night, finally, the telephone call came. The man in Chicago had done everything he could, but it was no use. A letter of rejection would arrive in the mail. My brother began to cry. My father, sitting in his soft gray club chair took him in his lap like a child and rocked him until he was finished sobbing.

During the next year, my brother worked and saved almost all his earnings. He had always wanted a big car and now he saw one that he really loved, a white Oldsmobile convertible with red leather interior. For a while, it seemed as if the medical obsession was replaced in part by the immediately realizable goal of a fancy car. The dollars in his savings account rose steadily toward the amount he needed.

One weekend in August, toward the end of basic training, I was given a pass home, one of those unaccountable pieces of good fortune the orderly room produced every once in a while. When I got to 1478 Walton Avenue, Mr. Roeder was standing in the lobby. He took my duffel bag and came up with me in the elevator, then followed me into the apartment, which was dark and empty and, for some reason, smelled faintly of vomit. As we walked back toward the bedroom my brother and I had shared for so many years the smell grew stronger, but still elusive. I stopped at the bathroom. The door was hanging off its hinges, the thin center panel shattered open.

"Someone get locked in?"

"They didn't tell you?" Mr. Roeder asked.

"Tell me what?"

"Nobody told you." He was silent. "Look, boy, I don't want to mix in. It's not right other people should get involved in family business. I don't want to say anything. You go right over to Morrisania Hospital. Jimmy is there. I thought they sent for you. They took him there this morning." There are six blocks between 1478 Walton Avenue and Morrisania Hospital. First comes 171st Street. On one corner is a traffic light; on the other, P.S. 64, where I attended kindergarten and grades one through six. Then there is 170th Street, our main shopping district. It is an IND subway stop at the Grand Concourse and is served also by the IRT elevated line which runs along Jerome Avenue. Next come Elliott Place, Marcy Place and Clarke Place, followed by 169th Street. Morrisania Hospital, a grim old city institution, occupies a square block beginning at 168th Street. Part of its area is taken up by a power house with a tall chimney. The building is made of dirty yellow brick and stone, stands higher than anything else around and would serve well in any movie as the exterior of a morgue.

My father was unconscious. His face was covered with grey stubble. His eyes were open but coated with an opaque slime. The lips chapped and broken. There was a dripping intravenous. About his wrists were gauze and cotton bindings tied to the bars of the bed. He was calling out in a voice that still possessed just enough ego in it to sound ever so slightly calculated, as if he knew we were listening and wanted to create a vivid effect.

"No good. No goddamned good. No good, Mama. No goddamned good at all."

We go through life unaware that it is a dream from which we wake level by level, never knowing which awakening, if any, is real. Not long ago I dreamed I was walking along a dirt road that wound off a hillside covered with thick stands of young trees whose leaves were dusty and dry in the heat of the sun.

I don't know where I was coming from or where I was going, but I was thirsty and hoped to find up ahead a place to drink. I walked around a bend and came upon a lion with a full red mane lying in the center of the road, his tawny pelt merging with the tan, powdery surface. It was one of those silent movie dreams in which fear has no voice because the sound track for it has been left out of the mix. I was afraid of the lion, but I had no way of letting myself know that I was afraid. All I knew was that I was walking down a road and had come upon a lion.

The lion stood, stretched and yawned in that perfectly human way all cats have and ambled off into the bush. Alone again on the road, I realized that this could only happen in a dream. As soon as I knew that I was dreaming, I woke up. I was in my own bedroom and my wife was sitting next to me.

"I've just had the strangest dream," I said.

"How do you know you aren't still dreaming?" she asked playfully.

"Because if I were still dreaming, I would wake up."

"Wake up," my wife said. "Wake up. The telephone is ringing." Again I woke and realized that I had been dreaming. My wife was standing over me holding the telephone. It was morning and I was in our bedroom. The landlord was wondering when I intended to pay the rent. This was reality.

My father, a big loser again and unable to pay the rent, had tried to put himself asleep permanently. The day before, my brother had come home to find him sitting disconsolately in front of the television set.

"The Yankees lost," he said.

"That's too bad," my brother answered. He had never noticed my father take any particular interest in baseball before and he was surprised at the depth of despair in his voice.

"I can't believe it," my father said. "The Yankees lost." The following morning, my brother woke to hear loud snoring from the bathroom. My mother, in her bathrobe, joined him at the door, which was locked.

"Daddy's in there," he said. "He's snoring very heavily, as if he's unconscious." She ran to the window and screamed for help. Mr. Roeder and one of the fat Fishes came running and broke down the bathroom door. In the tub, my father lay naked in a profound coma. He had taken enough sleeping pills to kill himself several times over.

Somehow he survived. When he finally woke, it was with a joy at being alive he had never shown before. While he was still in Morrisania Hospital my brother came and showed him his bankbook and told him the money was his. Transferred to Bellevue, he received his brothers and sisters like a prince recuperating from a battle wound and played mental chess with the psychiatrists who examined him. They had no idea of what to do with him. "I can't get a thing out of him," said one doctor. "He knows more about psychology than I ever will." My mother knew what to do: take him home. First she had to find a way to get him out of this prison hospital.

It was the kind of thing she was good at. Since she knew no rules but survival of her family and children and was sublimely confident of her own ability to judge what kind of treatment her husband ought to receive, she was not especially impressed by Bellevue's regulation that attempted suicides be held for possible commitment to a state hospital.

She was always her own Supreme Court when it came to the realities of life. When she was eighteen years old, her brother was arrested in Westchester County in the act of plundering a mansion. He had already been convicted of three felonies. Under the Barnes law, if convicted of a fourth, he could be sentenced to life imprisonment.

She went to see an important man in White Plains who told her that for $5000 he would probably be able to do something for her brother. Still married to the man with money who never came home, she had accumulated a considerable amount in savings, but not enough for this. She sold her diamonds, but still she was short. She had tickets printed to a benefit dance to be given in honor of her brother and sold them in bunches of fifty or a hundred to his friends, big shots in the Mob. The money was paid. Her brother was allowed to plead guilty and sentenced to seven years. A model prisoner, he did five and never went back in again.

Now, she found out that my father could be released immediately on the opinion of a private psychiatrist. Through sources known only to her, she found one who would be cooperative and we went to see him. He was an old Viennese man who had a dark office on West End Avenue. From the framed letters and diplomas hanging on his walls, I gathered that he did a lot of work for the Army and government agencies.

"So, Mrs. Siegel," the doctor said, "you want me to write a letter? I will be happy to do this for you and then I will see what we can do to help your unfortunate husband. For a beginning, it would be good for me to see him every day, an hour each day. Then, once his condition is stabilized, three times a week. Eventually, we cut that to once a week and finally, when he is recovered fully, I leave him to you."

"I'm not sure I understand you, Doctor."

"You're not sure you understand me? Why?"

"Is this treatment free?" she asked. "We are not rich people."

"Of course not," said the psychiatrist uneasily. "But here a man's life and happiness is at stake, is it not?"

"Can you guarantee that you're going to help him?"

"In life, my dear Mrs. Siegel, there are no guarantees. I will do my best for this unhappy man, but who can guarantee anything? How about three times a week? A beautiful, intelligent woman like you, I do my best to keep happy. Let us say, thirty dollars an hour?"

"Please, please," my mother exclaimed in a tone of exasperated irony. "For a man of your learning, Doctor, you don't seem to grasp the situation. My husband is a gambler. He gambled away all his money. If he had enough money to pay you ninety dollars a week, he wouldn't need a psychiatrist."

"One session a week?" the doctor offered.

"Doctor, maybe I am not making myself clear. There is no money at all for psychiatrists. All I need is a letter. My husband belongs at home with the security and love of his family."

"You are a strong-minded woman, Mrs. Siegel. I will go and see the patient and see what I can do. Maybe you are right. Maybe he will be better at home with such a wife as you than locked up in a state institution. Maybe I will examine this man and find that this is true. In this case, my fee for making this examination and writing my findings will be one hundred and fifty dollars."

"I'll give you fifty. That's all I can afford."

"Fifty dollars!" the psychiatrist said, raising his voice for the first time. "Are you crazy, Mrs. Siegel? Excuse me, but that is impossible. I cannot do this for fifty dollars. I am a professional man, Mrs. Siegel. I have a responsibility to conduct a thorough examination, to make a complete diagnosis, to write a report. I have to travel all the way downtown to Bellevue. I'm not a young man anymore. I must take a taxi. This is all time. This is all money."

"I'm sorry I troubled you, Doctor," my mother said, "but I heard that you were an understanding man. I see now that I was misinformed." She patted her hair, adjusted her hat, examined her perfect nails, put on her white gloves, and, infinitely slowly, picked up her handbag and rose to go.

"All right. All right." The doctor surrendered. "Sit down, please. One hundred dollars."

"Thank you, Doctor," my mother said. "I knew you would be kind."

"How did you know that he would settle for a hundred dollars?" I asked her as we came out. "I thought we were going to have to give him at least a visit a week for a couple of months."

"A hundred dollars is what they get," my mother said. "That's the right price. Don't you think I asked around?"

Soon my father was home in his own bed, newly shaven and barbered, wearing clean pajamas, weak but ready to begin all over again.

*M*y brother became a doctor and earned enough money to buy himself a succession of increasingly impressive cars, planes, apartment houses, an office building. My mother, through him, achieved respectability and financial security. I went back to school and emerged a writer. Like Moses before the Promised Land, my father was permitted to see his hopes about to be fulfilled. In the spring of 1959 he attended the graduations of his sons.

The following year, he and a partner swindled an exiled South American politician who was looking for high-profit investment opportunities. The partner was dissatisfied with my father's accounting of the proceeds. He sent his two strong young sons to collect the difference. There was a fight. My father stabbed one of the sons in the belly with a small pocketknife. My father wound up in the Tombs charged with attempted murder. The young man lay near death in St. Clare's Hospital.

"Why did you do it?" I asked my father, as if his face, still black and yellow and green from the beating he had taken, were not answer enough.

"They were killing me on my own territory. I had to do something. I couldn't let them get away with that. I wouldn't have been able to walk on the street. I'm an old man. I'm the oldest guy in the can. They call me 'Pop.' This is no business for old men. I want everyone to know that this is one old man who knows how to take care of himself."

We hired a criminal lawyer named Irving Mendelsson, a tall man who carried a briefcase full of candy and cigarettes which he handed out to clerks, elevator operators, guards, anyone else who worked in the criminal courts buildings. On my father's instruction, I borrowed $1000 for legal expenses from his older brother, telling him not to expect it back for a long time, if ever. An old prison friend who had just collected $20,000 in a personal injury settlement was good for another thousand. The man in the hospital recovered. The grand jury, after hearing the testimony of witnesses who told the truth the way they saw it, dismissed the charges.

You will understand exactly what kind of loan shark my father must have been from this: the people who came to speak in his behalf were his customers—a waitress, a carpenter, a man who once wrote for Life, a rodeo cowboy.

"Your father fed plenty of people around here," said the man who had once written for Life. "He was always a soft touch when someone was down and out. I was proud to go in there and testify for him. So would plenty of others if they were the kind who could come into court. We all love Jim on Eighth Avenue."

*B*y this time I was married and living in Jackson Heights, Queens. My brother was an intern at a hospital in Long Beach, California. One day in April, my mother called me at the office and told me that my father had not been home for two days. I called my brother and he came back to New York. A few days later, the police came to my mother's door. They had found my father's car. They needed the keys. My brother went with them. He identified my father's body, which lay decomposing in the trunk. The autopsy indicated suicide, acute barbiturate intoxication.

I went to the police station to reclaim the car, which was parked out in front of the building on a street overlooking the Harlem River. This is one of the most beautiful views in New York City. On the Manhattan side there is a lush park with a bell tower. A series of arched vaults supporting an elevated highway sits on the river. The car smelled foul.

The police refused to release the car. They wanted a letter of permission from the District Attorney. Before I left, I opened the doors and windows to air the vehicle. When I opened the trunk, the stench of death mugged me. It was a combination of shit, vomit, and garbage—and something else so subtle and attractive that the experience balanced on the exact borderline between pain and pleasure. I took out the rubber mat. Shiny black bugs crawled over the steel floor of the trunk.

During the days while I waited for the District Attorney's letter, I went back to the police station occasionally to air the car. Finally, after presenting the necessary documents, I drove it back to the garage of a family friend in the used-car business. There were no customers for a long time. There seemed to be no way to remove the smell. At last, a dealer offered $600. He planned to install completely new upholstery and repaint it. I took the money gratefully. That night, I called my mother and told her about the sale.

"Only six hundred dollars?" she said.

I see my father now in one of those pastel color movies that captures the past and holds it for us, to be played and replayed until the dyes fade, the ripple pattern of the sound track disintegrates, and this piece of the world that was returns to original, undifferentiated form, entering the endless void.

On this day he had just returned home from the hospital after his first suicide attempt. He and I were alone in his bed-room. Two windows faced the street. The sunlight was an afternoon yellow. The oiled French furniture, patterned in complicated herringbone marquetries of light and dark veneers, collected specks of dust, one speck at a time. He was lying in bed smoking a cigarette and telling me a story.

"I had a friend," my father said, "who got caught doing something wrong. He was sent to Sing Sing. At the reception center he didn't like something a guard told him to do. They got into a fight and he nearly killed the guard.

"They sent him to Dannemora as an incorrigible. He was assigned a job in the cotton shop. This was a spinning mill. In order to keep the threads from breaking, the cotton shop was kept damp. Since the prison was near the Canadian border, the weather was almost always cold. The combination of damp and cold caused fifty percent of the men who worked in the cotton shop to go into the con—come down with consumption, TB.

"My friend refused to go to work in the cotton shop. He didn't want TB. The warden gave him two weeks in solitary to think it over. The solitary confinement cells were small dungeons cut into the walls of the prison. Each one was six feet long, five feet high, and three feet wide. The only thing in it was a slop bucket. There was a trap at the bottom of the iron door for passing out the slop bucket and passing in bread and water. There was no heat. It was winter.

"At the end of the two weeks, they brought my friend to the warden. 'Will you go to work in the cotton shop?' 'No.' At that time, there was a rule that they couldn't keep a man in solitary more than two consecutive weeks. They gave my friend a shave, a shower, and a clean uniform, fed him three meals, and let him sleep in a regular cell overnight.

"In the morning, they took him to the warden. 'Ready to go to work in the cotton shop?' 'No.' He spent two more weeks in solitary. This time, the guards who came to take him to the warden had to help him walk. Again the same question. Again the same answer. Again a shave, a shower, a clean uniform, three meals, a regular cell for one night. Again solitary.

"At the end of the third two weeks in solitary, they had to take him out on a stretcher. The warden came to see him in the prison infirmary. My friend still refused to work in the cotton shop. The doctor told the warden that if they put him back in solitary, he would die. By this time, the whole prison knew the story. Gamblers were making book on whether or not my friend would go to work in the cotton shop. It was a test of will.

"If you were the warden, what would you have done?"

I didn't know.

"It was obvious my friend would rather die than work in the cotton shop. The warden couldn't kill him over something like that, but he couldn't give him another job either. It would have meant losing, and the one rule in running a prison is that the warden never loses.

"So what he did was duck it. He put my friend in a cell by himself. It had an exercise yard in the back. For the next eight years, the only people that my friend saw were the guards who brought him his food and took him out in the exercise yard once a day to do calisthenics. For eight years, my friend did nothing but read books." The story was over.

"You might want to write about something like that some day," he said casually.

On the way home from his funeral, my mother said, "He told me once that they thought he was so tough in that prison. 'I wasn't tough,' he said. 'I just didn't care whether I lived or died.' Did you know the Siegels never once visited him or wrote to him?"

In the bedroom, my father and I gazed at each other silently. From the street, there were the noises of children and the jingle of the Bungalow Bar truck selling ice cream. The Bungalow Bar truck had a body shaped like a little bungalow with a shingled roof and gabled windows. The ice cream was cheaper than Good Humor and not quite so good, but still good enough.

I went down into the street and bought ice cream for both of us, chocolate for me, strawberry for him, in large, waxed-paper cups. The curtains in the windows stand even now caught like sculpture in the instant of my eye, floating in a breeze that long ago died down and left them suspended. We ate the ice cream. For the first time since I could remember, I was not angry at my father for sloppiness while eating ice cream. But when he stubbed out his cigarette in the empty cup, I wanted to hit him in the mouth.

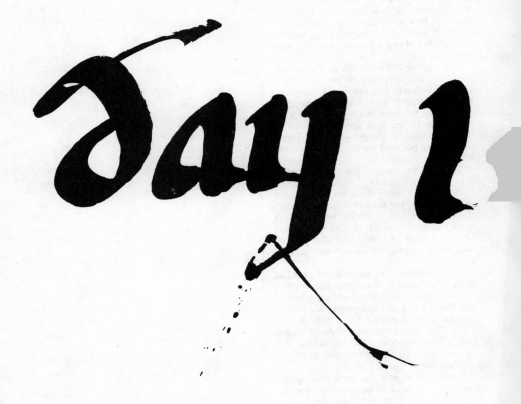

y. Day

remember the greedy
ones in the desert of
Sinai hoarding the
manna from heaven =

"give us this day our
daily bread" =

thinking too far ahead makes
me sick with worry. I see
the abyss more clearly
than the path...

In the Land
of Morning Calm,
Deja Vu

Naked, pistol in hand, Frazer, college graduate, poet, former child prodigy, in the eternally divided second of the lieutenant's inner thought and balancing decision, knew for certain that it had happened to him before. Once before he had stood on this off-limits beach on the River Han while Remsen looked on, while water flowed bearing mud and excrement into the sea and a second lieutenant of Engineers had walked into what might in this very second turn into his last thoughts on the painful side of time.

Of course, thought Frazer, as he snapped off the safety and deflected his gaze for one of the infinite moments of that infinite second to Remsen's face and the newly healing round bullet wound scarred on his hairless chest like some surrealistic lichen on a grey and breathing rock. Of course. First the secret; now the dream.

*I*t had begun even before the pipeline.

Though there was a truce, Frazer had not been in Korea more than a week and a half before he saw his first shot-torn corpse. That was when he was a photographer with the signal company in the 7th Division in Tong Du Chon. A photographer always went out to take pictures of soldiers who were killed by accident, or thieves, or each other, or themselves. The assignment was always given to the newest member of the photo platoon, not because of the horror, but rather because of the inconvenience; it was not pleasant to be awakened at four or five in the morning, to take a rattle jouncing jeep somewhere up the line to a huddle of dirty-looking tents and a quonset-hut mess hall, to take pictures of perhaps a headless GI who had put an M-1 in his mouth and blown his troubles the other side of time and then to have a soggy brown breakfast with a pallid criminal investigation man who had nothing better to talk about than some corpse he had found rotting in an abandoned bunker while flocks of glistening crows fought over the flesh.

It was after his first corpse that he had the dream for the first time.

Frazer's first corpse had been murdered, cut in half by bullets in an oblique line running from an inch or so above his left hip to a point six or seven inches from his right hip. The last bullet hole was like a grey and blue third nipple blooming on the soldier's chest.

"Christ," a CID man was whining when Frazer walked into the tent in which the wide-eyed corpse lay almost naked on a canvas cot, "I wish they would leave these corpses where they find them. They always got to move them."

"The medic did it," protested a fat, yellow-haired sergeant who was clearly wishing this had happened somewhere else far away. "He was still alive when they got to him. He was crying and praying and everything. What was they to do, leave him there and die?"

"Fuck the medics. They should of left him where he was." He turned to Frazer. "You the photographer?"

No, thought Frazer, I just carry this Army-issue Speed Graphic because I'm a camera fan. "Yes sir," he answered, not knowing then how to address the CID man, who wore no insignia of rank, just two gold U.S. initials on his fatigue lapels.

"Well take the pictures and let's get out of here. I ain't got all night to spend in this asshole."

While Frazer went about carefully setting up his flash guns and equipment and took his pictures the way he had been taught at photography school in Fort Monmouth, the CID man took down the details from a succession of cool or frightened GIs who did their best not to look at the dead man on the cot. The fat sergeant stood around listening and wringing his hands like a bereaved widow.

Before the picture-taking was over, the story was really finished. The rest of the witnesses the CID man heard were just corroboration. The dead soldier was a sentry who had challenged another GI who had come back to his tent late at night after drinking a great deal of beer in the battalion beer hall. Drunk and mean he had stumbled out to the latrine, only to be brought up short by the sentry.

"Halt. Who is there?" the sentry had challenged in formal Army style. The drunk kept walking at him. "Halt," the sentry called again, but the drunk kept walking. "Halt," the sentry said the third time and pointing his weapon at the drunk drew back the bolt and rammed a cartridge into the chamber, ready to fire.

"Piss off, you stupid bastard. It's me and I'm going to the latrine."

"Well for chrissake why didn't you say something. I was ready to blow your head off."

"You point that piece at me and I'll blow your ass off," answered the drunken soldier.

"Aw, come on, will you. Don't be such a prick."

"Get off my case, prick. You point that thing at me again and I'll fix your ass for good."

An hour or so later, the drunken GI went out to the latrine again, was challenged by the same guard, went back to his tent and got his grease gun, which is a kind of submachine gun firing .45-caliber slugs, and murdered the sentry. He was the last one to be brought into the tent. He was tall and thin and had silvery blond hair. His blue eyes and clean, sharp, regular features reminded Frazer of an actress he had seen. He was wearing wrinkled fatigues and dirty boots. His dog tags hung outside his fatigue jacket and where the silver chain crossed his yellowed T-shirt there was a greasy grey line of week-old body filth.

"All right, boy," said the CID man, suddenly now more gentle, more tired, "tell me what happened."

But all the boy did was put his face in his hands when he saw the body and began to weep long gagging sobs. The CID man looked at the two soldiers who had brought the silver-haired boy into the tent and then at Frazer, who was standing with his camera in hand waiting to be told what further to do.

"What are you looking at, goony bird," said the CID man to Frazer. "You finished with your pictures? Then get out of here and go develop them and stay out of my way."

During the next month or so, Frazer got more used to seeing dead soldiers. Perhaps he hit a streak of bad luck, but during that period it seemed to him there could not have been more deaths had there been a war.

There were so many ways for these soldiers to die. In Uijongbu, two master sergeants played "draw," like characters from Gunsmoke, and one shot the other and he died. A curly-haired corporal due to ship home in three days went into an uncompleted Butler building and put a carbine bullet through his ear. Pieces of his scalp dripped from the ceiling. His girl, a WAC, had written to tell him she was having a baby by another man.

A tall, chocolate-brown Engineers sergeant-first-class Frazer had met on the ship coming over went out in a boat to rescue three men trapped on a tank caught in a spring-flooded river. He brought off the first two men, but when he went to get the third the little boat broke up in the battering current. The bodies were washed up a few days later, jammed in with some debris by the edge of a conduit bridge.

An eighteen-year-old infantryman patrolling the pipeline that ran from Inchon up to the front caught a slickie boy tapping POL and got a .38-caliber slug in his chest for it. His death's-head face had a surprised look, as if to say, "Slickie boy you're supposed to run away, not shoot back." Two soldiers went to sleep inside the cab of a two-and-a-half-ton truck with the motor running to keep warm during a field exercise. Carbon monoxide let them sleep in each other's arms forever.

All of these deaths had to be recorded on film, delivered to a CID office in Eighth Army headquarters in Seoul and from there, Frazer felt, marked, measured, calculated and ordered into some scheme comprehensible only to the military, sent on to Washington where file girls on roller skates hid them in the depths of moldering files in the labrynthine subbasements of the Pentagon. There, that's explained, breathed the Army, which had a horrible fear of deaths in peacetime, that's explained, recorded, filed away and we will never have to think about it again — so Frazer imagined the mind of the Army reflecting briefly upon these photographs of headless soldiers traveling through its inner circuits.

Even before Frazer was transferred to the military intelligence detachment, he found out that it was not only the infantryman up on the line who checked in every once in a while with death's double-dealing timetable. It was, it seemed, a condition of the uniform, that it should attract various kinds of dangerous violence: children playing with powerful toys are bound to get hurt.

His first assignment after the death detail was to take pictures for Ordnance of a tank that for some mysterious reasons known not to its operator or even to those expert in the ways of armored vehicles had gone berserk while standing untended and

raced some half mile or more without a driver, toppling into a small ravine and there it lay on its side, spinning its steel tracks wildly and spitting smoke, flames and bullets of stone and mud until it ran out of gas. It was necessary, Ordnance thought, that the tank should be photographed from every angle before the vehicle was righted and towed off to be examined, tamed and repaired.

"Well, son," said a worried-looking major as he surveyed the site of the insane tank's final rest, "I want you to get up as close to it as possible after you get some long shots and then I want you to get inside and get me some pictures of the interior before we have the demolition boys clean it out."

But before he went down to make his close-ups and interiors, the demolition men, a grey old sergeant-first-class and a wintry-looking warrant officer with the narrow, controlled eyes and pale lips of those who have learned just how untrustworthy seemingly inanimate but violent tools can be, gave him a short briefing on how he should proceed.

"Number one: no flashbulbs. It's soaked with POL and napalm. Number two: no metal on you. Take off your belt, wristwatch, dog tags — anything else that could cause a spark." The warrant officer's tone was quite cheerful, nothing like what he would have expected from the war movies he had seen.

While Frazer stripped himself of the forbidden items, the sergeant began to tell him what he would find.

"The ammunition rack is broke open and there are live shells lying all around the interior and the outside of the tank. Try not to step on them. There's not much chance they'd go off if you did, but you want to be careful. There wouldn't be much of you left to send home to mom. Har-har!"

When Frazer was ready, the demolition men, the major and the medics and other soldiers took cover behind a temporary revetment built of sandbags about two hundred yards form the stricken tank. Very conscious of their eyes on him, but, for some reason, not especially frightened, he walked down slowly with his pants drooping and made his pictures. It occurred to him while he was taking time exposures inside the belly of the tank that it would be quite Chaplinesque if something should go

Tick tock tick tock tick tock
tick tock tick tock tick tock tick tock tick tock
tick tock tick tock tick tock tick tock tick tock
tick tock tick tock tick tock tick tock tick tock
tick tock tick tock tick tock tick tock tick tok
tick tock tick tock tick tock tick tock tick tock
tick tock tick tock tick tock tick tock tick
tock tik tok tik tok tick tock
tick tock tick tok

tick tock

can anyone count the hours away?

squirt. plop.
plunge.
splash.

wrong and while he was scrambling to safety his pants should fall down. It would get a big laugh — maybe even a bigger laugh if the crazy tank should right itself like an angry, wounded animal and chase him all over the countryside while he ran around trying to hold up his pants and take pictures.

When he came back to the bunker, though, he was sweat-soaked and trembling and eagerly drew at the polished silver flask of brandy the major offered him. Then he sat down on the ground and smoked a cigarette and watched the two demolition men set up their gear and go over a set of blueprints and sketches. The major bit his nails slowly, one by one, but for all the tension the demolition men evidenced they might have been discussing plans to erect a small and not especially complicated tent or quonset hut.

*N*ot too long after that, Frazer received orders to report to Eighth Army headquarters in Seoul for temporary duty of an unspecified nature and duration at the pleasure of the commanding officer. He was told, however, by the clerk who gave him his orders that he would be gone only a day or so for some sort of interview. Then he looked at him quizzically and leaned back.

"You some kind of commanist or something?" he asked in a very friendly manner.

"You think I am?" answered Frazer.

"I don't think nothing. I'm just an old clerk. But somebody sure is interested to know all about what's going on in your head."

"Like who?" The mysterious orders and the clerk's cat smile made him uneasy.

"Don't know as how I really can answer that. But there's been a couple of CIC fellas all the way from Japan in to see the captain. They asked some personal questions. Like was you a homosexual and so on."

"What did he tell them," asked Frazer, who was getting more and more uneasy.

"He told them how did he know, all he cared was you didn't get the clap off some gook whore and screw up the company VD record. When they asked him was you a commanist he said he figured all enlisted men is commanists, but you didn't seem to be no worse than the others. Then they

called me in and asked me what did I know and I told him you was a wild-eyed radical and peddled your ass every weekend down in Yung Dung Po." The clerk laughed. "Least that's what I should have told them. They would have liked that."

"Yeah, they would have liked that, all right. What do you think it's all about?"

"Hard to say, trooper, hard to say, but you look at them orders you'll see something very interesting."

Frazer studied the mimeographed sheet carefully. It looked pretty much like any other set of orders he'd ever seen — a list of names, dates, places men were to be at certain times, transportation priorities and so on.

"Doesn't mean anything to me," he said.

"Well, I'll tell you then. First of all, your name is the only one with rank specified. Second of all, these is all open orders, no duty specified. And third of all, every last order has top-priority transportation. Looks to me like you got yourself in with some mighty powerful people. You either going to be very happy or very sad when they get through with you."

*I*t was an interview before assignment in a military intelligence detachment. They needed a photographer for spot aerial-reconnaissance work, though they depended on the Air Force for the day-in and day-out surveillance of enemy activity across the demilitarized zone. Frazer, who had scored in the first percentile on the Armed Forces Qualification Test and received similarly high scores in a wide range of the aptitude tests, had been selected, he was told, because he seemed to offer the most promise as a generally useful member of the detachment. Did he want the assignment? Oh, yes, he did indeed. But on the way back, he thought of the rather fattish young captain who had interviewed him, and of the flat-eyed Korean soldier carrying a carbine who had picked him up without saying any word other than, "You Frazer? Come with me," when he called for him in the personnel office behind the old, red-brick Japanese barracks which now served the Eighth Army command in Seoul. There was something, somehow, the same between the two: as though they were sleeping with the same woman or sharing some secret. It was a silent hum that passed between them—they were humming on the same frequency, and he was not. When he thought of these two, who were the only members of his new outfit he had so far seen, Frazer worried a little—about the seemingly shared secret, the mysterious rapport—and he worried about what the company clerk had told him when he got his orders: very happy or very sad, powerful people. Maybe it would have been better to go on photographing corpses, accidents and newly arrived generals.

Yet at first it seemed he had made the right move, if, in fact, he had any choice in the first place. The detachment consisted of four men: Captain Green; an administrative sergeant-first-class named Philo who took care of the supply room and made the morning report; Remsen, a translator and interrogator, and, now, Frazer. Additionally, there was attached to the group a platoon of Korean troops who acted as drivers and bodyguards and were assigned the responsibility of the security of the detachment quarters. The Korean soldiers and their officers all wore insignia of rank, but the Americans wore only the gold U.S. initials on the lapels of their fatigues. Captain Green wore rank or not, as he pleased, usually not. For Frazer the experience of being in the Army without evidence of rank was exhilarating. He had, it seemed, been released from the general hierarchy. Still, it took a little while for him to get used to being saluted by soldiers and airmen, who were never quite sure what to do about these GIs with no rank, and it took him longer to get used to eating in the officer's mess. Would he be unmasked, he thought, and thrown out of the mess like an octoroon who passes for white in the South?

He quickly became intimate with Remsen. Remsen came from Iowa—a small town called Sidney, home of the world's largest outdoor rodeo. It was corn country and his father owned farms in Iowa, and Nebraska and was, it appeared, quite wealthy. Remsen had studied Chinese at Columbia University for a couple of years and then, grown tired of the misery and boredom of college life, the meaninglessness of his studies, enlisted. After basic training he was assigned to the Army Language School in Monterey. There he was taught to speak and read Korean with remarkable ease and fluency. But, peculiarly, instead of speaking it with an American accent, his Chinese intruded and Remsen spoke Korean with a Chinese accent, a source of great amusement to the Korean soldiers and to the whores in the village.

Remsen taught him how to read aerial photographs with a stereoscope, how to fire a .38-caliber pistol, how to spell his name in Korean and Chinese characters, and introduced him to a Chinese restaurant in Seoul which served Shanghai specialties and, occasionally, to Korean officers, spaghetti and meatballs. Frazer taught Remsen how to use a Speed Graphic, how to develop and print film, and how to stay in the village all night without Philo being able to catch them at it. They borrowed money from each other, used each other's whores and discussed with great detail and solemnity the different girls they had loved and what each one was like: much better, they agreed, than the Koreans but not quite as good as the Japanese girls in the little bars in Yoshiwara. Japanese girls spoke poetry—one, even, Donne's *Break of Day;* Korean girls smelled of kimchi, which is a kind of kraut, spiced and let ferment too long, and always had to go washee-washee though it was twelve degrees below zero outside.

Despite all this, however, Frazer still noticed that certain of the Korean soldiers and Remsen and Captain Green seemed to know something he didn't know. There was between them a flat kind of unpleasant communication which excluded not only Frazer but also Philo, but then Philo was a dud: Regular Army for the past ten years and before that a sailor in the Navy. Everybody disliked him because he was fat, Southern, stupid and mean. He never went to the village, saw every movie, couldn't read aerial photographs and spent most of his time counting uniforms in the supply room and building tiny HO-gauge model trains at night in the tent he shared with an Air Force sergeant who could have been his twin: both in appearance and mentality and in referring to the Koreans as gooks. It was not known whether the two liked each other or disliked each other, they neither spoke frequently to each other nor argued, but rather, Frazer thought, were like some long-married middle-aged couple who would have gotten a divorce years ago if they had thought of a good enough reason.

*F*razer began to understand about the secret slowly. One time, he was present at the interrogation by the South Korean intelligence men of a double agent who had been exposed. The interrogation took place in an isolated compound halfway between Seoul and Uijongbu. The barracks had been built before the war by the Japanese and were attractively made with dark, weather-worn shingles. They were surrounded and half-hidden by a fine stand of pine trees growing out of brown, needle-covered earth which had a pleasantly blurred and musty smell. The interrogation room was set up in the form of an amphitheatre, but the pit was lighted so that the prisoner could not see the observers who sat in the shadows. The interrogator's seat was a straight chair on a small platform. The prisoner would be seated on a stool facing him. Frazer, Remsen and Captain Green were met in the amphitheatre by Colonel Kim, a Korean intelligence officer who was approaching forty but showed no sign of age other than silver hairs mixed in with the black on his round, well-shaped head. They had met him before on a number of other occasions. Today he was wearing a civilian suit of grey worsted.

"This fellow," said Kim with a wave of his hand to indicate the prisoner, who had not yet been brought in, "is very tough, but he will be interesting."

"How did you get him?" asked Green.

"Very funny way. He had two boyfriends, one in Seoul, other one in Kaesong. Boyfriend down here found out about North Korean sweetheart and turned him in as a spy. CIC checked him out and found out he was Chinese agent before they found out he was one of our people too."

"Typical," said Green.

"Yes," said Colonel Kim and he smiled his best Korean intelligence political smile, "but things are happening. Soon there will be changes."

A buzzer sounded in the room and the men took their seats up in the dark. The prisoner was brought in. Doe-eyed, slight and intelligent-looking, he wore only skivvy shorts. Frazer looked around at the other men. They were leaning forward expectantly. He could hear their breathing and it seemed heavier. For a moment their attitudes and the nearly naked Korean down

in the pit reminded him of the skivvy show he and Remsen had gone to one night in Yung Dung Po. The atmosphere was somehow the same and he would have been only a little surprised if, instead of the crewcut Korean captain who walked into the center of the pit and sat down on the interrogator's chair, the same Korean whore he had seen that night had come in and begun to work with the prisoner the way she had with that Korean boy.

Something almost more interesting happened. As the interrogator looked on, one of the Korean guards took out a roll of adhesive tape and carefully taped up the prisoner's hand into a tight fist. Then while the other guard held the prisoner by the neck, he pushed him down to the floor. A third guard appeared and held the man's arm and fist out flat on the floor and then the guard slowly and methodically began stamping the prisoner's fist into a pulp with his heavy, brown, polished GI boot. Frazer stood up in his seat, but before he could do anything, if he indeed intended to do anything, Remsen put a firm hand around the upper part of his arm and without turning his face from the spectacle below pulled him down into his seat. After the guard had finished crushing the prisoner's fist, the man was permitted to rise and sit on the interrogation stool. While the prisoner's other hand was being taped, the interrogator gave him a cigarette, lit it for him very solicitously and then began to question him in what Frazer later learned was the form of address reserved for women and dogs.

"They do things differently than we," said Remsen afterward. "You learn not to get upset." He had continued to hold Frazer's arm throughout the interrogation.

"What happens after they get through with him?" Frazer asked. Remsen turned to their driver and said something to him in Korean. The soldier responded with the universal horrible grin and the universal gesture of the cut throat.

After that Frazer began again to have the dream regularly. And when they started working the pipeline, every fourth or fifth night he would awaken out of the dream. The waking into moving shadows, into the scuttle of rats in the wallpaper ceiling of a Korean hut or the grey board floor of the six-man tent he and Remsen occupied alone, was almost worse than the dream.

There were different versions, but the most disturbing seemed to take place in England: not the England of today but some timeless pre-Roman England where he walked aimlessly on a moss lawn that sloped down to a small stream. The lawn appeared to be a carefully kept thousand-year-old clearing, most of its perimeter a deep green forest in which leaves, mosses, ferns, soil and trees formed a menacing pattern of browns, blacks, blues and greens.

Very close to the edge of the forest was what appeared to be a small shrine or temple buried like a bunker in the sloping riverbank: an ancient quarried stone cave sunk into the earth by the passage of thousands of years of unremembered time. Frazer would walk stooping into the entrance, which was built of carefully dressed slabs of grey stone made to form a simple lintel and post doorway. Inside, at first there was nothing, just the moist stone walls and deeply umbrous shadows; then there was a presence which, hidden at first, expanded and filled the small room and grabbed at Frazer's heart with cobwebby tendrils of cold and invisible fog. *Brought here by murdering Druids,* Frazer's dreaming mind would think in terror and then he would be quite quickly awake, and simply, very simply and accountably, afraid just as he had been afraid of the dark as a little boy.

But then Remsen was shot and for a few weeks that Frazer slept alone in the tent, there were no more dreams. They had been out in the field working the pipeline, trying to develop the information that would enable the Army to close off the huge losses of fuel siphoned off every day by Korean thieves all along the route of the supply artery. The pipeline ran alongside the road from Inchon to just above Tong Du Chon, where it terminated in a fuel depot that served the 7th Infantry Division and the other assorted units strung throughout the American sector facing the DMZ. Each month tankers down in the port city of Inchon would pump fuel into the pipeline, some million and a third gallons of it. At the other end would arrive, in a good month, eight hundred thousand gallons. The balance was lost along the way.

Korean thieves would uncouple the joints in the pipeline and replace the fitting with one of their own making which had a concealed valve. At night a tube would be run from the valve into a five-gallon jerry can. Drip by drip, all night long, the can would fill up. Before dawn, the thief would return and pick up his full can of fuel. Three companies of infantry patrolled the pipeline twenty-four hours a day and managed to keep this petty form of thievery down to a reasonable level by shooting two or three Koreans a week.

Somewhere along the line, though, someone was stealing fuel from the pipeline in more substantial quantities and taking it off, Captain Green believed, in a twenty-thousand-gallon refueling unit stolen one night from the Air Force base at Kimpo, along with a ten-ton bulldozer. The Air Police recovered the bulldozer simply by following its tracks, but the refueling unit disappeared totally, turning up now only in hints and suggestions on aerial photographs, tracks on certain dusty roads that should not have had those tracks, casual remarks by low-level informers and more concrete tips by Captain Green's paid spies. Strangely, or, better, significantly, there was no news at all from any of the official or unofficial Korean army sources.

Significantly, because there were three places the fuel could be going: to the black market, to North Korea or to the gas-hungry Korean army. To the detachment, the third possibility seemed most likely, since it was American policy to keep the Republic of Korea army on a ten-day supply of fuel and a thirty-day supply of ammunition in order to reduce the possibility of war-hawk army leaders initiating their own independent attack on North Korea.

This theory was reinforced quickly. One night in an isolated village not far from an ROK armor unit to which Frazer and Remsen had traced the tracks of what might have been the refueling unit. Frazer had stepped out of his whore's warm hut to urinate and smelled on the air, mixed in with the odor of excrement the farmers used to fertilize the rice paddies, the very distinct fumes of nearby gasoline. He had hunted through the immediate outskirts of the village, sniffing like a dog until, in the midst of the strongest gas smell, he found a thatch-rooted shed built against the side of a hillside. Frazer opened the door of the shed and flashed his light into a huge, low cavern dug out of the mountain as far back as the torch carried into the darkness. It was filled with fifty-five-gallon steel drums stacked neatly on either side of a center aisle into which the flashlight shone like a locomotive headlight in a tunnel.

He went back to the hut to wake up Remsen. The two men had been detached temporarily to the armor unit, ostensibly to teach the officers some of the new techniques of combat intelligence. Remsen was sleeping with one of the two young whores they had been given earlier in the evening at a drinking party the Korean officers had thrown in honor of the good relations between the two intelligence men and the Army of the Republic of Korea.

Both girls were surprisingly good-looking with long straight black hair and white teeth. It was hard to tell their ages, but Frazer thought they could be no more than eighteen years old. One girl was able to speak English with some degree of communication, but the other, who nonetheless looked to be the more intelligent of the two, spoke none. While they sat around low tables, drinking, the Korean-speaking whore at first watched Remsen with a curiously appraising air. Then, as the powerful Korean moonshine began to take effect and the party got more and more hilariously nervous, Remsen became more and more amorous, touching the girl, speaking to her intensely in Korean, as though she really were a girl he had met at a cocktail party and was trying to convince her to come home with him. And, in fact, the young whore resisted him somewhat as though she were in fact what he pretended her to be. Then Remsen pulled out a roll of Korean money and waved it at her. She struck his hand aside and, with a peculiarly unpleasant laugh, coughed something short in Korean and pointed from Remsen to a very young, good-looking Korean officer with soft eyes and clear, delicate features. The officer blushed and after a momentary silence, in which all the Koreans seemed to be looking at Remsen, laughed. Remsen spoke quickly in Korean and pointed from his girl to Frazer's and they all laughed heartily.

"What did they say," asked Frazer of his girl, who had up until the beginning of this incident been translating the conversations amid floods of giggles.

"Oh, nothing. Just joke, Too hard to explain." And she put to his lips another glass of the Korean liquor and groped him expertly as he poured the liquid brimstone down his throat.

Now Remsen and his girl were lying uncovered on the sleeping platform but not in each other's arms; in fact, widely separated, as though they were avoiding unnecessary contact with each other. This seemed strange to Frazer, who enjoyed almost as much as the act itself sleeping spooned in the curled body of his bedmate. The girl was facing the wall and Remsen lay on his stomach on the side nearest Frazer. A nerve twitched down near his buttocks and a little ripple of muscle spasms ran up his back. Frazer reached down and touched him gently and spoke his name. Remsen awoke with a start and turned instantly, pulling out from beneath his pillow his pistol, which with almost no motion at all he pointed straight at Frazer's heart. Then his eyes cleared.

"You scared me," said Remsen and yawned and stretched. "What's up?"

"I found the gas."

"No shit! Where?"

Frazer told him. He put on his trousers and boots and the two soldiers went out to the shed. The girl still slept. When they got to the shed, they both hesitated simultaneously: something was wrong. In the absolute blackness of the cloudy, moonless night they both felt it like the peculiar, ominous presence that fills the air before an electrical storm. Then a voice barked in Korean. Remsen answered in Korean and started to walk forward, catching the first slug out of the blazing carbine in his chest.

*I*n the secret inquiry into the matter some weeks later, while Remsen lay in a Tokyo hospital with a mangled .30-caliber bullet hanging from his dog tags as a souvenir of the occasion, the Korean sentry who had shot him testified that he heard the Chinese-accented response and decided it was an infiltrator. Fortunately, he had been carrying a carbine, not an M-1. The lighter, lower muzzle-velocity slug, had given Remsen a chest wound, but it would not be too long before he was back on duty, if only on a limited basis.

To Frazer, the waiting time seemed interminable. Sometimes he even found himself making conversation with Philo while he constructed those tiny model trains. The sergeant was due to ship home pretty soon and it had been decided that until Remsen was sufficiently recovered to go on

I dreamed last night that I was drowning in a sea tide filled masses of people. I fought my way forward stepping on heads turning on a pavement of human faces until I reached the clear open water where I was at last alone — and afraid of sharks.

active duty again, once he got out of the hospital he would take over Philo's job. There was no question of his returning to the States, which they would at least have done for an infantryman. He was too valuable and still had eleven months of his overseas tour to serve. It might take that long to find a replacement among the Army's scarce Korean interpreters.

"That boy would be better off out of the Army altogether," Philo said one night.

What do you mean?" asked Frazer. "He's a good man." He was surprised at Philo's remark, which had come gratuitously in a conversation about the advantages of Army life. Frazer had been pretending as best he could to agree with the Regular Army sergeant's opinion that the Army was a good career for a man with drive, ambition and ability.

"I mean his kind don't belong. They always cause trouble. Him, Green, that little gook driver. They all candidates for Section Eights."

"His kind?" Frazer asked. Philo, as abruptly as he had opened the line of conversation, closed it by changing the subject to a long and rambling discussion about how to beat speeding tickets in speed-trap towns in Georgia. It had something to do with insurance companies putting up the bail but Frazer, disturbed and edgy, walked out in the middle of it and went over to the officers' mess for a glass of beer. He was very lonely.

By the time Remsen returned from Tokyo, the pipeline was closed. Although the refueling unit never had been recovered — Captain Green believed by now it had been sold to the North Koreans — it had been discovered in action in broad daylight. A group of GIs out hunting pheasant on pine-studded hillsides near Taejon had walked out of a covert of trees into a group of ROK sentries who immediately began firing. Seeking cover, the GIs returned the fire with their shotguns, possibly killing two or three of the ROKs, certainly injuring others. The ROKs retreated and one of the soldiers surreptitiously followed them down the hillside. In the valley was the highway, which at this point crossed a riverbed lying on still lower land. On the dry sandy bed of the river, itself something of a highway in the dry season, stood the refueling unit, a couple of Korean army jeeps and three five-thousand-gallon tank trucks. Soldiers were scrambling all over them, disconnecting the lines and dragging off their casualties. A Korean officer was talking urgently on an ANPRC-10 radio set, probably warning the roadblocks he had set up half a mile on either side of the site to stall the sparse early-morning traffic. It was clear what had been happening. The powerful pumps of the refueling unit were used to transfer the fuel quickly from the pipeline to the tank trucks wherever there was a suitable parking place. The whole operation was presumably timed precisely to the rounds of the US Army guards who patrolled the line. Green calculated that within a half hour the whole thing would have been begun and finished. It was an example of Korean criminal ingenuity at its most refined. Come the conflict next time around, those who knew about it joked, they would make resourceful soldiers. Strong protests were made to the Republic of Korea Chief of Staff, who promised an immediate investigation. The forthcoming report purported to show that the whole operation was planned and executed by Korean soldiers who were selling the fuel on the black market. All of them, it was said, were to be severely punished. It was as good an answer as any. In any case, the pipeline was closed by decision from Japan. Too many Koreans were being killed to keep it running. The troops were withdrawn from guard duty, but recalled when the pipeline itself began to disappear.

*D*espite Remsen's return, Frazer still felt the overpowering sense of uneasiness and loneliness he had experienced during his friend's absence. Whether the change was in him or in Remsen he could not tell. It was summer, late summer. All up and down the Korean roads stood high columns of dust. Soldiers coming in off the highways after even short trips were covered white with the pale fine grit. Their dark eyes burned out of white faces and the sweat from their armpits turned their uniforms to mud. It seemed to Frazer that he was gagging in this dust which stood miles high in an all-encompassing haze that ruined his aerial photos and made each bright, sun-hammered overcast day paradoxically and unbearably bright. Physical contact was repellent and the frequency with which they went to the villages at night became less and less. Instead, they lay around naked in their tent with the side walls rolled up and drank beer they had

chilled in the darkroom cooling unit, Remsen's red scar on his chest turning redder and redder as they drank more and more, his pale eyes brighter and brighter, following Frazer's every move in the tent. Once Frazer woke out of the dream into grey dawn to find Remsen awake sitting up on his cot staring at him reflectively with a look Frazer knew he had seen somewhere before but could not place.

"You were moaning again," said Remsen. He blushed in patches all over his white body, but his scar turned a paler pink. Behind him, a large calendar marked with crosses ticked off the long expanse of time ahead of them.

"It's a dream I have."

"I know."

"Do you?"

"Shit. Let's go to the beach today."

They had discovered the beach while they were working the pipeline. Far up in the Han River estuary it was surrounded and hidden by a stand of pine forest, miraculously saved from the destruction most of the other Korean forests had undergone in this section of the war. All over Korea there were thousands of hills with nothing on them except mud and rocks. Slowly they were being reforested with hip-high pines. The pines around the small sandy beach they had discovered on a set of aerials closed in an almost complete circlet. As a result, the beach was hidden not only from the road, which skirted along the edge of two high hills, but also, to a great extent, from the river as well. From certain angles, however, it was possible to observe the highway from the beach. This was important, because swimming in the Han was forbidden. The water was said to be polluted. But Frazer and Remsen, who had eaten the equally forbidden Korean food for months on the pipeline and in the villages with the whores, who had undergone discomfort, sometimes hardship, while breaking the Army's laws, were certainly not going to worry about breaking them for recreation.

They had been to the beach a few times. They usually brought a couple of girls along with them if it was a weekend and the girls brought food. They would bathe naked in the Han and make love on blankets in an abandoned bunker down near the water's edge. Farther down the river where the bridge crosses from Yung Dung Po into

Seoul, Korean bourgeoisie would be bathing on another beach with European bathhouses, brightly colored umbrellas, children, food-hawkers. Often when they crossed that bridge Frazer thought of the films he had seen of this very neighborhood made only a few years before: the American Army in retreat and thousands of Korean rufugees streaming out of Seoul attempting to cross the bridge until finally the demolition men blew it, crawling as it was with Koreans who had broken through the company of MPs stationed as a rear guard at the other end; or the road which paralleled the Han stacked with Chinese soldiers' bodies like an old-fashioned corduroy lumber road out west, with jeeps and trucks riding over them north, mashing the bodies into the mud. Even now, you could not dig there without turning up bones, uniforms, belt buckles and the rubber-soled sneakers the Chinese soldiers had worn instead of boots. On the beach beneath the bridge occasionally a human body or a piece of it would wash up, turned to adipocere and preserved by the cold running waters—once, Colonel Kim had told them, a perfectly preserved but swollen face still bearing the contorted expression of its death agony.

This time they went to the beach alone. It was afternoon by the time they got there and the sun was quite hot. They swam in the cold river, then lay panting on the blanket in the sun. Frazer, who was quite fair, had managed in the few times they were there to get something of a tan, but Remsen whose body was as white as death neither burned nor really tanned: his freckles grew larger and there appeared in his skin an undertone of tannish grey.

"Oh, this is good," said Remsen, lying on his back, his fingers lightly touching the scar on his chest. It had become a habit with him, touching the round raw scar.

"We should have brought some moose," said Frazer, using the GI argot for girls. Cold water and sun always aroused him.

"No, it's better without them. Don't you ever get tired of moose?"

"Is there something else?" The sun was powerfully bright. The whole clearing was quite still, waiting for something, each grain of sand picked out clearly, each pine needle frozen.

Remsen turned on his side and raised himself on his elbow. Frazer's face was turned toward the path to the road and Remsen.

"Don't you know?"

"I don't know anything." But of course he did know and he knew in that moment by the silence and the expression on Remsen's face and the slightly trembling muscles of his own abdomen that Remsen knew he knew, but would tell him anyway and initiate him finally into the secret. Tentatively, almost shyly, Remsen moved toward Frazer who lay passive on the sand.

a lieutenant of Engineers was standing at the path leading from the road into the clearing, his eyes swollen wide with astonishment and something like horror. Frazer looked up to the highway. An empty jeep stood there. The officer was alone. Frazer reached for his pistol as the lieutenant walked down into the beach. How long had he been standing there? Frazer exchanged a look with Remsen. He knew instantly what he would do and they had agreed without a word or sign passing. Meaningless anyway, thought Frazer, If the lieutenant said one word out of the way he was going to shoot him through the heart, and then they were going to strip his body and bury it in the bunker. It would not be the first time that an officer had been mysteriously shot in Korea, nor the first time one had disappeared to be found perhaps years later, possibly identifiable by his teeth. It was the dry hot season and the body would corrupt quickly, its death smell merging easily into the other smells of the Korean countryside, absorbed lightly into the still present, never transmuted sickish sweet smell of death which hung over the country like the tall, interminable haze. The two naked men stood up.

"Is there something I can do for you lieutenant?" said Frazer quite calmly, pointing the pistol at the officer's heart. And as he looked into the young, green, innocent officer's eyes, he knew what the answer would be. I have been here before: this beach, this river, these trees.

Of course, thought Frazer, as he snapped off the safety and deflected his gaze for one of the moments of that infinite second to Remsen's face and the newly healing round bullet wound scarred on his chest like a surrealistic lichen on a breathing rock. Of course. First the secret. Now the dream.

sunday, april 26, 19

sumerian surmises
at the edge of summe
an ~~illumination~~
at sunset:
remembering the
first golden days
of Daylight
Savings
Time

my first
memory of spring
awninged green
and gold afternoons,
the yellow sun in
the little kitchen
honey and apple
juice ~ so much
time to
play

temp
12°

Bank
Balance:
$275.41

and the birdsong
night

Another Dawn

It was a beautiful room; there was no doubt about that. One wall was a window, facing out onto a fresh lawn which sloped down to a small stream. On the other side of the stream was a mossy dark bank of woods, perhaps the outer edge and beginning of a forest.

The walls were white. So white, in fact, and so reflective of the clear quanta of brilliant sunlight that Frazer's eyes revolted and closed reflexively, retaining on the interior of his eyelids, it seemed, the reversed colors of the wooded window scene. He had, after all, only just awakened as he had not so many times awakened before in a room and bed that were not his own.

How nice, he thought, to wake up in this lovely bright room with this lovely bright girl beside me. Carefully he brushed from his ticklish chest skin the electrical ends of her full black, loose curtain of straight polished hair. Brown and naked, she stirred sleepily against him and said something incomprehensible and pleasantly murmurish: a whispered thought from the whisper of her sleeping dream.

How nice, he thought, to wake up in this Japanese decor and woodland splendor, but what do I do for an encore?

He decided to study the room in order to avoid having to think about the encore. He moved himself up in bed and looked around. I am, he thought, undoubtedly the luckiest fellow on earth to be able to consummate a love affair in such stylish surroundings. A tribute to my good taste, discretion, and luck. Cigarettes. On the night table were cigarettes. He lit one with a match from an Italian-made matchbox with a gimmicky rubber band closing device and the advertisement of The New Starlite French Restaurant.

Still the girl slept. It is her savage simplicity, he thought, enjoying his own sarcasm. They're born with it. Oh, the rhythm of our bodies beating time. But monkeys have to be taught how to make love. Nobody, mused Frazer, in his silent mind, is born with anything except a skinful of cells and chromosomes fighting for a chance to screw up your life. Still, it would be nice to think she was born with it. It would make things so much easier: primitive attraction and all that, no need to think about love or encores, just go down to the quarters and grab off a good, hot, meaningless piece of tight, wet gash.

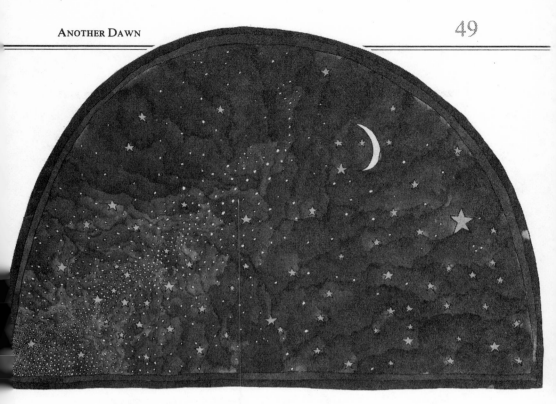

How it had started out in the first place was that he had written a note that might have appeared at the beginning of a story in a slick magazine; though if there was anything he wanted to avoid it was to become the kind of character who inhabits stories in slick magazines.

Up until now, he had avoided it quite successfully. Instead of living in Manhattan, he lived in Jackson Heights; instead of working for a stockbroker or a bank or a publisher, he was a rather highly paid (considering the work and his abilities) socio-economic analyst in a firm which provided various kinds of manufactured facts to producers of contraceptives, suppositories, and patent remedies for women's complaints.

His specialty was suppositories. And he knew they wouldn't even mention that in a story in a slick magazine, though the ads on the facing pages might feature detailed instructions for use and provide accurate and interesting diagrams showing the proper method of insertion. And, of course, when he wrote notes to girls he made sure the proposed relationship had certain socio-

logical significances he didn't want to think about too much. In this, the slick magazines shared his feeling, but for different reasons, mostly commercial and geographic in origin.

Anyway, there he was, assigned to investigate the commercial possibilities of cannabis in the event of a future change in the law and social structure of America, when he saw her. He was in a somewhat foolish mood. For three days he had been reading through scores of recondite and dusty journals searching out the history of intoxicating and exhilarating drugs for the benefit of a tobacco company executive who was forthrightly looking forward to the eventual demise of the cigarette industry.

His assignment: to establish the nature and location of research materials which would enable a fullscale feasibility projection of (a) the economics of commercial marijuana production, (b) the public-relations factors required for the engineering of appropriate legal and social change, and (c) the time-money investment factor versus finding a cure for cancer.

Giddy with the logical insanity of his

I will never get to see it but I have
faith in the ultimate creation of
a study of the handwriting of jules
siegel. siegel scholars please note. ah,
how i love you guys and gals even
before you are born. remember that
you are my children, conceived at
the moment i began to fuck your
ancestors' brains.

i am a master of the art of self=
congratulation.

a guy in omaha, a working man,
told mel that he was married but
felt guilty because he still liked to
jerk off. "that's what it's all about,"
mel told him (says he told him, that
is), "why should you feel guilty about
making love to yourself?" good question! my friend bennett levine used to
say, "99% do it — and the other one % are
liars." the voice of the chochm is a heard
again speaking a chochma. why
doesn't i.b.singer write about instead
of philip roth? notice the mistake.
that's why. he doesn't lose control.
have to respect that as much as
you may hate it.

at last we begin to hit pay dirt!

rah!

★

rah!

3=40

research topic and somewhat intoxicated by the exciting dust of his own depravity, he had looked up from The Journal of Applied Ecstatics into the black irises and dark skin of a perfect girl whose momentarily unfocussed eyes stared at a spot some four inches inside his skull. Before her on the oaken library table was a fat, dusty, occult-looking volume bulging into his peripheral vision.

He looked down at it and read the chapter heading upside down: "Counterpoint and Symbol in *Paradise Lost*. James Whaler." His eyes went back to her perfect face, but quickly turned in flustered retreat to a now totally meaningless paragraph on the page in front of him. Her change of focus had precisely pinpointed on his frozen corneas and her irises were dilated in a full, frank, and exciting stare.

For the next hour they sneaked stares at each other between grabs at half-cooked gobs of turgid information in their respective texts. It seemed to Frazer that one of the varnished putti in the baroque ceiling of the reading room had snapped off a well-aimed dart right into his medulla oblongata. Old-fashioned enough to believe in Cupid's arrows, he was still too enlightened to think that beefy pump, his heart, could be the center of this hand-grenade emotion.

Her left hand, cradled in her lap, was hidden from him. The right hand long, slightly bony fingers, tipped with carefully manicured, strong, ivory-colored nails. At last the beautiful left hand came up out of the recesses and turned a page. No ring. No diamond solitaire. No signal of captivity. Oh perfect olive girl whose naked, ever-so-slightly trembling hand betrayed her knowledge and perhaps response to Frazer's radiating heat waves of desire.

When she got up to pick up a new book from the call desk, he reached over and copped the call slip from her book. On it would be her name, address, and reason for living. Palming the slip, he rose and collecting up his closely written index cards went down to the Automat to eat, relax, and reflect upon this fortuitous hand of cards Fortuna's deal had thrown into the game.

*F*razer had been coached in the techniques of cafeteria galanterie by his friend Mixolydian, a bearded Hungarian novelist, who had, by inferring he

was an escaped Hungarian Freedom Fighter, often in Frazer's presence made connections Doris Day-Rock Hudson comedies would have avoided as unlikely. Mixolydian, for example, had picked up a Lithuanian girl during the intermission of *La Dolce Vita*, disappeared with her into a hotel across the street, and returned her to her frantic, unbelieving boyfriend before the movie was over. As Mixolydian had slipped back into his seat Frazer had asked him, "What is she telling her boyfriend?" A fat Fellini fan in the seat in front of him turned around and gave him a dirty look.

"That she went to the ladies' room to lie down." Frazer had attempted unsuccessfully to choke back an admiring giggle.

The instruction in cafeteria technique had taken place in the garden of the Museum of Modern Art while bearded art students picked their noses and fell in love.

"First," said Mixolydian, "we are going to go into the cafeteria here and buy a cup of coffee. Then we are going to walk around and look for two pretty girls sitting at a table where there are two empty seats."

"Suppose there aren't any?"

"Don't be stupid. Why do you think there is a cafeteria?"

"So hungry people will have a place to eat?" Frazer volunteered, knowing it was probably not the right answer.

"For that, they can go to Lindy's. The reason there is a cafeteria is the same reason there is a Museum of Modern Art."

"To look at pictures?" Frazer offered, wondering if he had perhaps forever lost the line of reasoning.

"Americans!" Mixolydian sighed with particularly Hungarian despair. "So that young women will have a place to meet young men, idiot. Ergo, there will be not only girls but empty seats."

"Oh."

"Now, to continue, we will find a table with two pretty girls who will have made sure to keep two seats empty for us and we will walk up to them and say, 'Pardon me, but are these seats taken?' and then we will sit down, drink our coffee, and make conversation and then we will take them to your apartment and make love to them."

"Look, can we try this out first. You know, like a dry run." Frazer had never attempted to pick up girls before in a cafeteria.

Mixolydian looked at him for a moment

with the fond regard a mother gives a backward child.

"Suppose I play a girl in a cafeteria who lets you sit down, what would you do next?" Mixolydian asked.

"Make conversation."

"Oh yeah? What's your opening line?" Frazer shrugged helplessly. He hadn't thought about that.

"Your opening line is 'Are you waiting for someone?' All right, try again."

"Are you waiting for someone?"

"Yes, My fiance as a matter of fact." Frazer punched his friend in the arm and despaired of ever learning the cafeteria technique. Mixolydian laughed. But later, in the cafeteria, it worked out exactly as he said it would, and Frazer spent the night in the arms of a Barnard girl who confessed to him at four o'clock in the morning that she couldn't stand Ferdinand Leger and had come to the museum really to meet a young man.

It was the first time she had allowed herself to be picked up, she said. Frazer swelled with pride at his accomplishment. And soon he was privileged again to hear her tell him wildly how good, good, good it all was. Some months later, almost out of gratitude, he married her, but after a year he grew tired of her and, when she asked him for a divorce so she could marry some childhood sweetheart of hers who had turned up from the Midwest with a satchel full of money and a patent leather hairdo, he had agreed without much trouble. He understood she was divorced again now and that she wondered why he never called her anymore.

*1*n the Automat, Frazer looked about expectantly for his dark angel. Nowhere was she to be seen. Crestfallen, he stood on one foot, like an Ivy League stork, trying to decide whether to go to the steam table for a delicious Chopped Sirloin Steak or to the banks of little windows for Sandwiches, Cakes, Salads, and Coffee and Milk.

"Excuse me," said a female voice behind him in the tone reserved for the slow, retarded, lame, and blind. Frazer turned around. It was she. Cupid twisted the dart and robbed him of voice. He fled back through the revolving doors over to the Algonquin where he was greeted effusively by the headwaiter, who evidently took him for someone else and seated him immediately.

Bolstered by some stout, Frazer reflected more calmly on his situation. He pulled out the call slip and studied it. It said: "Diane Carver, 1100 Edgecombe Ave. Author: Donald Dorian. Title: *The English Diodatis*. Class Mark. VV-208-p." Attached to the slip was one of those little stickers which tell the various reasons why books are not available. Checked was "missing." So, thought Frazer, a literary girl; therefore, a literary approach. He called for some stationery and, in his neat clear script, wrote:

"Dear Miss Carver: You will perhaps think it strange to receive this note from a stranger, but, then, since it is perhaps as strange for me to write it as for you to receive it, we will already have something in common.

"The reason for the note is simple: that we should remedy this sorry state of affairs in which I find that all I know about you is that you are doing research on John Milton, and all you know about me is that I am some kind of lunatic who writes notes to strange girls.

"I hope that your number is in the telephone book. If it is not, perhaps you will be kind enough to drop me a note and tell me where you can be reached. You will, it is possible, remember me as the one who sat across from you in the library today and stared at you constantly."

Then he wrote his address and signed the letter, addressed the envelope, inserted the letter, sealed it, got up, and paid his bill, leaving the waiter too much of a tip, and mailed the note in a polished, carved, ornate, bronze mailbox between the elevators. It was not until he was out on the street that he realized that he had forgotten to put a stamp on it.

Her telephone number, information told him, was unlisted.

Nonetheless, the letter arrived, though Frazer spent the next two days deciding the whole thing was beneath his dignity. Stay out of compromising situations, said his mind to him, stick with your own kind. Call up the blonde girl from Barnard who lay in your arms all night so many nights and still wants nothing more than to share your bed and, occasionally, a meal at the Four Seasons and a pair of tickets to the theatre. It was not, he thought, exactly pleasant to have spiteful little boys screwing around with your glands and hormones, causing you to write notes to strange girls.

He was particularly worried about having written the note. It was one thing to stare at girls in the library or think about making conversation in automats, but, somehow, did it seem quite *normal* to write notes? It was more like what some crank might do, some nut who actually believed that by the overpowering force of his personality apples would drop off limbs in faraway orchards and golden girls would tumble into waiting arms. Such people

imported from Germany, as was the cologne he splashed all over his body after his shower. He clipped his toenails and manicured his fingernails and brushed his teeth vigorously with a toothpaste designed to keep teeth decay-free. His toothbrush had a rubber tip on it for massaging the gums and this he did carefully, for fear of the calculus that might, some day, cause these useful, handsome, bony teeth of his to fall out of his head like leaves from an autumn tree.

Thus scrubbed, shining, deodorized, and perfumed, dressed in a suit of 12-ounce

I wonder if there is any one who collects trip books. It would be no stranger than collecting paintings.

should be locked up, thought Frazer, and he wondered if, indeed, his honey-colored passion might not take fright like the skittish doe she was and call the police to rid her of this stalking hunter in the city forest. It would serve him right.

On the third day he arrived home from his office and found in his mailbox a small white envelope addressed in a rather large and regular script. The note inside had engraved gray initials at the top. It said:

"Dear Mr. Frazer: I'm sorry, but I don't usually go out with strange men. But since you now owe me 5¢ postage due and I'm a poor working girl, perhaps you will find some way to reimburse me."

And then she gave him her telephone number and added a neat postscript, "You *did* stare mercilessly, impertinent man."

So he called her anyway. And it turned out that she had a little girl and couldn't go out too much because of the expense of baby sitters, but he would be welcome to come up to her apartment some evening if he didn't mind simply sitting around talking and listening to records. Mind? No, he wouldn't mind at all.

On the afternoon of the appointed day, Frazer began his preparations by picking up his shirts from the Chinese laundry. Custom-made were the shirts, and when, like Antony, he had shaved three times over, the shaving lotion he applied to his skinned but now baby-smooth face was

English worsted, wearing boned leather shoes and long wool socks that stayed up miraculously and neatly without garters, Frazer stepped out into the night air feeling somewhat like the Green Knight out looking for the Green Giant: he might lose his head, but that was the bargain and who knew what honor might result? In a moment of inspiration he stepped into the liquor store and bought a bottle of cold champagne and then in a big comfortable Checker cab sped off into the falling evening on his exhilarating and lonely quest. He had not even bothered to ask Mixolydian for advice.

She lived in an apartment building on Edgecombe Avenue, one of those huge buildings put up before the First World War, when money bought heavy soundproof walls and concrete floors covered with walnut parquet, big rooms with fireplaces and many baths, kitchens with gigantic pantries. It had seen its best days, but even now was still elegant and, perhaps, a little bit pretentious, despite the fact that most of the apartments had been cut in half.

The neighborhood had run down, but, to Frazer's experienced and sophisticated eye, it was still pretty good.

In her building, the carpeting in the lobby was a little worn but clean, the brass on the elevator doors was carefully polished and had fresh white lines of Noxon sticking in the cracks like accidental caulking. The elevator man wore a gray uniform with the address of the building embroidered in gold thread on his breast pocket. Before he would take Frazer up he called the apartment to get permission.

"Come in," she said. Frazer, who had stood there looking at her for a couple of heartbeat moments, smiled, stepped over the threshold, and held out his spangled and giftwrapped bottle of *Lanson 1953.*

"Here," he said, "I thought we should begin by celebrating."

"Oh, aren't you sentimental. How nice. How very nice. I love champagne." And, looking up at him, she gave him now the bright clear smile of instant rapport. "Let me put it in the refrigerator." She took his hand as she led him into the kitchen, and when he turned her again to look at her and they examined each other happily for a few silent seconds they laughed together, short delicious laughter like that of children sharing a secret. He would have leaned over to kiss her and taken the chance of spoiling or starting everything, but, as if she sensed his thought, she moved almost accidentally away, chattering lightly about the champagne.

The evening was successful, too successful. They listened to records, of which she had a huge collection, looked at art books, talked to each other about each other.

She had been divorced about a year. Her husband, who made a great deal of money, had let her keep the apartment and paid the rent as part of the divorce settlement. She worked as a secretary to a professor of English at Columbia and was studying for her master's in English at night.

He told her about the Barnard girl who had been his wife and about his job and the marijuana assignment, and they laughed together again at the foolishness of the depraved world outside. He told her he thought she was beautiful, and she told him she had never met anyone so clever before. So engrossed were they that they almost forgot the champagne.

"Are you hungry?" she asked.

"Starving. I forgot to eat dinner."

"Let's have caviar and toast and drink the champagne."

In the kitchen, she told him about her husband, a fairly famous jazz musician.

"I was living in Chicago. You know: 17 years old, first year in college, hating

my parents. He was playing a club downtown, visiting with his aunt—my mother's cousin. He had some kind of English car and a big dog and a lot of money; the whole thing. And, of course, he was so much older and dignified and, you know, hip, that I thought he wouldn't even look at me. But we went to the beach, and I guess he looked at me and well—" she laughed a little, indicating her body, which was a bit better than the better photographers' models.

"So you got married."

"I didn't know what else to do. Here I was just out of braids practically, and this sporting life takes me over. You know, I hadn't even let a boy touch me *there* and suddenly I was in bed with him. He had to teach me everything, and then I just wanted to get away from home and all. We got married about a month later, and I thought my mother didn't know anything, but we were waiting for the car to come and we were alone, and she said to me, 'Diane, if you ever get so you want to come home, don't let anything stop you.' When I did go home after we split, she told me she had seen us one night on the living room couch when we thought she was asleep." She drank down the rest of her glass of champagne and stood up. "Let's go back into the living room."

On the way, she stopped to look in at her daughter. She beckoned Frazer into the room. He sat down on the bed facing the child's and looked down into the sleeping little girl's face. Her mouth was open just a trifle. She had her mother's straight, black hair, but her skin was a shade darker, rather more tawny than olive. Her small regular features were calm, dreamless, unafraid . . . innocent.

He came so rarely into contact with innocence. Had he ever been innocent himself? He sensed a powerful force streaming through the room like a magnetic field, emanating from the child's innocence and inexorably tying him to this young woman who stood above him with her hand draped over his shoulder, her eyes, he felt, watching his face rather than the child's.

He could almost verbalize what he felt: leave and never see her—miss the experience; sleep with her soon—part in tears; marry her later—live in sorrow. All possibilities seemed, he thought, to be bringers of unhappiness, in exchange for which they held out this overpowering and beautiful emotion which he felt pressing up upon him like a black, soundless, slick-surfaced · but terribly turbulent tide.

When they walked into the living room he was melancholy.

"Come sit on my lap," he said with such ease and naturalness that he thought it was the champagne speaking, but realized with some slight surprise and small admiring fear that it was himself. He held out his arms, and she curled herself against his body, looking at him silently with alert expectant eyes. He could feel a slight tremor in her hands.

"What's to become of us, Diane?"

"What do you mean?"

"I mean, what's to become of us all. Your daughter, me, you, all those people out in the street, the gangs in the park, the cops beating them on the head, the guys who stood on the other corner and stared at me when I got out of the cab. All of us, Diane. What's going to happen to all of us?"

"You learn not to think about it."

"And that's the answer. Don't think about it?"

"Please, just for now, don't think about it . . ."

They kissed. First a short dry kiss, a little bit awkward. Then a softer kiss somewhat longer in which her lips opened a little beneath his and moved on his mouth. Then a long, hot, exciting, deep kiss in which they tasted each other's mouths, and his hands, moving lightly against her breasts, felt the sharp and delicate flutter of her rapid, animal heart.

When he went home his body was excited and unrelieved. His back ached down near his butt, and his mouth was beginning to dry out in anticipation of the hangover of a half-bottle of champagne on a practically empty stomach. She had stood in the doorway, her hair falling over her face and her sweater rumpled, and they had kissed again and again until finally she had pulled away and said, "I don't usually kiss my dates on the first night."

"Well, look. If I promise not to kiss you, will you let me sleep with you?"

"Go away, you silly boy. Go away and let me think about that tonight."

"Goodnight, Diane."

"Goodnight . . ."

They saw each other regularly in the weeks after that. But it was an uncon-summated love affair. "We can't do it here in the house," she'd say as they lay on the couch almost naked, fearful of the child's waking, and she wouldn't come to his apartment at first. When she did come, she was suffering, she claimed, from miasmic fears of pregnancies and abortions and, despite Frazer's protestations of great technical competence in matters of birth control, they merely lay in each other's arms naked through the night like Tristram and Iseult. But, somehow, despite the real pain that often resulted from this unrelieved almost adolescent passion, he secretly seemed to prefer it this way. As long as they didn't take that final knowledge, final step, they were free to part—no promises, no vows, or so he had thought on the few occasions when he let himself think about anything but experiencing the emotion.

Because he knew what it was all about, that it wasn't false chastity but perhaps the suddenly renewed virginity that makes even a prostitute fight an alien rapist in an occupied country, he couldn't bring himself to press her as hard as aching veins were urging him.

When he did press her, bitter things happened. On the night in which she had come to his apartment, he had made a steak, which they ate with a bottle of wine and a green salad. She praised his cooking; later he praised her unclothed body which he held in his hands and touched with his mouth like a piece of tender fruit he had been forbidden to bite.

"You know," he said, "you have the most beautiful breasts in the world."

"No I don't. They're not big enough," she complained, indicating her smallish but round globes, which had the slight lovely droop and big aureoles that come from bearing a child and nursing it. He bent over her and kissed first one nipple then the other.

"I think they're beautiful. You'd rather look like a cow? And they taste delicious. And I love the rest of you, too." He ran his hands over her buttocks, then more exploratively.

"Stop that. What do you like the best?"

He raised on his elbow and looked at her. "I like your skin the best, because it's clear and clean and it's you."

"So strange, you like it, but I wish I could strip it off my body!" And she turned from him and wept.

A few days later Mixolydian called and invited him to a party. "Bring a friend," he said. "It's going to be Fasching in New York."

She had sent the child out to Chicago to visit with her mother, who had been pleading for some time to have her grandchild with her for a while. Frazer had rented a car to take the little girl to the airport and kept it in anticipation of a drive on the weekend.

Alone now, it seemed to be understood between them that tonight they would finally enjoy each other in totality. But the anticipation put them both on edge and often during the evening she lapsed into that peculiar, hard drawl she used when she wanted to put him for some period of time outside her world, to drive home to him how different their worlds really were.

To the party, she wore a cream-colored, floor length, empire dress deeply cut at the bosom, and her long hair was bound up in a smart French knot. When they walked in the door there was a clearly distinguishable drop in the noise level, then a sudden rise. A band was playing dance music, uniformed waiters were circulating good liquor, and on the huge half-lit terrace overlooking Central Park couples were dancing. On long tables were piled platters of food, and behind one stood a mustachioed chef in tall hat and white uniform carving a gigantic brown roast into thick, bloody slices. People were eating, laughing, telling stories, dancing, drinking, smoking cigars, pipes and cigarettes, making eyes at each other, and beginning or contemplating all kinds of mockery, mayhem and murder. They looked for Mixolydian.

"*Edmeg au shegimet,*" said Frazer when he found him, "you dirty Hungarian refugee."

"*Ozopod fossa,*" answered Mixolydian, who took great pride in the number and variety of disgusting Hungarian expressions he had taught his friend, "Fascist bastard." And he looked down into Diane's bosom with the friendly appreciative manner of a connoisseur and good friend. Evidently he liked what he saw, for he looked quickly at Frazer and said, "Are you going to introduce me to this beautiful young lady or do I have to dishonor her modesty by introducing myself?"

"Diane Carver, meet Zoltan Mixolydian. He is a disreputable Hungarian drunk and

not to be trusted with anything valuable."

"I'm sure it's a lie," said Diane, "I'm really pleased to meet you, Mr. Mixolydian. I think your book was marvelous . . . "

"Come quick. Tell it to my publisher. And call me Tom." He linked his arms with theirs and hustled them over to where his publisher, the host, was listening to his lawyer expound on their latest case in the obscenity courts.

"What can I do with a book like this?" declaimed the lawyer, waving his drink dangerously. "Personally, I think it's plain dirty. I mean, after all, there is a limit."

"Please, Mr. Rainbow," said Mixolydian, "you are talking about a work of art, with great literary and social merit and, above all, commercial success. We writers must eat, you know. Books banned by customs never make the best seller list. What's the name of the book this time?"

"You, you son-of-a-bitch, what the hell do you know about artistic merit? What do you think, that because some poor slob in New Jersey gets arrested for selling a book to a teen-ager that makes it automatically art? You guys are all alike. You take a couple of chapters out of Krafft-Ebbing, fill them in with underprivileged dope addicts and homosexuals, and you think it's art. I think it's dirty."

"Well then, why do you seem to specialize in these matters?" asked Mixolydian. "Surely there are enough corporations in trouble with the SEC for you to make a living without contributing to the moral decline of Western civilization?"

"Because I have the misfortune to be on retainer to this guy here," the lawyer said, indicating the publisher, who grinned proudly, "and he has found the magic formula for success: Find a good dirty book with an international reputation, line up the editor of the Paris Review and a few literary geniuses from Yale, Harvard, and Northwestern, and bring out a new edition with a foreword by Edmund Wilson. Result: The copies the teen-agers and sex-starved don't buy are snapped up by the readers of the New Leader."

"My dear Rainbow," said Mixolydian, "surely you don't expect us to believe that you will handle these cases purely because of your relationship with this vulgar gentleman. Where is your integrity? Are you so easily selling your soul for a mess of porridge?"

1:36 a.m. Saturn was favorably aspected yesterday. Today Mars and Uranus are in good aspect = a good time for getting things started or finished [mars gives energy]; and [through Uranus, the planet of change] for dealing with novel ideas, studying the occult and astrology, working with imagination, experimentation with ESP.

"It's birthright and pottage."

"Excuse me. Sometimes I have trouble with your English language," said Mixolydian, who, in fact, had not spoken more than a few sentences of Hungarian, excluding curses, since he was eight or nine years old. "Nonetheless, you know what I mean."

"Yes, I know what you mean." Rainbow paused and drank deeply from his glass, which appeared to be filled with a great deal of whiskey and very little soda. To Frazer, who with his arm about Diane watched and listened silently, it seemed that perhaps the lawyer had had a great deal to drink already.

The lawyer wiped his mouth with the back of his hand. "Let me tell you," he said, "let me tell you. I do it because I am the only honest person in this whole bunch. I love this country. I love the law. You see what it is, the law. It is a great structure. It reflects our best image of ourselves and our worst.

"And the law says there shall be freedom of speech, which I think really means that you, Zoltan Mixolydian, can go out on a street corner and say 'shit' if you like as long as you carry a sign that says, 'I say dirty words,' so that people can avoid you

if they want. The law really means freedom of speech, because if it doesn't mean it then this fag who wrote a letter to a friend telling him how much better he liked making it with him than with his wife really can be arrested. And they can persecute this comedian, what's his name, in Chicago because he makes dirty jokes about Christianity. And the racists can take Ginzburg to court because he puts out a magazine in which appears for the first time in the whole history of the world a picture of a black man and a white woman pressed up against each other . . ."

Everybody looked at Diane and Frazer. "Oh well," said Mixolydian, breaking the momentary silence as Rainbow blushed violently, embarrassed at his own vehemence and, he thought, his own lack of discretion and tact. "I suppose you are right. Myself, I feel that people with dirty minds are entitled to read. It's better for them than watching television, anyway. You know my newest book don't you? It will be the world's best-selling novel—*1001 Things To Do With Girls*."

Everybody laughed, and Frazer grabbed a drink from a waiter who had been standing bug-eyed listening to the conversation. Mixolydian turned his attention to a cute, short-haired, little girl in a villagey dress who had been waiting patiently for him to notice her and pick her up. Which he did, and, before long, the two couples were making their way tortuously to the dance floor. The Hungarian managed to brush her breast as he took her in his arms and moved into the dance. The girl smiled knowingly and leaned up and whispered into his ear.

Frazer and Diane danced silently at first. The band played a fox trot. She leaned her head against his shoulder in the melancholy way she had when things were moving through her secret mind.

"What's the matter?" he asked.

"Nothing. Really nothing. But you see how it is. Do you want this forever?"

"I don't know what I want. Shall I lie to you and tell you, 'Yes. Anything. Forever,' when I don't really know?"

"No, I don't want you to lie to me, but I thought maybe you would surprise me, that you would be more than you can ever be."

"You're not fair."

"The world isn't fair, boy. It isn't fair that we should be separated by a couple of thousandths of an inch of skin, but that's the way it is. That's the way it really is. Go tell Rainbow about this, and let him do something in court. No structure of the law for us. We're outside the law."

"Yes, we are. We're alone. Look at the rest of them. Individuals. Moving around like aimless molecules bouncing off each other. They should call it the Brownian Dance. But we've escaped . . ."

"Escaped into what?"

"We're out in the universe. Look at the stars—dust, sparkling dust. We're moving together on the same orbit, and the rest of those stars are standing there aimlessly watching us take off in a perfect pattern of time and space."

"You talk too much. All it is is statistics. You hang around long enough, anything will happen, even a fluke like this. But it never lasts." And as the band began a mambo she took up the lead and he followed her into an intricate series of steps called The Chase.

They left early.

"Where are we going?" she asked in the car, lolling back and letting the wind blow her hair as she unpinned it.

"To my place."

"Oh?" She looked at him somewhat speculatively, a trace of anticipatory smile tugging lightly at the edges of the annoyed lines gathering about her mouth.

"I want to change." His shirt and suit had become somehow too confining for him. "Then we'll got for a drive. Maybe get a hamburger or something."

"Well, then, after you've changed I want to come back to my place and change, too."

At his apartment, she settled herself on his couch and lazily leafed through a copy of Glamour while she waited for him to dress.

In his bedroom he stripped and put on a pair of tight blue jeans, a soft worn shirt, and an old cashmere sport jacket cut a long time ago in Hong Kong.

"There's a review of Tom's book in here," she said when he came out of the room. She looked at him in frank appraisal, "You know you're really not bad looking at all. Why you're almost as handsome as Mixolydian."

"I'll break your neck." And he grabbed her with mock violence, tearing the magazine out of her hand. "It's a lousy review. It only says the novel is the greatest literary event of the year. He's unhappy because it didn't say of all time."

"Why are you so jealous of him?"

"I'm not jealous of him personally. I'm just envious because he makes girls on the first night out and I have to fool around with crazy chicks like you."

"Poor baby. Let momma make it better," she said, groping him with sarcastic tenderness. He was annoyed and moved sharply to get up, but instead she pulled him down again and kissed him, searchingly, coolly, slowly, with infinite relaxation and absence of urgency as though she were merely tasting him like a gourmet tasting wine. He put his hand up into her dress, touching the flesh above her stocking.

"No," she said. "Not now. I want to change."

"Diane, please—don't be afraid of me. I love you."

"You've never said that before. Say it again."

"I love you."

"You're lying."

From her apartment, they drove up the West Side Highway. A huge sign on the other side of the Hudson flashed SPRY. The roller coaster of an amusement park was outlined in lights. Farther up were the Palisades, cliffs of basalt formed sometime ages ago, he guessed, when the flow of lava met the river and froze. Then came the new luxurious apartment houses of Riverdale, middle-class giants standing oppressively and somehow self-consciously on the riverbank among the small ruins of bygone estates and palaces.

Soon they were speeding up the Saw Mill River Parkway into the populated wilderness of the far suburbs. It was a clear moonless night. Spring had come only a few days before with sudden warmth as

stronger, I used to have an unhappy love affair like this every day or every week anyway. In fact, I still have them. When you are in the office working, I'm home making love to my secretary."

"You're probably telling the truth. Have you ever made it with a colored girl?"

Frazer turned to look at her. Her face was quite innocent and composed, but had an expression of rather prurient curiosity sneaking around the corners of her mouth and eyes.

"No," he lied. "I have never made it with a colored woman, and why do you have to ask questions like that?"

The Gentle 57 25 The Unexpected

though the season would fly headlong into summer wihout pause for the gentle days he had longed for throughout the dismal snowless winter.

At first they were silent. Then she recited poetry:

"Nymphs and shepherds, dance no more . . ."

"*Arcades*. Milton." he said.

"How clever you are. Did you know that Housman called them the most significant and melancholy words of poetry in the English language."

"Why?"

"Because they made the hairs on his face stand up if he recited them while he was shaving. Something like that. Do you really think we are suited to each other?"

"Yes I do."

"How do you know?"

"Because you make the hairs on my face stand up when I'm shaving. I figure you'll save me ten dollars worth of shaving cream a year."

"You're a bad guy. You like me all right, but it has nothing to do with the hair on your face. How many other girls have you made love to?"

"None. You're the first one."

"Don't fool with me; tell me the truth."

"I have made love to many girls. In fact, when I was an adolescent and much

"Because most boys have their first time with colored girls. That's the role of the colored race, you know, to provide white boys with sexual experience so they can be good lovers for their lily-white wives. When was the first time for you?"

"Look, what difference does it make?" He was being roasted, he felt, for something he had never done. My God, he thought, I've never even *thought* the word colored for most of my life.

"Oh none, none at all baby. Don't mind me. Just drive the car."

He slowed the car down and looked around. Somehow they had wound up on the New York State Thruway. Above them on a hill were the night-softened pagoda-like shapes of a famous motel.

"Look," he said, pulling the car up onto the greensward by the highway, "let's go back and forget the whole thing. I leave you alone and you leave me alone."

"Is that what you want?" She looked at him with shimmering eyes, about to cry.

"No, baby, you know that isn't what I want. It's just that you're digging at me. If I didn't love you, I wouldn't care, but I do love you, and you're cutting my heart out."

"You really love me, Frazer?"

"Yes, I really love you." And he took her in a long langorous kiss, tears running down her face and mixing into their mouths so that the taste of the kiss was salt. He stroked her breasts and her flanks and pressed his open mouth against her neck, his face wet with her bitter flowing tears. "I love you and I will always love you and I will defend you against the world," he whispered into her neck and he was no longer sure that the tears he felt were hers alone.

"Then take me someplace and make love to me and make me forget there's a difference between us." She pulled a tissue out of her pocket and wiped her face and blew her nose and smiled at him and reached over and grabbed him in the crotch.

"Hey, hey," he said, and ground the car into gear, ripping out onto the highway leaving two black tracks of raped turf on the mall.

So they had wound up in the fancy motel, where Frazer had to tip the desk man ten dollars to give them the "last" thirty-dollar room. But it was a beautiful room. They couldn't have asked for more.

In the room, Frazer lay expectantly on the bed waiting for her. The drapes were drawn, and it was very dark. All he could see of her was the shadow of her form as she stepped out of her clothing and hung it neatly in the closet and then went into the bathroom for interminable moments. Strange, he thought, that he should wind up making love in Oriental decor again, remembering what had actually been his first time, in Korea, when Mixolydian, who had been assigned to a public-relations post in Seoul, had taken him, country boy, raw recruit, from a military intelligence detachment up near the DMZ to a good whorehouse where he wouldn't get a dose of clap.

He had made love with his boots on to a small girl who seemed no more than 16 years old. She had said to him before he began, "Take it easy, GI. I had a long day." And he had taken it easy, but it wasn't much at all. Later, in Japan, smart sensitive Japanese girls had taught him love's pleasure, but he couldn't remember any of those faces, just the pretty Korean girl in the good whorehouse who had gently taken his virginity without knowing he was offering it to her, while Mixolydian laughed in another room as two whores made love to him at once.

Diane came back into the room, and

before she turned out the bathroom light he saw again how beautiful her body was and loved the clear, clean, olive tone of her smooth supple skin, and there was no time at all for talk or thought.

Only later, as they stood naked on the balcony outside the big window, watching the first pink touch of dawn stroke the night sky, did he say, "Baby, I love you. It's too soon, but baby baby I love you and I want it to be forever and I've never said it like this before."

And they went back into bed, and she made him pretend she was his nigger whore and held his fifty dollars in her hand until she dropped them by the side of the bed while she did all kinds of interesting and exciting things to him, and he did similar things to her, and their hearts exploded, and they slept.

On the floor now lay the fifty dollars, but she was sleeping still as the sunlight spilled into the white room, and Frazer smoked his cigarette and lay there and thought.

He closed his eyes again and measured his slow breathing against the rapid rising and falling of the girl's breasts. She slept so deeply, yet her breaths outnumbered his. Strange, it always struck him, that their delicate respiration should be so much quicker than a man's. Perhaps it was the reason for the basic discordance. Yet last night, and now the memory was defined, it seemed they hit rhythms that for some incalculable moments synchronized their movements against another movement, against the headlong plunge of galaxies in space, so that when the rhythm exploded and the stars broke he felt for just a moment they had touched a universal pulse and died in it.

Forever, thought Frazer. He had said forever, and, well, maybe he meant it, maybe he meant it, indeed. He snuffed out the cigarette. He turned to her and pressed his face close into her hair and fell asleep again, drifting down into a deep pool while a hollow echoing thought followed him down. It seemed to be Mixolydian's voice calling after him, "But what about an encore, boy, what about an encore?" But Frazer slept, and the sunlight poured into the white room while in the black edge of the forest outside strange dark birds sang mournful melodies of death.

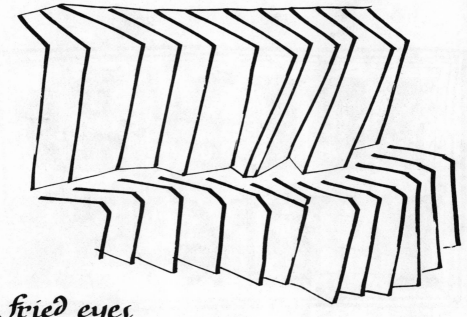

fried eyes,

Space 24

not space village

The Big Beat

Snapping, crackling, her body wired directly into 1100 watts of amplifiers through which the Yardbirds were pouring crazy electronic sounds you never heard before in your life, the blonde girl with pleurisy and all kinds of terrible troubles was finally, once and for all, alive.

All evening she had been moping around with dead marble eyes, choking out awful racking coughs, and languishing through dinner, drinks, marijuana, amphetamines, brilliant conversation—everything. Downbeat to the depths of her sorrowful soul, she wasn't moving out of her depression for anything but massive shock treatments in a class-A mental hospital.

But then at midnight at a party in the Hollywood Hills, in a room as big as a small garage, the music had begun. It was like standing in front of howitzers—blast after blast of wonderful noises crushing the hot cigarette air into some kind of supercharged electronic plasma that reverberated through the blood, creeping into every dead cell, flushing out poisons that could have devastated entire cities if unleashed in concentrated form. And there she was—without pleurisy, without thought, without, in fact, anything but shock waves of rhythm and blues—*alive.*

It is, of course, the sound of the big beat and, like everything else important, it sneaked into the country and took over while I was out of town. In the thirteen months of 1955-1956 I spent in Korea sleeping with whores, dreaming about the deliciousness of life in America—television, ice cream, fresh milk, paved roads, central heating, white-limbed girls who did it willingly for nothing—we kept hearing about it, but there was no place in Seoul you could find the sound they were calling rock and roll. We knew something was happening, but we didn't know what it was.

Then I was back home and a bump-and-grind maniac with a guitar was screaming "Don't Be Cruel," and the little beautiful girls with their skinny legs and tight round behinds were going crazy over what led to 110 million Elvis Presley records by 1965. Rock and roll accounted for eighty percent of all the records on the Top 40 list.

Since then, there has been no retreat. Divisions of commando units with names like Wayne Fontana and the Mindbenders, the Supremes, the Ronettes, the Shirelles, the Four Seasons, Cannibal and the Head-hunters, the Nightcrawlers, Paul Revere and the Raiders, the Lovin' Spoonful, The Rascals marched into the radio stations and set up command posts for the big revolution.

Despite deadly counterattacks by Bing Crosby fans hurling mind-destroying *White Christmas* LPs, they have not been ousted. The forces of counterrevolution have been defeated. In 1965 the instrument of surrender was signed by the Government of the United States and Murray the K led occupation armies into the White House. Victory day was officially celebrated on national television with a 90-minute rock and roll show sponsored by the poverty program.

It is easily the best thing that has ever happened to America, and in marvelously strange ways it is tied in with a whole network of psychic changes in the matrix of our society: integration, psychoanalysis, Zen Buddhism, LSD, draft-card protests, war babies. It is as if the electronic amplifiers and the flat guitars are wired right into some kind of homogenous Zeitgeist surging through the minds of everybody under forty and blasting out along the airwaves.

For the teenagers, to whom it really belongs, it is just another part of their way of life, something they do very naturally, like making love or wearing ankle-length Granny dresses. The war is far away; money comes easily; there is no memory of a time when it was not like this. But for those who remember the terrible, arid years of Eisenhower, the crew-cut college campuses with the serious, so serious GIs, the married students, the silent fraternity of McCarthy-pertrified academics, this music-filled air of today is clean and sparkling as wet grass. Contraceptive pills and prosperity and rock and roll have given us freedom. A generation made dead has come alive.

To understand you have to go back to the black slaves who brought it over. Forty-five million of them died in the passage from Africa to the New World, and the survivors who got here were as close to being dead as any forcibly transported people in history, only there was no real chance for recovery. Give them good red beans to eat, water, better living quarters than even the crew, and still they insisted on dying. It was costing a lot of money.

Then somebody discovered that if you made the slaves sing and dance they somehow stayed alive. Just plain exercise was no good—it had to be the Twist, the Jerk and the Watusi, only the real originals. The result has been described by Daniel Mannix and Malcolm Cowley in their book *Black Cargoes:*

After the morning meal came the joyless ceremony called "dancing the slaves." "Those who were in irons," says Dr. Thomas Troccter, surgeon of the 'Brookes,' in 1783, "were ordered to stand up and make what motions they could, leaving a passage for such as were out of irons to dance around the deck."

Dancing was prescribed as a therapeutic measure against suicidal melancholy and also the scurvy—although in the latter case it was a useless torture for men with swollen limbs. While sailors paraded around the deck, each with a cat-o-nine-tails in his right hand, the slaves "jumped in their irons until their ankles were bleeding flesh."

Music was provided by a slave thumping on a broken drum or an upturned kettle or an African banjo if there was one aboard, or perhaps by a sailor with a bagpipe or a fiddle. The slaves were also told to sing. Said Dr. Claxton after his voyage in the 'Young Hero', "They sing but not for their own amusement. The captain ordered them to sing and they sang songs of sorrow. Their sickness, fear of being beaten, their hunger and the memory of their country are the usual subjects."

Through all kinds of evolutionary changes it is this music you are hearing on WMCA, KHJ or any of the Top 40 stations throughout the country. It gave birth to Dixieland, and Orson Welles recognizing the irony of the rich dancing to misery, put it in *Citizen Kane* in a nighttime picnic scene in which gowned and sequined ladies dance with tuxedoed men as a black man wails, "It can't be love, because it feels so good," while Kane and his idiot wife argue in a nearby tent.

But Dixieland today is a curiosity for banjo parlors like Your Father's Moustache in Greenwhich Village or McGoo's on Hollywood Boulevard. Instead, in the Ondine, Arthur, Whisky A Go Go, Daisy, Rudolf Nureyev is Frugging Sybil Burton's brains out.

What happened to produce this great

noise of the Sixties is that in the late Twenties and early Thirties Dixieland music became big-band music, and it began to die. Huge bands with instrumentation like a symphony orchestra only heavier on the brass and including that concert-hall anathema, the saxophone, toured the country stirring up trouble. Glenn Miller, Glen Gray, Woody Herman, the Dorsey Brothers, Harry James and Benny Goodman took the jazz of improvization and forced it into the locomotive rolling beat of the big band, riding steadily along in a powerful drive along tracks as carefully planned and arranged as any railroad. This was the only really nationally popular adult music of the Thirties, Forties and, before the rock revolution, the Fifties.

But, as brilliant, slick and beautiful as the big band was, it was also death on the real feeling of jazz which is constant change through improvization. And it was no place for the great performer to show how marvelous he was. What was the fourteenth saxophone player in Glen Gray's Casa Loma Band supposed to do, hang a flag on the bell of his axe so that his girlfriend could tell he was playing? The result was the small groups of the postwar period—combos of bass, piano, clarinet or sax, vibes and so on. When Shelly Mann, Dave Brubeck, the Modern Jazz Quartet, Thelonious Monk, Bud Powell, Max Roach, Dizzie Gillespie or Charlie Parker blew, you knew who was blowing.

But what they were blowing was ice chipped and breaking into stunningly brittle and yet liquid glissandos of abstract sound. They cut down to the heart of jazz in one way, but at the same time they were doing something very strange and dead, like what the Bauhaus did to modern architecture, and then, as the progressive jazzmen went further and further into outer space, like what the abstract expressionists did to painting. There was nothing but color and line and if there was any melodic organization it was so subtle that only computers could discover it.

It was the music of the cool, and the college kids of the late Forties and early Fifties were so cool you could hardly believe they could walk and talk. The drug of choice for all these icy babies was always an opium derivative—one nice flash of warmth and then you were so removed, so confident, so nice and lovely and far

away that anything that was reaching you was nothing, just nothing at all. Even your own thoughts were totally refrigerated, glacial.

During this same terrible time, teenage music and popular music were degenerating into something so awful that Hieronymous Bosch would have had difficulty making it graphic. The major sources of hits seem to have come from three areas: Broadway shows, motion-picture musicals and the novelty factories of Tin Pan Alley.

I have completely blocked most of them out of my mind, and it would take hypnotic suggestion of the most powerful persuasion to bring them back. But among the more incredibly traumatic which have stayed with me, I seem to remember things like "Flatfoot Floogie (with Floy, Floy)," "Mairzy Doats," "The Anniversary Waltz," "Racing with the Moon," "Dance Ballerina Dance," "Josephina Please Don't Leana upon the Bell," "That's My Desire," "I Left My Heart at the Stage Door Canteen," and "The House I Live In."

But fortunately there was another kind of music bubbling around. In fact, there were three other kinds of popular music which occasionally sneaked onto the hit parades of the time: rhythm and blues, country and western, and the aforementioned and dread "pop."

There was also a beginning kind of folk-trend, but it was very ethnically and socially oriented, with great emphasis on the gypsy songs of Transylvania, the 17th century roots of "Barbara Allen," and the proletarian role in mass revolutionary songs of economic yearning. It was very much a specialty and if there were twelve records sold off college campuses, it would have been announced in the Proceedings of the Modern Language Association.

Of these, it is rhythm and blues, with overlays of country and western, and finally, within the past several months, folk that has become the music of our time. Slowly, and then with increasing speed and force, as Dixieland became bigband jazz and then went into a manneristic phase in which songs were created out of pure shellac by people who had studied under Irving Berlin and flunked out, rhythm and blues outflanked everybody and successively conquered country and western, pop, and folk.

First it was Deep South blues with the

added massive rhythms of gospel music, but then, after the war, came the electric guitars, bass and drums. Muddy Waters, Chuck Berry, Bo Diddley and John Lee Hooker were just driving everybody who was listening crazy. In Cleveland, Alan Freed was listening and then he was playing it on white stations and calling it "rock and roll," other people called it "race" or "sepia," but once white people began to hear it, it started to move.

Slowly it began to infiltrate the white market. Teen-age music was not so homogeneous that it could not find a place for the thrilling sounds of rock and roll. The first real rock and roll breakthrough took place in 1954 when "Hucklebuck," "Long Gone," "Pink Champagne," all by the Crows, smashed through.

But to a great extent the "race" songs that made the hit parade were reworked by white performers. Hank Ballard's "Work with Me Annie" was redone almost note for note as "Dance with Me Henry" by Georgia Gibbs. Chuck Berry's "Maybelline" was sung by Pat Boone and became a hit.

In 1954, Bill Haley's "Rock Around the Clock" started to take off and went on to become the best-selling nonseasonal record of all time with a total sale to date of more than 15 million copies. But nobody was taking it very seriously. The full assault had not yet begun.

Then, in 1956, came Elvis. It started out to be a big year for foreign instrumentals, with things like "Lisbon Antigua," "The Poor People of Paris," and "Portuguese Washerwoman" doing the big job and one-third to one-half the chart covered by rock and roll numbers. What Presley did was combine country and blues into something so wild that millions of kids all over the country and in foreign lands just wigged out, and from then on it was really all over. "Heartbreak Hotel" was number one on all three charts—the first time it had ever been done—and the walls were down.

They have never been successfully rebuilt, although for a while it looked as if the Philadelphia sound promoted by Dick Clark and his singing midgets was going to do the work that armies of enraged adults found impossible. It is very possible that, if the Beatles and Motown Records had not come to save our souls, the whole rock and roll thing might have been put right out of business by Frankie Avalon, Fabian, Bobby Rydell, Rickie Nelson and all the other pompadour shakers.

Counterattacks by Chubby Checker and the Twist held the fort and, then, in the nick of time, arrived the Beatles, with longer hair than anyone had worn since Prince Valiant, electronic instruments that made echo chambers seem like using the loud pedal on the piano, and songs that struck terror and joy into the hearts of the world.

The Allied invasion of Normandy was not more successful, and the Beatles were followed by landing parties from Liverpool and other parts of England. Charging out of the LSTs were the Animals, the Dave Clark Five, the Rolling Stones, Herman's Hermits. Until only a little while ago, it was this British sound that dominated American radio—slicing air time up with teams of singers of Motown Records' Detroit sound of modified soul music, the kind they used to call sepia or race and the kind that really produced the whole thing in the first place.

The response to the rock and roll groups is clearly unlike anything that has ever happened before in American culture, except the movie craziness of pre-TV. In its overpowering intensity, it cuts across age, class and educational lines with such strength that it frequently threatens to break out and swallow the performers. During the summer, the Dave Clark Five followed the Beatles into New York. You would have thought that the kids would have been exhausted by two full days of orgasmic Beatle delight. But, no, at the end of their stay the Dave Clark Five were wrecked and exhausted from fighting off mobs of admirers.

The reaction of a certain kind of adult to all this frightening stuff has been maybe predictable, but also maybe a little excessive—unless you measure the reaction in terms of the force of the music.

"Uncivil, rude," said Agnes De Mille about the Frug. "Shameful," "degrading," "immoral," cried teams of Senate Republicans led by Gordon Allcott of Colorado after CBS broadcast Murray the K's *It's What's Happening, Baby* in behalf of the poverty program.

When the Beatles were awarded the OBE for singlehandedly almost solving the British balance of payments problem by making music England's single largest export, Colonel Blimps from Australia to

the black citizen exclaimed gleefully
as he pointed Billy the wrong way
                                        home
    "Go to Memphis
         take a lot of reds
    buy yourself
         some fine new threads —
    that's entertainment"
         = Hobo song.

London turned in their medals, something they never bothered to do when the salami manufacturers or beer merchants received the award in the past.

But there were other adults who were loving it. For, beginning with the Twist, the music of the big beat began to infiltrate the world outside the teenage subculture.

So warmly have adults embraced the teen beat that 40 percent of all the Top 40 records are bought by persons over 20. A New York City rock and roll station estimates its adult audience at better than 50 percent. A firm which sells carpeting finds it necessary only to advertise on WMCA to get bundles of leads for its salesmen. North American Newspaper Alliance, a feature syndicate serving nearly 200 newspapers, released a ten-part series on rock and roll and, according to the service's editor, Sid Goldberg, the pickup in the newspapers was "unbelievable." Serious articles appear all the time in Holiday, Esquire, The New Yorker, and, for all anyone knows, Commonweal.

Rock and roll provides a continuing source of news because, like art and to a lesser extent literature, it is always chang-

ing and the change is so breathtakingly fast that there is always something new to report on and respond to.

Yet it is not only variety that rock and roll has going for it in the adult world. There was plenty of variety in the teenage music of the Forties and Fifties. There were fads ranging then from Tex-Mex and rockabilly to calypso and folk singing. It's just that the variety was lifeless and terrible. Now, not only is the new music increasingly more interesting and sophisticated in both sound and lyric but also it seems to be part of something much more important finally breaking through into our mass culture—the idea that it is possible to be alive.

For those raised in the atmosphere of deadness of the postwar period, for this Silent Generation of the Age of Anxiety there has got to be some way of coming into contact with feeling and life, especially now that there really is life going on all around in teen-agers who don't know about the necessity to play dead.

So now, the drugs are amphetamine and LSD—one a powerful energizer, the other a hallucinogen which dissolves the ego defenses and brings the mind directly in contact with a whole new set of perceptions of the way the world might be. These are up drugs, and the search is now for up experiences; not the down drugs and the down experiences of ten years ago. And the same feeling of active release that is brought by LSD can also be triggered by other means, as Zen Buddhists, Chassidic Jews and Freudian psychoanalysts have known for a long time.

One of the ways is through music, and what better music is there than the music that kept a whole race of people alive for better than 300 years of the worst dehumanizing torture human beings have ever known?

But being alive means being subject to the shocks of life, and there are those who still prefer the old ways, the passive Muzak of the "good" music stations. Nowhere was this residue of resistance better demonstrated than when rock and roll forces began invading the sacred territory of folk music.

It started when an American group named the Byrds recorded Bob Dylan's "Tambourine Man," complete with swishy Buddy Holly intonations. Within minutes, there was nothing you were hearing but Bob Dylan—80 different versions of his songs. And then, in one of those incredible, treacherous things that can only happen in America, there was Dylan himself, the pure folksinger, the boy who made the citybillies respectable, playing an electric guitar with four guys backing him up on organ, drums and other guitars.

First he did it at Newport, and then, as if to show he wasn't fooling around, showed up at Forest Hills with all the equipment and all those fellows. And he was brilliant. You have to picture this open stadium with green grass and a striped tent big enough for a circus at one end, in front of which there was a stage. Under a storm-cloud sky that looked like some kind of special LSD experience, Dylan, dressed in blue sport jacket, tieless, wearing boots, came out first and played alone and everybody was loving it.

Then, after the intermission, came the group and the people started to cheer and boo. Little boys—"frenzied kamikaze squadrons," Jack Newfield called them in the Village Voice—ran out on the field and dodged cops, as if to prove that they were accepting Bob Dylan right into the R and R pantheon of crazy-makers.

But about twenty percent of the audience was booing and there were even some terribly nasty remarks yelled out. "You scumbag," one enraged fan howled. "Aw c'mon," Dylan answered. In an expensive box a college-age guy with crewcut hair and a bored girl friend screamed, "Sellout." Asked what he was angry about, this SS youth in a tartan plaid jacket replied, "We came here to listen to Dylan, not a big band." At that moment there were a total of five people on the bandstand—Dylan and four accompanists on guitars, drums and organ.

During the following months, Dylan's own "Like a Rolling Stone" shot up to the top of the charts and was followed by "Positively Fourth Street," with "Ballad for a Thin Man" making a strong showing in between. Folklike sounds were all over the Top 40, not only the pure protest stuff, like Barry McGuire's "Eve of Destruction," but also socially-oriented things like the Animals' "We Gotta Get Out of this Place," Billie Joe Royal's "Down in the Boondocks," the McCoys' "Hang on Sloopy" and Sonny Bono's "Laugh at Me." Even Joan Baez was there with "There but for Fortune" by Phil Ochs. At the same time, electronic equipment was infiltrating all the folk-music coffeehouses in Greenwich Village, accompanied by unamplified screams of anguish from diehard purists.

Maybe it is because many of the old-timers were schooled in the hair-splitting Marxist Lenin-Trotsky-Stalin battles of the Thirties, but they just did not want to hear anything about this revisionist electrically amplified music. It is more difficult to explain the revulsion of the younger folk-music performers and fans. Judy Henske, whose husband's Modern Folk Quartet went rock not too long ago and changed its name to Your Friends, said, "They want to be museum pieces before they're twenty-five." She caught part of it, but there seems to be more.

Part of it has to do with the fact that many college students, who form the main folk audience, think rock and roll is kid stuff.

But there was also beneath it all the sniff of something very strange and weird—unresolved anti-Negro prejudice which has been boiling beneath the surface of music in America for a long time. On the one hand, there seemed to be among the folk fans the unexpressed emotion that the Negro sound of rock and roll was dumb and dirty, unfashionable.

Among the professionals, on the other hand, the feeling was almost, but not quite, explicit. It has to be remembered that, despite all the crap about talent having no race, popular music has been pretty much a segregated area of American life. The white performer frequently is the victim of a kind of reverse Jim Crow perpetrated by people who still want to hold on to the belief that Negroes have a natural sense of

needed, you only have to look at Billboard's 1965 special section on religious music. Up front, from page 10 to 65, are the white gospel groups. In the back of the bus are the Negro gospel singers, and there is nowhere in the magazine where the two are drinking out of the same water fountain.

But despite the controversy, and whatever the reasons, Dylan's arrival in rock and roll may be the harbinger of magnificent new things to come. It is, already, a surprisingly smart bunch of people who are writing and performing the big beat. Jackie

Bill Graham = a man who took a name like Millard Fillmore and made it mean something quite different. We ought to get closer to him, if possible, and see if something healthier can be created out of the ashes of Auschwitz.

rhythm. Because most of the important jazz innovations have, in fact, come from Negroes—mainly because they have greater depth and experience in the medium—white jazzmen have tended to feel inferior.

Negroes, for their part, have for many years seen their own music making white people famous and wealthy, with whole record companies built on simply stealing "race" music and putting it across in the national pop market with white performers.

The resulting mutual antipathy has been real and substantial, edging to the surface in remarks like the one Albert Grossman, Dylan's manager, made when I asked what he thought the main influence of the Beatles had been. "They proved that it was all right to be white," he answered. It is also revealed in the statement one surfer rock and roll performer made to a national weekly magazine: "We play white music."

It is also a fact that there has never been any nationally famous integrated rock and roll group other than the Crests, who made "Sixteen Candles" and a few other fairly important records and are now no longer around. If further evidence is

De Shannon, the Four Tops, Chad Stuart, Peter Asher come on in bursts of intellect that would be laughed off the set on Broadway. And they have responded with intelligence to this highly intellectual and metaphysical poetry that Bob Dylan has introduced into the popular music of teen-agers.

Says Jackie De Shannon, who has written hits for everybody and had two lovely ones of her own in the past several months, "Dylan twisted my head all around. He made me realize that you didn't have to write only 'my boy friend's gone' songs. You could write things with meaning and emotion. I don't know if I like what he's been doing lately—all these weird lyrics—but I think he is one of the most important things that's ever happened to popular music."

What is so important about Dylan is that he is a poet, sometimes a lousy one, but more than frequently as good a one as we have had around in years. It is even possible that he may help revive the whole art of poetry in the United States, where it has been dead ever since T.S. Eliot and the New Critics put their frigid hands out and

Enslaved
to a scriptural habit as
the radio plays, Leon Russell
sings "A Hard Rain's Gonna Fall."

Bob Dylan

was the first Top 40 star to
try the role of prophet.

Young Girls

led the poets into the groves of the academy, effectively sealing them off from the possibility of any experience except sitting around with college teachers.

Yet poetry wasn't always that way. The poems of Elizabethan and Jacobean times were almost always set to music, and many of them were the most popular songs of their time. One composer, Henry Lawes, wrote music for both Shakespeare and John Milton. The early poems of John Donne were set by John Dowland and Alfonso Ferrabosco the Younger. But it is 300 years since anyone bothered to write poetry for popular music audiences, and it may turn out to be one of the great cultural treats of the 20th century to find out that it is going to happen again while we sit around and listen.

The teen-agers, meanwhile, aren't worrying about any of this, but just wolfing down everything anybody with talent is willing to throw at them. What they will be going for next, though, they're not telling, and there is nobody around who can predict it. Folk-rock may have already had its brief day and be done, and just over the horizon of the ionosphere there is probably some kind of strange and wonderful thing that no one even knows about.

In the air there is talk of a rock and roll musical by The Beatles, another by Dylan, a rock and roll *Othello* by Jack Good. Meanwhile, the clever people argue and discuss and come to conclusions, but as 16 editor Gloria Stavers says, "When the babies dig the beat something happens and everything freaks out. Until they decide what they dig, there's no use talking about it."

with heavy duty hardware.

hard
rain

plink   plunk

magnetized

1953 Chevrolet with
dual pipes lowered
in the rear with 14 inch
wheels and 1957 Plymouth
fenders = white niggers
first hot rod.

Bob Dylan

Quick and little, Bob Dylan scrambled from the safety of a rented gray sedan and ran for his dressing room through a wildness of teenage girls who howled and grabbed for his flesh. A cordon of guards held for a moment against the over-whelming attack. Then it broke and Dylan disappeared beneath yards of bell-bottoms and long hair. After a brief struggle he was rescued by one of his assistants, who methodically tore small and large girls off him, but it was too late. With a pair of enormous shears, a giant blonde girl has snipped a lock of the precious Dylan hair and now was weeping for joy.

"Did you see that?" said Dylan in his dressing room, his pale face somewhat paler than usual. "I mean did you *see* that?" repeated Dylan, who tends to talk in italics. "I don't care about the hair, but she could have killed me. I mean she could have taken my eyes out with those scissors."

This is Bob Dylan's year to be mobbed. Next year it will probably be somebody else. But this year Bob Dylan is the king of rock and roll, and he is the least likely king popular music has ever seen. With a bony, nervous face covered with skin the color of sour milk, a fright wig of curly tangles, and dark-circled hazel eyes usually hidden by large prescription sunglasses, Dylan is less Elvis or Frankie and more some crippled saint or resurrected Beethoven.

The songs he writes and sings, unlike the usual young-love pap of the airwaves, are full of dark and, many insist, important meaning; they are peopled with freaks, clowns, tramps, artists and mad scientists, dancing and tumbling in progression of visionary images mobilized to the massive beat of rock and roll. They often make very little logical sense, but almost always they make very good poetic sense. According to a recent poll, college students call him the most important contemporary poet in America.

He is certainly the only poet who gets his hair snipped off by shrieking teenage girls, but Dylan has always been a defier of categories. His first fame was as a folk singer and folk-song writer. Last year he modified his style to what has been labeled "folk-rock," a blend of serious, poetic lyrics and rock and roll music, which has brought him his greatest commercial success but has alienated some purists who were his early fans. He is a singer whose voice has been compared to the howl of "a dog with his leg caught in barbed wire"; a performer whose stage presence includes no hip wiggling or even, until recently, any acknowledgment of his audience; a public figure whose press conferences are exercises in a new kind of surrealism in which reporters ask, "Are you planning to do a movie?" and Dylan answers, deadpan, "Yes, I'm going to play my mother."

Yet, Bob Dylan, at the age of 25, has a million dollars in the bank and earns an estimated several hundred thousand dollars all look to for approval, the one we're all eating our hearts out about, the one who proved you could make it with the kids without any compromises. If I didn't admire him so much, I would have to hate him. In fact, maybe I do hate him anyway."

Born Robert Zimmerman, May 24, 1941, in Duluth, Minn., Dylan is a product of Hibbing, Minn., an iron ore mining town of 18,000 inhabitants about 70 miles from the Canadian border. The Southwestern accent in his singing voice is apparently acquired; he speaks without it. His father is a pros-

Bob Dylan is a man standing barefoot on a red hot griddle singing slowly.

a year from concerts, recordings and publishing royalties. He is even more popular in England and Europe than in America. Four hours after tickets went on sale for his recent London concerts at Albert Hall, the SOLD OUT sign was put up, and at one time five of his LP albums were selling in the top 20 in London. One paperback book on him has already been published; a hard-cover book about him by Robert Shelton, folk critic of The New York Times, will be published this winter; a third book of photo-graphs and text by Daniel Kramer is scheduled for winter publication. A two-hour documentary of his English tours will soon be released for theater showing; he is about to begin production of his own movie; ABC-TV has signed him for a television special. A book of his writings, *Tarantula*, is to be published by Macmillan late this summer, with a prepublication excerpt to appear in the Atlantic Monthly.

And although he is still not nearly so popular as the Beatles, who have sold near-ly 200 million records in four years, his artistic reputation is so great that in the recording business Dylan is ranked as the No. 1 innovator, the most important trend-setter, one of the few people around who can change radically the course of teen music.

"Dylan," says Phil Ochs, a folksinger friend of his, "is the king. He's the one we perous, witty, small (five-foot-six), cigar-smoking appliance dealer. His mother, a deeply tanned, attractive woman, is des-cribed by acquaintances as extremely intel-ligent, well informed and very talkative.

Dylan has a brother, David, 20, who attends St. Olaf College on a musical scholarship, and in the family it was always David who was thought of as "the musical one." Abe Zimmerman remembers buying a piano ("Not an expensive one," he says) when Bob was ten. Bob took one lesson and gave up in disgust because he couldn't play anything right away. David, then five, be-gan taking lessons and has been playing ever since.

Despite his initial impatience, Bob Zim-merman soon taught himself how to play the piano, harmonica, guitar and autoharp. Once he began to play the piano, says Mrs. Zimmerman, he beat the keys out of tune pounding out rock and roll. He also wrote—not only music but also poetry. "My mother has hundreds of poems I wrote when I was twelve years old," says Dylan.

As an adolescent, Dylan helped his father in the store, delivering appliances and sometimes attempting to make collections. "He was strong," Abe Zimmerman recently told an acquaintance. "I mean he could hold up his end of a refrigerator as well as kids twice his size, football players.

"I used to make him go out to the poor

sections," Mr. Zimmerman said, "knowing he couldn't collect any money from those people. I just wanted to show him another side of life. He'd come back and say, 'Dad, those people haven't got any money.' And I'd say, 'Some of those people out there make as much money as I do, Bobby. They just don't know how to manage it.'"

In more than one way the lesson was well taken. Dylan today, while professing not to know anything about his wealth, appears to be a very good manager of money, careful sometimes to what might be considered stinginess.

Dan Kramer recalls having to meet him at a hotel. "I called him," he says, "and asked if he wanted me to bring anything up for him. 'A container of tea,' Bobby said. I said, 'Bobby, they have room service in the hotel; you can have it sent up.' He thought about that for a couple of seconds and then said no, room service was too expensive." This was in 1965, the year that Dylan became a millionaire.

But Dylan learned more than frugality in the depressed areas of Hibbing. He learned, as Abe Zimmerman hoped he would, that there were people who knew nothing about middle-class life and middle-class values, people whose American dream had become a nightmare of installment debt. He seems to have felt a blood tie with them, based on a terrifying sense of his own peculiarity.

"I see things that other people don't see," he says. "I feel things other people don't feel. It's terrible. They laugh. I felt like that my whole life.

"My friends have been the same as me, people who couldn't make it as the high-school football halfback, Junior Chamber of Commerce leader, fraternity leader, truck driver working their way through college. I just had to be with them. I just don't care what anyone looks like, just as long as they didn't think I was strange. I couldn't do any of those things either. All I did was write and sing, paint little pictures on paper, dissolve myself into situations where I was invisible."

In pursuit of invisibility, Bob Zimmerman took to running away from home. "I made my own depression," he says. "Rode freight trains for kicks, got beat up for laughs, cut grass for quarters, met a waitress who picked me up and dropped me off in Washington." He tells of living with car-

nivals, of some trouble with police in Hibbing, of entertaining in a strip joint.

Be that as it may, he managed to finish high school at the appropriate time and even earned a scholarship to the University of Minnesota. Then the middle-class college boy from Hibbing began to remake his life and his image radically. He moved from his fraternity house to a downtown apartment. He began singing and playing the guitar and harmonica at Minneapolis's Ten o'Clock Scholar for two dollars a night; it is said that when he asked for a raise to five dollars, he was fired. He became Bob Dylan, and has since changed his name legally. This was not in tribute to Dylan Thomas, as the widely circulated legend maintains, but for some reason which he doesn't feel compelled to explain seriously.

"Get that straight," he says. "I didn't change my name in honor of Dylan Thomas. That's just a story. I've done more for Dylan Thomas than he's ever done for me. Look how many kids are probably reading his poetry now because they heard that story."

Dylan also gave up his very conventional college-boy dress — for his first professional appearance in Minneapolis he had worn white buck shoes — and began to develop his own personal style. At first, he was influenced by the uniform of folksingers everywhere — jeans, work shirt, boots, collar-length hair. Now that he's a rock and roll star, the uniform has changed. The boots are still part of it, but the jeans are now tight slacks that make his legs look skinnier than they are. The work shirt has been replaced by floppy polka-dot Carnaby Street English shirts with oversized collars and long, puffed sleeves. Sometimes he wears racetrack-plaid suits in combinations of colors like green and black. His hair seems to get longer and wilder by the month.

In December, 1960, Dylan gave up on Minnesota and took off for New York to try rock and roll, then in an uncertain state and dominated by clean-cut singers like Fabian and Frankie Avalon. It was not an auspicious time for someone who looked and sounded like Bob Dylan.

"I tried to make it in rock and roll when rock and roll was a piece of cream," he says. "Elvis had struck, Buddy Holly was dead, Little Richard was becoming a preacher, and Gene Vincent was leaving the country. I wrote the kind of stuff you write when you have no place to live and you're very wrapped up in the fire pump. I nearly killed myself with pity and agony. I saw the way doors close; the way doors that do not like you close. A door that does not like you needs no one to close it. I had to retreat."

Retreat for Dylan was folk music and Greenwich Village. He was strong medicine for both—nervous, cocky, different from anyone else around.

Arthur Kretchmer, a young magazine editor, remembers meeting Dylan at a party: "There was this crazy, restless little kid sitting on the floor and coming on very strong about how he was going to play Holden Caulfield in a movie of *Catcher in the Rye*, and I thought, 'This kid is really terrible'; but the people whose party it was said, 'Don't let him put you off. He comes on a little strong, but he's very sensitive—writes poetry, goes to visit Woody Guthrie in the hospital,' and I figured right, another one. I forgot all about him until a couple of years later he was famous and I wasn't. You can't always be right about these things, I suppose." Both Kretchmer and his wife are now Dylan fans.

Says Robert Shelton, whose book about Dylan is to be published this winter, "He was so astonishing-looking, so Chaplin-esque and cherubic, sitting up on a stool playing the guitar and the harmonica and playing with the audience, making all kinds of wry faces, wearing this Huck Finn hat, that I laughed out loud with pleasure. I called over Pat Clancy (an Irish folk-singer, one of the Clancy Brothers) and he looked at this cherub and broke into a broad smile and said, 'Well, what have we here?' "

Not too long after that, Shelton wrote a laudatory review in the New York Times of a Dylan performance. About the same time, Columbia Records executive John Hammond met Dylan at the home of folksinger Carolyn Hester, whom Dylan was going to accompany on a new record Hammond was producing. Without hearing him perform, Hammond offered Dylan a two-year contract with Columbia, and immediately hit a snag.

Dylan, a minor of 20, refused to admit to having any living relatives who could sign for him. "I don't know where my folks are," he told Hammond. "I think I've got an uncle who's a gambler in Nevada, but

I wouldn't know how to track him down." Taking another chance, Hammond finally let the boy execute the contract himself.

The young folksinger's first LP was called *Bob Dylan*. It cost $403 to produce and sold, initially, 4200 copies. By way of comparison, Dylan's most recent record as of this writing, *Highway 61 Revisited*, has sold 360,000 in the United States. All together, it is estimated that 10 million Dylan records have been sold throughout the world. His songs have been recorded in more than 150 other versions by performers ranging from Stan Getz to Lawrence Welk, and the royalties, Dylan admits, have made him a millionaire.

In achieving this success, Dylan has had powerful allies. Not the least of these was Billy James, a young Columbia public relations man who is now the record company's West Coast artist-relations director. It was through James' efforts that Dylan got his first taste of national publicity, but the singer's past was to come between them. In 1963, when Dylan was entering his first flush of fame with "Blowin' in the Wind", a song which became an unofficial anthem of the civil-rights movement and a major popular hit, Newsweek revealed that Bob Dylan was Robert Zimmerman and went on to suggest that not only was Dylan's name a fake but it was rumored another writer had created "Blowin' in the Wind." One part of the story was false—Dylan was the author of the song; but the other part, of course, was true: Bob Dylan was Robert Zimmerman.

Dylan was infuriated by the article and blamed Billy James for it. For two years the two did not speak. James won't talk about the incident at all, but people who know both of them say that Dylan attempted to get the public relations man fired. Two years later, they met at a party and Dylan was all friendship again. When James mentioned the Newsweek affair, Dylan put an arm around him and said, "Thousands of people are dying in Vietnam and right at this minute a man is jumping off the Empire State Building and you got *that* running around in your head?"

One of the great factors in Dylan's early success was his profound ability to articulate the emotions of the civil-rights revolution, which was developing its peak of power in the early Sixties. Recognition of this talent came in dramatic form at the

Newport Folk Festival of 1963.

Although he had already appeared once on the program, which is a sort of Hall of Fame of folksinging in action, he was called back to the stage at the end of the final concert. Accompanied by a stageful of folk stars, from Pete Seeger, the gentle "king" of folk music, to Joan Baez, the undisputed queen, Bob Dylan sang "Blowin' in the Wind" to an audience of 36,000 of the most important folksinging fans, writers, recording executives and critics.

"How many roads must a man walk down before they call him a man?" they sang. *"Yes, 'n' How many seas must a white dove sail before she sleeps in the sand? Yes, 'n' How many times must the cannon balls fly before they're forever banned? The answer my friend, is blowin' in the wind, The answer is blowin' in the wind."* *

Recorded by Peter, Paul and Mary, "Blowin' in the Wind" was Dylan's first major hit, and very quickly there were 58 different versions of the song, by everyone from the Staple Singers (a screaming gospel version) to Marlene Dietrich. Almost overnight Dylan was established at the top of the folk music field. Here at last, sighed the folk critics and the civil-rights people, was a songwriter with the true "proletarian" touch, one who could really reach the masses. For two years, Dylan was the musicial spokesman for civil rights, turning up in Mississippi, in the march on Washington, at the demonstrations and rallies.

"I feel it," said Joan Baez, whom Dylan had met before Newport, "but Dylan can say it. He's phenomenal."

For a while, Joan and Bobby were to be inseparable, the queen and crown prince of folk music. When Dylan went to England for a concert tour, Joan Baez went with him. As much as anyone's, it was her voice and authority which helped to create the charismatic reputation of Bob Dylan the folksinger.

These days Dylan and Baez are not as close as they used to be. When the rough cut of *Don't Look Back* was screened in Hollywood this spring, Baez was everywhere on the film, in the limousine, at the airport, singing in the hotel room. After the screening, Dylan said to the film editor, "We'll have to take all that stuff of

* © 1962 by M. Witmark & Sons.

Joan out." He hesitated and then added, "Well, it looks as if she was the whole thing. She was only there a few days. We'll have to cut it down."

Far more important to Dylan, however, was Albert Grossman, who took over Dylan's career and, to a great extent, his life. He is not only Dylan's manager, but also his confidant, healer and friend. Until recently, in fact, Dylan had no home of his own. He lived in Grossman's New York City apartment or the manager's antique-filled country home in Woodstock, N.Y.

He appears to be only vaguely aware of the extent or nature of his wealth, leaving the details to Grossman. "When I want money," Dylan says, "I ask for it. After I spend it, I ask for more."

Dylan has had his effect on Grossman, too, however. "I used to remember Albert as a nice-looking businessman, the kind of middle-aged man you would meet in a decent restaurant in the garment center," says Gloria Stavers, editor of 16. "Then, a while after he signed Dylan, I met him again. I couldn't believe it. I just couldn't believe what had happened to him. He had long gray hair like Benjamin Franklin and wire-rimmed spectacles, and he was wearing an old sweatshirt or something and Army pants. 'Albert,' I screamed, when I finally recognized him. 'Albert, what has Bobby done to you?'"

A measure of Dylan's relationship with his manager is found in the tone and style he uses in talking to Grossman. Even in the most ordinary conversation, Dylan can be almost impossible to understand. He is often vague, poetic, repetitive, confusing. But his flow of imagery can be startlingly precise and original, and the line of his thought brilliantly adventurous, funny and penetrating. So, in describing his music he will say, "it's all math, simple math, involved in mathematics. There's a definite number of Colt .45s that make up Marlene Dietrich, and you can find that out if you want to."

This kind of talk is not useful for more than a few situations. Nonetheless, it is the way Dylan speaks to fans, disk jockeys, reporters, acquaintances, and frequently, friends. It is not the way he speaks to Grossman. Then his voice often goes into a kind of piping whine, the voice of a little boy complaining to his father.

Thus, after a concert on the West Coast,

at three o'clock in the morning, Dylan was told by a visitor that his voice was not heard over the blast of the electronically amplified instruments. Grossman lay dozing on the hotel bed, his tinted glasses still on, a slight smile of repose on his heavy face.

cially demanding nor temperamental, even when things don't quite go according to schedule.

Last spring, for example, a concert in Vancouver was an acoustical disaster. The arena still smelled strongly of its last guests

Excessive pumping of the creative well induces first exhaustion, then regeneration. I am at that point in my cycle called Bringing In the Sheaves.

"Al-*bert*," Dylan cried, "Albert, did you hear that? They couldn't hear me. Al-*bert*, I mean they couldn't *hear* me. What good is it if they can't hear me? We've got to get that sound man out here to fix it. What do you think, Albert?"

Grossman stirred on the bed and answered soothingly, "I told you in the car that the volume was too high. Just cut the volume by about a third and it'll be all right." Grossman went back to sleep, very much like an occidental Buddha, snoring lightly. Dylan was satisfied.

Grossman's formidable managerial talent is displayed most clearly when Dylan is on concert tour. From Grossman's New York office, the logistics of moving the singer and his crew from concert to concert halfway around the world are worked out with an efficiency that makes the whole operation seem effortless.

On the road the Dylan entourage usually consists of Dylan, his road manager, a pilot and co-pilot for the 13-seat two-engine Lodestar in which the group travels over the shorter distances (tourist-class commercial jets are used for overseas and transcontinental travel), two truck drivers who deliver the sound equipment and musicians' instruments from stop to stop, a sound man and five musicians—two guitarists, a drummer, pianist and organist. Grossman flies out from time to time to hear a concert or two and then returns to New York. On foreign tours he usually stays with the group throughout the trip.

Dylan's people are protective and highly attentive to his wants, and Dylan himself, given his status as a star, is neither espe-

—a stock exhibition. It was perfectly round, with a flat dome that produced seven echoes from a sharp handclap in the center. Large open gates let sound leak out of the hall as easily as if the concert were held in the open air. Although Dylan's $30,000 custom-designed sound system filled eight large crates with equipment, it could never fill this gigantic echo chamber with clear sound. To add to the problem, one of the small monitor speakers placed on stage to enable the musicians to hear themselves play, was not working.

Dylan's concerts are divided into two halves. During the first, in which he played his acoustic guitar into a stage microphone, the sound was patchy; in some spots it was perfect, in others it was very bad. In the second half, however, in which rock and roll songs were played on the amplified instruments and electric guitars, the music was a garble of reverberation, and Dylan's voice was totally scrambled by the echo. The sound man sweated and twirled his knobs, but it was no use. At one point Grossman ran up to the stage to tell Dylan he was "eating the mike," that is, getting too close to the microphone and contributing to the electric jumble. The musicians, deprived of the monitor, watched each other tensely as they tried to keep their beat by observation rather than sound.

"Man, that was just terrible," Dylan said when he came offstage and hurried into the waiting car. "That was just awful. I mean that was worse than Ottawa, and Ottawa was the worst hole in the universe." He turned to each person in the car and asked them separately. "Wasn't that worse than

Ottawa, and wasn't Ottawa the worst hole in the universe?" Everyone agreed that it was worse than Ottawa.

"That was really worse than Ottawa, and Ottawa was the worst, terrible, miserable hole in the entire universe," Dylan repeated, with a certain satisfaction. "Worse than Ottawa," he mused, and then, laughing, turned around and said, "And anyone who doesn't think it was worse than Ottawa can get out of the car right now."

Later he and Grossman discussed the problem again, and it was agreed that the fault lay in the arena, not in the equipment. In a better hall or a theater there would have been no trouble. Dylan's concern now was with the halls in which he was booked in Australia.

"Albert, it's no good in those arenas," he said. "I just would rather forget about arenas and play theaters. To hell with the money, I mean I would much rather have a good show. Are we going to play any arenas in Australia?"

"We have to," Grossman answered. "We haven't any choice, Bobby. There just aren't enough big concert halls or theaters there. It's not America. The country is still undeveloped."

"Well, all right," said Dylan. "I mean if we have to, but I wish we could play theaters and halls. I mean that place was worse than Ottawa and—" "Ottawa was the worst hole in the universe," someone chimed in.

"Yeah. The worst in the universe. And this was worse."

At no time, perhaps, was Dylan's closeness with Grossman more important than in 1965, the year Dylan turned from folk music to rock and roll. He had by this time cut three more albums, two of them, *The Times They Are A-Changin'* and *Freewheelin' Bob Dylan,* outstandingly successful, not only in sales but in acclaim from the critics and the civil-rights activists. But he came back from a stunningly successful English tour with a feeling of *malaise* and a desire for change.

"After I finished the English tour," he says, "I quit because it was too easy. There was nothing happening for me. Every concert was the same: first half, second half, two encores and run out, then having to take care of myself all night.

"I didn't understand; I'd get standing ovations, and it didn't mean anything. The

first time I felt no shame. But then I was just following myself after that. It was down to a pattern."

In his next album, *Bringing It All Back Home,* Dylan broke the pattern. Instead of playing either conventional "protest" as it was understood then, or using the traditional folk music modes, he electrically amplified his guitar and set surrealistic verses to the rock and roll beat.

Ironically, it was one of the album's few non-rock songs that brought Dylan his first great success in the pop market. "Mr. Tambourine Man," recorded by the Byrds in a hard-rock version complete with falsetto, was a massive hit.

"When 'Mr. Tambourine Man' broke, we didn't know anything about Bob Dylan," says "Cousin Brucie" Morrow, a disk jockey on WABC Radio, New York. "Oh, I remember a few years ago we'd listen to a single of his. It didn't seem to fit the sound then, so we didn't play it. That was all I knew about Bob Dylan until the Byrds hit with 'Tambourine Man.' Then everyone was asking, 'Who's this Bob Dylan?' It's the only time I can remember when a composer got more attention for a hit than the performers did."

Then when Dylan released his new single, "Like a Rolling Stone," and his new album, *Highway 61 Revisited,* the folk fans knew Bobby was going to be a teenage idol, and if he was a teenage idol he wasn't theirs anymore. For people who had thought they owned Bob Dylan it was a bitter disappointment, and Dylan lost a great many people he thought were his friends. "A freak and a parody," shrieked Irwin Silber in the folk music magazine Sing Out! At the Newport Folk Festival of 1965, Dylan was booed off the stage. At his Forest Hills concert in September, the audience listened attentively through the first, folk, half of the program and then began to boo when the musicians came out for the rock portion. This time Dylan did not walk off the stage as he did at Newport, but fought his way through the performance, supported by 80 percent of the crowd. "Like a Rolling Stone" finally put Dylan across as a rock and roll star. He wrote it in its first form when he came back from England. "It was ten pages long," he says. "It wasn't called anything, just a rhythm thing on paper all about my steady hatred directed at some point that was honest. In the end it wasn't hatred, it was telling someone something they didn't know, telling them they were lucky. Revenge, that's a better word.

"I had never thought of it as a song, until one day I was at the piano, and on the paper it was singing, 'How does it feel?' in a slow motion pace, in the utmost of slow motion following something.

"It was like swimming in lava. In your eyesight, you see your victim swimming in lava. Hanging by their arms from a birch tree. Skipping, kicking the tree, hitting a nail with your foot. Seeing someone in the pain they were bound to meet up with.

"I wrote it. I didn't fail. It was straight." "Like a Rolling Stone" climbed rapidly to to the top of the charts. It was followed by "Positively 4th Street" and then by "Ballad of a Thin Man," and Dylan's lead was soon followed by other songwriters released from the inane bondage of the "I Love You, Teen Queen" straitjacket. Soon the airwaves were full of songs about the war in Vietnam, or civil rights, or the general disorder of the world and society in America. It was quickly labeled "folk-rock," and the kids wolfed it down and are still listening to it.

Along with the teenagers, Dylan got a surprising bonus audience — the adult hip intellectuals who had just found out about rock and roll. National magazines began writing favorably about both Dylan and rock, and rock concerts became the social events of the intellectuals' seasons. Allen Ginsberg said, "He writes better poetry than I did at his age . . . . I'd say he's a space-age genius minstrel more than an old library poet . . . " One Sunday, the magazine sections of The New York Times and The New York Herald-Tribune simultaneously published long articles on the poetry of Bob Dylan, complete with learned analyses and exegeses of the most fashionable academic - journalist - sociological kind.

Dylan's reaction is predictably thorny. "The songs are not meant to be great," he said. "I'm not meant to be great. I don't think anything I touch is destined for greatness. Genius is a terrible word, a word they think will make me like them. A genius is a very insulting thing to say. Even Einstein wasn't a genius. He was a foreign mathematician who would have stolen cars."

Some of his recent songs have brought him new criticism: it has been claimed that the lyrics of "Mr. Tambourine Man" and his latest hit, "Rainy Day Women 12 and 35" ("Everybody *must* get stoned!"), are all about drugs and drug experiences. Grossman denies it. Dylan won't talk about his songs. "Don't interpret me," he says. Talking about drugs, he is typically elusive. "People just don't need drugs," he says. "Keep things out of your body. We all take medicine, as long as you know why you're taking it. If you want to crack down on the drug situation, the criminal drug situation takes place in the suburban housewives' kitchens, the ones who get wiped out on alcohol every afternoon and then make supper. You can't blame them and you can't blame their husbands. They've been working in the mines all day. It's understandable."

During the past year Dylan has got married, fathered a son, Jesse Byron Dylan, and bought a townhouse in Manhattan's fashionable East 30's. Typically, he has attempted to keep all of this a secret. When his wife, a beautiful, black-haired girl named Sara Lownds, visited him in Vancouver and attended his concert, Dylan was faced with a problem: two disk jockeys were coming up to the dressing room to interview him; how was he to hide his wife from them? "Sara," said Dylan, opening a large closet, "when they arrive I want you to get in here." His wife looked at him quizzically but stepped reluctantly toward the open door. Dylan began to laugh, but it is a mark of the seriousness of his desire for privacy that his wife was ready to get into the closet.

The only thing anyone now will predict for certain is that Dylan will change. "I'll never decay," he says. "Decay is when something has stopped living but hasn't died yet, looking at your leg and seeing it all covered with creeping brown cancer. Decay turns me off. I'll die first before I decay."

Hideous laughter

alone like
a stone

reading
old
books

entering
the season
of

sadness
and
madness

where
will you go now?

x

x

x

sinister

all around

all about it

all
alone
exept
for the
Devils

tell me
all about it

retreat

cold light

headache

I am
a ghost,

Docile android

windows

The Subcontractor

When Elva Cole lost her way on the Hollywood Freeway somewhere between Highland Avenue and Civic Center Interchange she tried to remain very calm. She was a small, pretty, timid young redhead who had only recently passed her driving test. This was the first time she had ever soloed on the freeway.

She would not have risked it but the voice on the telephone gave her no choice. She had to come downtown immediately to discuss a matter of the most urgent importance regarding her late husband's estate, the man had said, giving her the route in a tone that allowed no questions.

Now she was lost and frightened. She had never wanted to come to California, never wanted to learn how to drive, never wanted to be on a freeway. Bob Cole had brought her here and talked her into taking driving lessons. In the days after he died of one of those sudden coronaries that begin to cut men down as they enter their thirties, she had continued the lessons because she had nothing else to do. She knew no one here. Her own parents were both dead. Her brother, an executive with a computer company, was stationed in Tokyo. He had come to Los Angeles for the funeral and left a few days later.

Only this morning she had received a letter from him. He was going to be back in the States soon. He hoped that she was keeping her chin up. He knew that she was brave, he wrote, and he was sure that she would be back on top again. He advised her to count her blessings: she was young, trim, good-looking and had no worries about money. She had read the letter over and over again and resolved to pull herself together.

The decision to chance the freeway was her first act in the new outlook. It had not turned out well at all. Agitated by the mysterious phone call, she was filled with anxiety. Teenagers in open convertibles cut ahead of her at high speeds, laughing and sounding arrogant horns. Great trailer trucks overtook her impatiently as she tried to keep her speedometer precisely at forty. They blasted clouds of suffocating fumes and exploded loud noises.

A black panel truck followed her closely. A man on a motorcycle swerved in front of her, herding her car toward the wall. She pulled frantically at the wheel. Her car bucked and skidded. She heard a crumpling

shriek. She saw a woman lying bleeding on a car seat. A black panel truck was parked nearby. Two men with stretchers approached. A man on a motorcycle spoke into a microphone. The motor fumes became an anesthetic.

When she awoke, she was choking. There was a hard piece of plastic or rubber in her mouth and her face was covered with a mask. Her arms and legs were strapped down and doctors in pale green surgical costumes were doing something to the lower part of her body. She gagged and struggled as an acid edge of vomit rose in her throat.

"I told you to keep her down lower," said one of the doctors. "The director won't like it if he finds out she woke up. You better knock her out and bag her." A nurse handed the doctor a vial which looked like a penicillin bottle. He filled a hypodermic syringe. There was a bee sting pain in her arm. Her lungs stopped working. She tried to drag in air, fighting to keep breathing, but her chest would not move. The doctor squeezed a black rubber bag near her head and gasoline fumes flowed through the mask into her mouth and throat. The desire to struggle left her.

There were mirrors surrounding the light above her head. She could see her bare thigh. It had been sliced open from groin to knee. The red muscles oozed trickles of blood. Bunches of shiny forceps held the wound open. The doctor rummaged around in her thigh and pulled out a torn tube that looked like the pink hose of an enema bag.

A door opened at the end of the room and a little man in a checked sport jacket and a very skinny tie walked into the light. A stethoscope several sizes too large for him hung around his neck.

"Too much blood," he said. "Much too much blood. We want you to make it dramatic, but this is excessive."

"Can't help it," said the probing doctor. "When you bring them in like this, I have to do the best I can. Sometimes you just have to search around in these things."

"These are the best cases I can afford," said the little man, looking at the scene through a blue monocle. "I'm just a subcontractor. Get on with the work. And put her under. It looks very bad when they're awake on the table. Did you ever see Ben Casey operating on a conscious patient? Put her to sleep."

"She's lost a lot of blood," said the doctor

who was rhythmically squeezing the black bag. "Your men really banged her up. If I let her go too far under, we may have trouble bringing her back. I want to keep her very light. That way she'll last longer. Saves money in the long run when they last longer, doesn't it?"

"Spare me the technical details. Just get it over with and make it look right. This is costing plenty." He disappeared into the darkness beyond the operating table.

The doctor at her head peered into her eyes and made an adjustment on the hissing tanks with one hand as he continued to pump the bag with the other. The auto fumes piled up in her chest and the scene disappeared. Once again she was driving on the freeway. Pine-covered hills were barnacled with pastel stucco apartment houses and private homes. A tall French chateau with whipped-cream turrets and towers stood on the heights, illuminated by floodlights. Its neon sign announced, ROOMS WITH BATH. She had been driving forever. If she could only get off the freeway she could stay overnight at that hotel.

A sign appeared ahead of her: CIVIC CENTER. In an agony of desperation, she pressed down on the brakes, bringing the car almost to a halt. A blast of horns reverberated. A trailer truck zoomed by with crushed fenders and doors hanging from its high grill. The dark air was filled with the noxious odors of truck exhaust. The lights blanked out into a flat black mist.

"Please," she moaned, "please, no more operations. Please have mercy. Please let me see my brother."

She opened her eyes. She was in a hospital room. A very pale, beautiful girl in a white nurse's costume was sitting at her bedside.

"Please, Miss," Elva Cole whispered, "some water." The girl jumped nervously. She seemed bewildered by the request. "Please," Elva said, "just something to wet my lips."

"Well, I . . . I guess it's all right," the nurse said in a throaty, singing voice. Elva drank greedily, then rested back, examining the girl. She was magnificently beautiful, with bronze hair, white skin flushing pink and honey, large breasts fighting the starched white uniform bib. The eyes were tawny green, almost yellow, heavily accented with make-up. They reminded Elva of the eyes of the bosomy

girls in tight pants she saw shopping in Ralph's 24-Hour Supermarket late at night.

"Where am I?" she asked.

The girl hesitated, then answered in that thrilling voice, sounding somehow as if she were speaking memorized lines. "In the hospital, of course. You've had a very serious accident, but you're all right now."

"Has anyone notified my brother?"

"Your brother?" the girl repeated very nervously, her voice rising in pitch.

"Yes, my brother. He's in computers. In Tokyo. You have to send him a cable right away." Tears came to Elva's eyes as she thought of her brother.

"Why, why, I mean I'm sure he's been notified," the girl said. "I guess he just hasn't gotten here yet. Or maybe they haven't been able to reach him," she ventured uncertainly. "I better get the director," she said and ran out of the room with a graceful, skipping motion that made her round buttocks bounce.

After a few moments, voices approached the room. Men shouting. No, just one of them was shouting. The other was answering calmly, quietly.

"Goddamn you," the loud voice cursed in the hallway, "I told you, no goddamned relatives. No relatives. Do you know what this will mean if he recognizes her? A brother. Jesus Christ. A goddamned brother in Tokyo. We'll have to destroy the whole sequence. This is going to break me. We'll never survive this one. We're finished."

"Don't get irrational," the other voice soothed. "He'll never recognize her. It's only a pilot. He'll never see it."

"We don't know that yet, do we? We don't know that at all. He's in computers. That's heavy advertising. We've got to dig this thing through immediately and find out who he is. You told me your people were absolutely reliable. Goddamned idiots. I told them, no relatives. Well, it's too late for complaints now. We're on deadline. Maybe we can salvage a —"

The little man walked in with a nervous young man who carried a clipboard. The little man was wearing a doctor's white coat, stethoscope tubes peeping out of a pocket. A red pain was throbbing up out of her thigh. Black nausea rose in her throat.

"Well, hello there," said the little man kindly. "How are you today? Feeling a little woozy?" He took her pulse and examined her eyes.

"Where's my brother?" Elva whispered hysterically, almost unable to speak because of the pain and the terror. "I want my brother. What kind of place is this? Why don't you want any relatives?"

"This is a hospital, Mrs. Cole. Your brother is on his way. He'll be here soon. We had trouble reaching him in Tokyo. It's so hard to find people so far away, you know. But we're in touch with him now."

"I'm very upset, doctor," said Elva, tears flowing freely from her eyes. "My brother's going to be angry with me. I wrecked the car. I've been so depressed since I lost my husband. Now I'm in the hospital and everything seems so strange."

"Of course, you're upset," said the little man. "Who wouldn't be? I'm going to give you something to make you sleep and when you wake up everything will be all right. You're just upset and confused." He continued talking in that soothing tone of his as he jabbed a needle into her arm.

"Yes, I am very upset," said Elva. "I've always been a very excitable person and I knew I shouldn't drive on the freeway but the man said it was about Bob's estate and since I lost him I haven't been able to . . ." She stopped talking. She was very tired, too tired to speak. She closed her eyes.

"Of course," said the little man, holding her hand. "Now you just go to sleep. Everything's going to be all right. Just go to sleep." Emma opened her eyes. The beautiful nurse was there. She tried to smile at the girl. Poor thing, Elva thought, probably new, inexperienced. Once again, the darkness came. Once again she was on the freeway. Once again there was an accident. Once again she began to waken.

The lights were powerful. The snout of a television camera was aimed at her body, which was open from throat to navel. Machines pumped blood through her. Gas tanks hissed. Her throbbing heart was exposed and bleeding, a fat, thumping piece of red meat.

"Ahhhhh" Elva screamed, strangling on the plastic bit.

"Put her under," yelled the little man.

"I can't take her down too deep," said a voice behind her. "We'll lose her."

"Do what I say or you'll be back where I found you." The voice was commanding, cold, cruel, filled with unspeakable inference.

"Don't threaten me," said the doctor.

"I'm sorry," the little man said, suddenly soothing again. "It's just the pressure. The budget. The deadline. We've got to meet the deadline or we lose everything. This has never been done before. Realism. Absolute realism. But the big bastards make the money. I'm just a subcontractor. Try to understand my problems."

"I'll do what I can," said the doctor. Fumes filled Elva's nose and mouth.

Now, again, she was driving on the Hollywood Freeway between Highland Avenue and Civic Center. The round Capitol Records tower was on her right. Everything was pale, faded, gray. No more awakening now, she thought, as the windshield slowly dimmed. Exactly like a television being turned off, the last white dot of light in the center disappeared.

(by candlelight last night)

Memories of failing light:
falling all the way through the
inner darkness, too frightened to
cry out; speaking out of the dream
in nonsense garble; Aztec terror
patterns

If you are afraid of the dark, how
are you going to feel when you see
the light?

Clear skies, cloudy eyes

Pretty girls better watch out for
witches and wolves.

People with loud voices should
practice whispering.

We are all ecology freaks until
it comes to buying bio-degradable
soap.

"Go out and earn some more money;
other people are paying for your
wife's Crest."

The old righteous hippie bullshit
turns me off faster than Billy
Graham

There are many brands of poison.

"Do not meddle in the affairs of the wizards for they are subtle and quick to anger."

Teeny-weenies who think they are heavies have short, unhappy lives.

Goodbye Surfing, Hello God!

It was just another day of greatness at Gold Star Recording Studios on Santa Monica Boulevard in Hollywood. In the morning four long-haired kids had knocked out two hours of sound for a record plugger who was trying to curry favor with a disk jockey friend of theirs in San Jose. Nobody knew it at the moment, but out of that two hours there were about three minutes that would hit the top of the charts in a few weeks, and the record plugger, the disk jockey and the kids would all be hailed as geniuses, but geniuses with a very small g.

Now, however, in the very same studio a Genius with a very large capital G was going to produce a hit. There was no doubt it would be a hit because this Genius was Brian Wilson. In four years of recording for Capitol Records, he and his group, the Beach Boys, had made surfing music a national craze, sold 16 million singles and earned gold records for 10 of their 12 albums.

Not only was Brian going to produce a hit, but also, one gathered, he was going to show everybody in the music business exactly where it was at; and where it was at, it seemed, was that Brian Wilson was not merely a Genius — which is to say a steady commercial success — but rather, like Bob Dylan and John Lennon, a GENIUS — which is to say a steady commercial success and hip besides.

Until now, though, there were not too many hip people who would have considered Brian Wilson and the Beach Boys hip, even though he had produced one very hip record, "Good Vibrations," which had sold more than a million copies, and a super-hip album, Pet Sounds, which didn't do very well at all — by previous Beach Boys sales standards. Among the hip people he was still on trial, and the question discussed earnestly among the recognized authorities on what is and what is not hip was whether or not Brian Wilson was hip, semi-hip or square.

But walking into the control room with the answers to all questions such as this was Brian Wilson himself, wearing a competition-stripe surfer's T-shirt, tight white duck pants, pale green bowling shoes and a red plastic toy fireman's helmet.

Everybody was wearing identical red plastic toy fireman's helmets. Brian's cousin and production assistant, Steve Korthoff was wearing one; his wife,

Marilyn, and her sister, Diane Rovelle—Brian's secretary—were also wearing them, and so was a once-dignified writer from The Saturday Evening Post who had been following Brian around for two months.

Out in the studio, the musicians for the session were unpacking their instruments. In sport shirts and slacks, they looked like insurance salesmen and used-car dealers, except for one blonde female percussionist who might have been stamped out by a special machine that supplied plastic mannequin housewives for detergent commercials.

Controlled, a little bored after 20 years or so of nicely paid anonymity, these were the professionals of the popular music business, hired guns who did their job expertly and efficiently and then went home to the suburbs. If you wanted swing, they gave you swing. A little movie-track lushness? Fine, here comes movie-track lushness. Now it's rock and roll? Perfect rock and roll, down the chute.

"Steve," Brian called out, "where are the rest of those fire hats? I want everybody to wear fire hats. We've really got to get into this thing." Out to the Rolls-Royce went Steve and within a few minutes all of the musicians were wearing fire hats, silly grins beginning to crack their professional dignity.

"All right, let's go," said Brian. Then, using a variety of techniques ranging from vocal demonstration to actually playing the instruments, he taught each musician his part. A gigantic fire howled out of the massive studio speakers in a pounding crash of pictorial music that summoned up visions of roaring, windstorm flames, falling timbers, mournful sirens and sweating firemen, building into a peak and crackling off into fading embers as a single drum turned into a collapsing wall and the fire-engine cellos dissolved and disappeared.

"When did he write this?" asked an astonished pop music producer who had wandered into the studio. "This is really fantastic! Man, this in unbelievable! How long has he been working on it?"

"About an hour," answered one of Brian's friends.

"I don't believe it. I just can't believe what I'm hearing," said the producer and fell into a stone glazed silence as the fire music began again.

For the next three hours, Brian Wilson recorded and re-recorded, take after take, changing the sound balance, adding echo, experimenting with a sound effects track of a real fire.

"Let me hear that again." "Drums, I think you're a little slow in that last part. Let's get right on it." "That was really good. Now, one more time, the whole thing." "All right, let me hear the cellos alone." "Great. Really great. Now let's *do it!*"

With 23 takes on tape and the entire operation responding to his touch like the black knobs on the control board, sweat glistening down his long, reddish hair onto his freckled face, the control room a litter of dead cigarette butts, Chicken Delight boxes, crumpled napkins, Coke bottles and all the accumulated trash of the physical end of the creative process, Brian stood at the board as the four speakers blasted the music into the room.

For the 24th time, the drum crashed and the sound effects crackle faded and stopped.

"Thank you," said Brian, into the control room mike. "Let me hear that back." Feet shifting, his body still, eyes closed, head moving seal-like to his music, he stood under the speakers and listened. "Let me hear that one more time." Again the fire roared. "Everybody come out and listen to this," Brian said to the musicians. They came into the control room and listened to what they had made.

"What do you think?" Brian asked.

"It's incredible, incredible," whispered one of the musicians, a man in his 50s, wearing a Hawaiian shirt and iridescent trousers and pointed black Italian shoes. "Absolutely incredible."

"Yeah," said Brian on the way home, an acetate trial copy or "dub" of the tape in his hands, the red plastic fire helmet still on his head. "Yeah, I'm going to call this 'Mrs. O'Leary's Fire' and I think it might just scare a whole lot of people."

As it turns out, however, Brian Wilson's magic fire music is not going to scare anybody—because nobody other than the few people who heard it in the studio will ever get to listen to it. A few days after the record was finished, a building across the street from the studio burned down and, according to Brian, there was also an unusually large number of fires in Los Angeles. Afraid that his music might in fact turn out to be magic fire music, Wilson destroyed the master.

"I don't have to do a big scary fire like that," he later said. "I can do a candle and it's still fire. That would have been a really bad vibration to let out on the world, that Chicago fire. The next one is going to be a candle."

A person who thinks of himself as understanding would probably interpret this episode as an example of perhaps too-excessive artistic perfectionism. One with psychiatric inclinations would hear all this stuff about someone who actually believed music could cause fires and start using words such as neurosis and maybe even psychosis. A true student of spoken hip, however, would say *hang-up,* which covers all of the above.

As far as Brian's pretensions toward hipness are concerned, no label could do him worse harm. In the hip world, there is a widespread idea that really hip people don't have hang-ups, which gives rise to the unspoken rule (unspoken because there is also the widespread idea that really hip people don't make *any* rules) that no one who wants to be thought of as hip ever reveals his hang-ups, except maybe to his guru, and in the strictest of privacy.

In any case, whatever his talent, Brian Wilson's attempt to win a hip following and reputation foundered for many months in an obsessive cycle of creation and destruction that threatened not only his career and his future but also his marriage, his friendships, his relationship with the Beach Boys and, some of his closest friends worried, his mind.

For a boy who used to be known in adolescence as a lover of sweets, the whole thing must have begun to taste very sour; yet, this particular phase of Brian's drive toward whatever his goal of supreme success might be began on a rising tide that at first looked as if it would carry him and the Beach Boys beyond the Beatles, who had started just about the same time they did, into the number-one position in the international pop music fame - and - power competition.

"About a year ago I had what I consider a very religious experience," Wilson told Los Angeles writer Tom Nolan in 1966. "I took LSD, a full dose of LSD, and later, another time, I took a smaller dose. And I learned a lot of things, like patience, under-

standing. I can't teach you or tell you what I learned from taking it, but I consider it a very religious experience."

A short time after his LSD experience, Wilson began work on the record that was to establish him right along with the Beatles as one of the most important innovators in modern popular music. It was called "Good Vibrations," and it took more than six months, 90 hours of tape and 11 complete versions before a three-minute-35-second final master tape satisfied him. Among the instruments on "Good Vibrations" was an electronic device called a theramin, which had its debut in the soundtrack of the movie *Spellbound,* back in the Forties. To some people, "Good Vibrations" was considerably crazier than Gregory Peck had been in the movie, but to others, Brian Wilson's new record, along with his somewhat earlier LP release, "Pet Sounds," marked the beginning of a new era in pop music.

"They've Found the New Sound at Last!" shrieked the headline over a London Sunday Express review as "Good Vibrations" hit the English charts at number six and leaped to number one the following week. Within a few weeks, the Beach Boys had pushed the Beatles out of first place in England's New Musical Express' annual poll. In America, "Good Vibrations" sold nearly 400,000 copies in four days before reaching number one several weeks later and earning a gold record within another month when it hit the one-million sale mark.

In America, where there is none of the Beach Boys' California-mystique that adds a special touch of romance to their records and appearances in Europe and England, the news had not really reached all of the people whose opinion can turn popularity into fashionability. With the exception of a professor of show business (right, professor of show business; in California such a thing is not considered unusual) who turned up one night to interview Brian, and a few young writers (such as The Village Voice's Richard Goldstein, Paul Williams of Crawdaddy!, and Lawrence Dietz of New York Magazine) not too many opinion makers were prepared to accept the Beach Boys into the mainstream of the culture industry.

"Listen man," said San Francisco music critic Ralph Gleason who had only recently graduated from jazz into Bob Dylan and

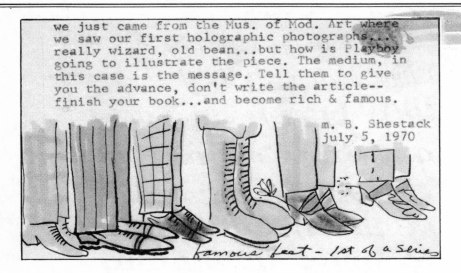

we just came from the Mus. of Mod. Art where
we saw our first holographic photographs...
really wizard, old bean...but how is Playboy
going to illustrate the piece. The medium, in
this case is the message. Tell them to give
you the advance, don't write the article--
finish your book...and become rich & famous.

m. B. Shestack
july 5, 1970

famous feet - 1st of a series

was apparently not yet ready for any more violent twists, "I recognize the L.A. hype when I hear it. I know all about the Beach Boys and I think I liked them better before, if only for sociological reasons, if you understand what I mean."

"As for the Beach Boys," an editor of the Saturday Evening Post chided his writer, who had filed the world's longest Western Union telegram of a story, "I want you to understand that as an individual you can feel that Brian Wilson is the greatest musician of our time, and maybe the greatest human being, but as a reporter you have got to maintain your objectivity."

"They want me to put him down," the writer complained. "That's their idea of objectivity—the put-down."

"It has to do with this idea that it's not hip to be sincere," he continued, "and they really want to be hip. What they don't understand is that last year hip was sardonic—camp, they called it. This year hip is sincere.

"When somebody as corny as Brian Wilson starts singing right out front about God and I start writing it—very *sincerely,* you understand—it puts them very uptight.

"I think it's because it reminds them of all those terribly sincere hymns and sermons they used to have to listen to in church when they were kids in Iowa or Ohio.

"Who knows? Maybe they're right. I mean, who needs all this goddamn intense sincerity all the time?"

What all this meant, of course, was that everybody agreed that Brian Wilson and the Beach Boys were still too square. It would take more than "Good Vibrations" and *Pet Sounds* to erase three-and-a-half years of "Little Deuce Coupe"—a *lot* more if you counted in those J.C. Penney-style custom-tailored, kandy-striped sport shirts they insisted on wearing on stage.

Brian, however, had not yet heard the news, it appeared, and was steadily going about the business of trying to become hip. The Beach Boys, who have toured without him ever since he broke down during one particularly wearing trip, were now in England and Europe, phoning back daily reports of enthusiastic fan hysteria—screaming little girls tearing at their flesh, wild press conferences, private chats with the Rolling Stones. Washed in the heat of a kind of attention they had never received in the United States even at the height of their commercial success, three Beach Boys—Brian's brothers, Dennis and Carl, and his cousin, Mike Love—walked into a London Rolls-Royce showroom and bought four Phantom VII limousines, one for each of them and a fourth for Brian. Al Jardine and Bruce Johnston, the Beach Boys who are not corporate members of the Beach Boys' enterprises, sent their best regards and bought themselves some new clothing.

Dream of the beginning one upon a time when everything ~~~~

Was fresh and new and time did not yet exist in the mind of man. Oh rich sea of souls swimming through love without end toward destinations uncharted and unknown, Survey this little universe of ours and find it more complicated than any map-maker could imagine, ⎯ Fine lace figuring every last detail with rippling feathers of liquid crystal.

"I think this London thing has really helped," said Brian with satisfaction after he had made the color selection on his $32,000 toy—a ducal-burgundy lacquered status symbol ordinarily reserved for heads of state. "That's just what the boys needed, a little attention to jack up their confidence." Then, learning that he wouldn't be able to have his new car for three months, he went out and bought an interim Rolls-Royce for $20,000 from Mamas and Papas producer Lou Adler, taking possession of the automobile just in time to meet his group at the airport as they returned home.

"It's a great environment for conducting business," he explained as his friend and former road manager, Terry Sachen, hastily pressed into service as interim chauffeur for the interm Rolls-Royce, informally uniformed in his usual fringed deerskins and moccasins, drove the car through Hollywood and to one of Brian's favorite eating places, the Pioneer Chicken drive-in on Sunset Boulevard.

"This car is really out of sight," said Brian, filling up on fried shrimp in the basket. "Next time we go up to Capitol, I'm going to drive up in my Rolls-Royce limo. You've got to do those things with a little style. It's not just an ordinary visit that way—it's an arrival, right? Wow! That's really great—an *arrival*, in my limo. It'll blow their minds!"

Whether or not the interim Rolls-Royce actually ever blew the minds of the hardnosed executives who run Capitol Records is something to speculate on, but no one in the record industry with a sense of history could have failed to note that this very same limousine had once belonged to John Lennon; and in the closing months of 1966, with the Beach Boys home in Los Angeles, Brian rode the "Good Vibrations" high, driving forward in bursts of enormous energy that seemed destined before long to earn him the throne of the international empire of pop music still ruled by John Lennon and the Beatles.

At the time, it looked as if the Beatles were ready to step down. Their summer concerts in America had been only moderately successful at best, compared to earlier years. There were ten thousand empty seats at Shea Stadium in New York and 11 lonely fans at the airport in Seattle. Mass media, underground press, music-industry trade papers and the fan magazines were filled with fears that the Beatles were finished, that the group was breaking up. Lennon was off acting in a movie; McCartney was walking around London alone, said to be carrying a giant torch for his sometime girl friend, Jane Asher; George Harrison was getting deeper and deeper into a mystical Indian thing under the instruction of sitar-master Ravi Shankar; and Ringo was collecting material for a Beatles museum.

In Los Angeles, Brian Wilson was riding around in the Rolls-Royce that had once belonged to John Lennon, pouring a deluge of new sounds onto miles of stereo tape in three different recording studios booked day and night for him in month-solid blocks, holding court nightly at his $240,000 Beverly Hills Babylonian-modern home, and, after guests left, sitting at his grand piano until dawn, writing new material.

The work in progress was an album called *Smile*. "I'm writing a teen-age symphony to God," Brian told dinner guests on an October evening. He then played for them the collection of black acetate trial records which lay piled on the floor of his red imitation-velvet wallpapered bedroom with its leopard-print bedspread. In the bathroom, above the wash basin, there was a plastic color picture of Jesus Christ with trick effect eyes that appeared to open and close when you moved your head. Sophisticate newcomers pointed it out to each other and laughed slyly, almost hoping to find a Keane painting among decorations ranging from Lava Lamps to a department-store rack of dozens of dolls, each still in its plastic bubble container, the whole display trembling like a space-age Christmas tree to the music flowing out into the living room.

Brian shuffled through the acetates, most of which were unlabeled, identifying each by subtle differences in the patterns of the grooves. He had played them so often he knew the special look of each record the way you know the key to your front door by the shape of its teeth. Most were instrumental tracks, cut while the Beach Boys were in Europe, and for these Brian supplied the vocal in a high sound that seemed to come out of his head rather than his throat as he somehow managed to create complicated four and five part harmonies with only his own voice.

"Rock, rock, Plymouth rock roll over,"

Brian sang. "Bicycle rider, see what you done done to the church of the native American Indian . . . Over and over the crow cries uncover the cornfields . . . Who ran the Iron Horse . . . Out in the farmyard the cook is chopping lumber; out in the barnyard the chickens do their number . . . Bicycle rider see what you done done . . ."

A panorama of American history filled the room as the music shifted from theme to theme; the tinkling harpsichord-sounds of the bicycle rider pushed sad Indian sounds across the continent; the Iron Horse pounded across the plains in a wide-open rolling rhythm that summoned up visions of the old West; civilized chickens bobbed up and down in a tiny ballet of comic barnyard melody; the inexorable bicycle music, cold and charming as an infinitely talented music box, reappeared and faded away.

Like medieval choirboys, the voices of the Beach Boys pealed out in wordless prayer from the last acetate, thirty seconds of chorale that reached upward to the vaulted stone ceilings of an empty cathedral lit by thousands of tiny votive candles melting at last into one small, pure pool that whispered a universal *amen* in a sigh without words.

Brian's private radio show was finished. In the dining room a candle-lit table with a dark blue cloth was set for ten persons. In the kitchen, Marilyn Wilson was trying to get the meal organized and served, aided and hindered by the chattering suggestions of the guests' wives and girl friends. When everyone was seated and waiting for the food, Brian tapped his knife idly on a white china plate.

"Listen to that," he said. "That's really great!" Everybody listened as Brian played the plate. "Come on, let's get something going here," he ordered. "Michael — do this. David — you do this." A plate-and-spoon musicale began to develop as each guest played a distinctly different technique, rhythm and melody under Brian's enthusiastic direction.

"That's absolutely unbelievable!" said Brian. "Isn't that unbelievable? That's so unbelievable I'm going to put it on the album. Michael, I want you to get a sound system up here tomorrow and I want everyone to be here tomorrow night. We're going to get this on tape."

Brian Wilson's plate-and-spoon musicale never did reach the public, but only because he forgot about it. Other sounds equally strange have found their way onto his records. On *Pet Sounds,* for example, on some tracks there is an odd, soft, hollow percussion effect that most musicians assume is some kind of electronically transmuted drum sound — a conga drum played with a stick perhaps, or an Indian tom-tom. Actually, it's drummer Hal Blaine playing the bottom of a plastic jug that once contained Sparklettes spring water. And, of course, at the end of the record there is the strangely affecting track of a train roaring through a lonely railroad crossing as a bell clangs and Brian's dogs, Banana, a beagle, and Louie, a dark brown weimaraner, bark after it.

More significant, perhaps, to those who that night heard the original instrumental tracks for both *Smile* and the Beach Boys new single, "Heroes and Villains," is that entire sequences of extra-ordinary power and beauty are missing in the finished version of the single, and will undoubtedly be missing as well from *Smile* — victims of Brian's obsessive tinkering and, more importantly, sacrifices to the same strange combination of superstitious fear and God-like conviction of his own power he displayed when he destroyed the fire music.

The night of the dining-table concerto, it was the God-like confidence Brian must have been feeling as he put his guests on his trip, but the fear was soon to take over. At his house that night, he had assembled a new set of players to introduce into his life game, each of whom was to perform a specific role in the grander game he was playing with the world.

Earlier in the summer, Brian had hired Van Dyke Parks, a super-sophisticated young songwriter and composer, to collaborate with him on the lyrics for *Smile.* With Van Dyke working for him, he had a fighting chance against John Lennon, whose literary skill and Liverpudlian wit had been one of the most important factors in making the Beatles the darlings of the hip intelligentsia.

With that flank covered, Brian was ready to deal with some of the other problems of trying to become hip, the most important of which was how was he going to get in touch with some really hip people. In effect, the dinner party at the house was his first hip social event, and the star of the evening, so far as Brian was concerned, was Van Dyke Parks' manager, David Anderle, who showed up with a whole group of very hip people.

Elegant, cool and impossibly cunning, Anderle was an artist who has somehow found himself in the record business as an executive for MGM Records, where he had earned himself a reputation as a genius by purportedly thinking up the million-dollar movie-TV-record offer that briefly lured Bob Dylan to MGM from Columbia until everybody had a change of heart and Dylan decided to go back home to Columbia.

Anderle had skipped back and forth between painting and the record business, with mixed results in both. Right now he was doing a little personal management and thinking about painting a lot. His appeal to Brian was simple: everybody recognized David Anderle as one of the hippest people in Los Angeles. In fact, he was something like the mayor of hipness as far as some people were concerned. And not only that, he was a genius.

Within six weeks, he was working for the Beach Boys; everything that Brian wanted seemed at last to be in reach. Like a magic genie, David Anderle produced miracles for him. A new Beach Boys record company was set up, Brother Records, with David Anderle at its head and, simultaneously, the Beach Boys sued Capitol Records in a move to force a renegotiation of their contract with the company.

The house was full of underground press writers. Anderle's friend Michael Vosse was on the Brother Records payroll just scouting TV contracts and performing other odd jobs. Another of Anderle's friends was writing the story on Brian for The Saturday Evening Post and a film crew from CBS-TV was up at the house for a documentary to be narrated by Leonard Bernstein. The Beach Boys were having meetings once or twice a week with teams of experts briefing them on corporate policy, drawing complicated chalk patterns as they described the millions of dollars everyone was going to earn out of all this.

As 1967 opened it seemed as though Brian and the Beach Boys were assured of a new world of success; yet something was going wrong. As the corporate activity reached a peak of intensity, Brian was becoming less and less productive and more and more erratic. *Smile,* which was to have

been released for the Christmas season, remained unfinished. "Heroes and Villains," which was virtually complete, remained in the can, as Brian kept working out new little pieces and then scrapping them.

Van Dyke Parks had left and come back and would leave again, tired of being constantly dominated by Brian. Marilyn Wilson was having headaches and Dennis Wilson was leaving his wife. Session after session was canceled. One night a studio full of violinists waited while Brian tried to decide whether or not the vibrations were friendly or hostile. The answer was hostile and the session was canceled, at a cost of some $3,000. Everything seemed to be going wrong. Even the Post story fell through.

Brian seemed to be filled with secret fear. One night at the house, it began to surface. Marilyn sat nervously painting her fingernails as Brian stalked up and down, his face tight and his eyes small and red.

"What's the matter, Brian? You're really strung out," a friend asked.

"Yeah, I'm really strung out. Look, I mean I really feel strange. A really strange thing happened to me tonight. Did you see this picture, *Seconds?*"

"No, but I know what it's about; I read the book."

"Look, come into the kitchen; I really have to talk about this." In the kitchen they sat down in the black and white houndstooth-check wallpapered dinette area. A striped window shade clashed with the checks and the whole room vibrated like some kind of op art painting. Ordinarily, Brian wouldn't sit for more than a minute in it, but now he seemed to be unaware of anything except what he wanted to say.

"I walked into that movie," he said in a tense, high-pitched voice, "and the first thing that happened was a voice from the screen said 'Hello, Mr. Wilson.' It completely blew my mind. You've got to admit that's pretty spooky, right?"

"Maybe."

"That's not all. Then the whole thing was there. I mean my whole life. Birth and death and rebirth. The whole thing. Even the beach was in it, a whole thing about the beach. It was my whole life right there on the screen."

"It's just a coincidence, man. What are

you getting all excited about?"

"Well, what if it isn't a coincidence? What if it's real? You know there's mind gangsters these days. There could be mind gangsters, couldn't there? I mean look at Spector, he could be involved in it, couldn't he? He's going into films. How hard would it be for him to set up something like that?"

"Brian, Phil Spector is not about to make a million-dollar movie just to scare you. Come on, stop trying to be so dramatic."

"All right, all right. I was just a little bit nervous about it," Brian said, after some more back and forth about the possibility that Phil Spector, the record producer, had somehow influenced the making of *Seconds* to disturb Brian Wilson's tranquillity. "I just had to get it out of my system. You can see where something like that could scare someone, can't you?"

They went into Brian's den, a small room papered in psychedelic orange, blue, yellow and red wall fabric with rounded corners. At the end of the room there was a juke box filled with Beach Boy singles and Phil Spector hits. Brian punched a button and Spector's "Be My Baby" began to pour out at top volume.

"Spector has always been a big thing with me, you know. I mean I heard that song three and a half years ago and I knew that it was between him and me. I knew exactly where he was at and now I've gone beyond him. You can understand how that movie might get someone upset under those circumstances, can't you?"

Brian sat down at his desk and began to draw a little diagram on a piece of printed stationery with his name at the top in the kind of large fat script printers of charitable dinner journals use when the customer asks for a hand-lettered look. With a felt-tipped pen, Brian drew a close approximation of a growth curve. "Spector started the whole thing," he said, dividing the curve into periods. "He was the first one to use the studio. But I've gone beyond him now. I'm doing the spiritual sound, a white spiritual sound. Religious music. Did you hear the Beatles album? Religious, right? That's the whole movement. That's where I'm going. It's going to scare a lot of people. "Yeah," Brain said, hitting his fist on the desk with a slap that sent the parakeets in the large cage facing him squalling and whistling. "Yeah," he said and smiled for the first time all evening. "That's where

I'm going and it's going to scare a lot of people when I get there."

As the year drew deeper into winter, Brian's rate of activity grew more and more frantic, but nothing seemed to be accomplished. He tore the house apart and half redecorated it. One section of the living room was filled with a full-sized Arabian tent and the dining room, where the grand piano stood, was filled with sand to a depth of a foot or so and draped with nursery curtains. He had had his windows stained gray and put a sauna bath in the bedroom. He battled with his father and complained that his brothers weren't trying hard enough. He accused Mike Love of making too much money.

One by one, he canceled out the friends he had collected, sometimes for the strangest reasons. An acquaintance of several months who thought he had become extremely close with Brian showed up at a record session and found a guard barring the door. Michael Vosse came out to explain.

"Hey man, this is really terrible," said Voss, smiling under a broad-brimmed straw hat. "It's not you, it's your chick. Brian says she's a witch and she's messing with his brain so bad by ESP that he can't work. It's like the Spector thing. You know how he is. Say, I'm really sorry." A couple of months later, Vosse was gone. Then, in the late spring, Anderle left. The game was over.

Several months later, the last move in Brian's attempt to win the hip community was played out. On July 15th, the Beach Boys were scheduled to appear at the Monterey International Pop Music Festival, a kind of summit of rock music with the emphasis on love, flowers and youth. Although Brian was a member of the board of this nonprofit event, the Beach Boys canceled their commitment to perform. The official reason was that their negotiations with Capitol Records were at a crucial stage and they had to get "Heroes and Villains" out right away. The second official reason was that Carl, who had been arrested for refusing to report for induction into the Army (he was later cleared in court), was so upset that he wouldn't be able to sing.

Whatever the merit in these reasons, the real one may have been closer to something John Phillips of the Mamas and Papas and

Consulting
the Oracle

Sunday
nov 22
10 am.
28 Preponderance of
58 the Great
The
Joyous = "Under

certain conditions, intimidation without
gentleness may achieve something momentarily but not for all time. When, on
the other hand, the hearts of men are
won by friendliness, they are led to
take all hardships upon themselves
willingly, and if need be will not shun
death itself; so great is the power of
joy over men."

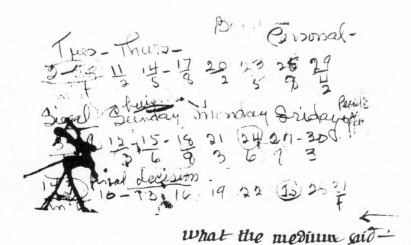

what the medium said →

a Monterey board member suggested: "Brian was afraid that the hippies from San Francisco would think the Beach Boys were square and boo them."

But maybe Brian was right. "Those candy-striped shirts just wouldn't have made it at Monterey, man," said David Anderle.

Whatever the case, at the end of the summer, "Heroes and Villains" was released in sharply edited form and *Smile* was reported to be on its way. In the meantime, however, the Beatles had released *Sergeant Pepper's Lonely Hearts Club Band* and John Lennon was riding about London in a bright yellow Phantom VII Rolls-Royce painted with flowers on the sides and his zodiac symbol on the top. In Life magazine, Paul McCartney came out openly for LSD and in the Haight-Ashbury district of San Francisco George Harrison walked through the streets blessing the hippies. Ringo was still collecting material for a Beatles museum. However good *Smile* might turn out to be, it seemed somehow that once more the Beatles had outdistanced the Beach Boys.

Back during that wonderful period in the fall of 1966 when everybody seemed to be his friend and plans were being laid for Brother Records and all kinds of fine things, Brian had gone on a brief visit to Michigan to hear a Beach Boys concert. The evening of his return, each of his friends and important acquaintances received a call asking everyone to please come to the airport to meet Brian, it was very important. When they gathered at the airport, Brian had a photographer on hand to take a series of group pictures. For a long time, a huge mounted blow-up of the best of the photographs hung on the living room wall, with some thirty people staring out—everyone from Van Dyke Parks and David Anderle to Michael Vosse and Terry Sachen. In the foreground was The Saturday Evening Post writer looking sourly out at the world.

The picture is no longer on Brian's wall and most of the people in it are no longer his friends. One by one each of them has either stepped out of the picture or been forced out of it. The whole cycle has returned to its beginning. Brian, who started out in Hawthorne, Calif., with his two brothers and a cousin, once more has surrounded himself with relatives. The house in Beverly Hills is empty. Brian and

Marilyn are living in their new Spanish Mission estate in Bel-Air, cheek by jowl with the Mamas and Papas' Cass Elliott.

What remains, of course, is "Heroes and Villains." And there is also a spectacular peak, a song called "Surf's Up" that Brian recorded for the first time in December in Columbia Records Studio A for a CBS-

TV pop music documentary. Earlier in the evening the film crew had covered a Beach Boy vocal session which had gone very badly. Now, at midnight, the Beach Boys had gone home and Brian was sitting in the back of his car, smoking a joint.

In the dark car, he breathed heavily, his hands in his lap, eyes staring nowhere.

"All right," he said at last, "Let's just sit here and see if we can get into something positive, but without any words. Let's just get into something quiet and positive on a nonverbal level." There was a long silence.

"OK, let's go," he said, and then, quickly, he was in the studio rehearsing, spotlighted in the center of the huge dark room, the cameramen moving about him invisibly outside the light.

"Let's do it," he announced, and the tape began to roll. In the control room no one moved. David Oppenheim, the TV producer, fortyish, handsome, usually studiously detached and professional, lay on the floor, hands behind his head, eyes closed. For three minutes and 27 seconds, Wilson played with delicate intensity, speaking moodily through the piano. Then he was finished. Oppenheim, whose last documentary had been a study of Stravinsky, lay motionless.

"That's it," Wilson said as the tape continued to whirl. The mood broke. As if awakening from heavy sleep the people stirred and shook their heads.

"I'd like to hear that," Wilson said. As his music replayed, he sang the lyrics in a high, almost falsetto voice, the cameras on him every second.

"The diamond necklace played the pawn," Wilson sang. ". . . A blind class aristocracy, back through the opera glass you see the pit and the pendulum drawn."

"Columnated ruins domino," his voice reached upward; the piano faltered a set of falling chords.

In a slow series of impressionistic images the song moved to its ending:

I heard the word:
Wonderful thing!
A children's song!

On the last word Brian's voice rose and fell, like the ending of that prayer chorale he had played so many months before.

"That's really special," someone said.

"Special, that's right," said Wilson quietly. "Van Dyke and I really kind of thought we had done something special when we finished that one." He went back into the studio, put on the earphones and sang the song again for his audience in the control room, for the revolving tape recorder and for the cameras which relentlessly followed as he struggled to make manifest what still only existed as a perfect, incommunicable sound in his head.

At home, as the black acetate dub turned on his bedroom hi-fi set, Wilson tried to explain the words.

"It's a man at a concert," he said. "All around him there's the audience, playing their roles, dressed up in fancy clothes, looking through opera glasses, but so far away from the drama, from life — 'Back through the opera glass you see the pit and the pendulum drawn.'"

"The music begins to take over. 'Columnated ruins domino.' Empires, ideas, lives, institutions — everything has to fall, tumbling like dominoes.

"He begins to awaken to the music; sees the pretentiousness of everything. 'The music hall a costly bow.' Then even the music is gone, turned into a trumpeter swan, into what the music really is.

"'Canvas the town and brush the backdrop.' He's off in his vision, on a trip. Reality is gone; he's creating it like a dream. 'Dove-nested towers.' Europe, a long time ago. 'The laughs come hard in Auld Lang Syne.' The poor people in the cellar taverns, trying to make themselves happy by singing.

"Then there's the parties, the drinking, trying to forget the wars, the battles at sea. "While at port a do or die.' Ships in the harbor, battling it out. A kind of Roman Empire thing.

"'A choke of grief.' At his own sorrow and the emptiness of his life, because he can't even cry for the suffering in the world, for his own suffering.

"And then, hope. 'Surf's up! . . . Come about hard and join the once and often spring you gave.' Go back to the kids, to the beach, to childhood.

"'I heard the word' — of God; 'Wonderful thing' — the joy of enlightenment, of seeing God. And what is it? 'A children's song!' And then there's the song itself;

"I haven't had any dope in 3½ years," said Brian.

the song of children; the song of the universe rising and falling in wave after wave, the song of God, hiding the love from us, but always letting us find it again, like a mother singing to her children."

The record was over. Wilson went into the kitchen and squirted Reddi-Whip direct from the can into his mouth; made himself a chocolate Great Shake, and ate a couple of candy bars.

"Of course that's a very intellectual explanation," he said. "But maybe some-

●

● *Mechanical Dreams, automatic handwriting, banking into another turn in the same old cycle. Nothing makes any sense — but why should it. Are you tired of my sadnesses? Think of how I must feel, trapped in motionless immortality over and over again. There are no reasons for my moods*

times you have to do an intellectual thing. If they don't get the words, they'll get the music. You can get hung up in words, you know. Maybe they work; I don't know." He fidgeted with a telescope.

"This thing is so bad," he complained. "So Mickey Mouse. It just won't work smoothly. I was really freaked out on astronomy when I was a kid. Baseball, too. I guess I went through a lot of phases. A lot of changes, too. But you can really get into things through the stars. And swimming. A lot of swimming. It's physical; really Zen, right? The whole spiritual thing is very physical. Swimming really does it sometimes." He sprawled on the couch and continued in a very small voice.

"So that's what I'm doing. Spiritual music."

"Brian," Marilyn called as she came into the room wearing a quilted bathrobe, "do you want me to get you anything, honey? I'm going to sleep."

"No, Mar," he answered, rising to kiss his wife goodnight. "You go on to bed.

I want to work for a while."

"C'mon kids," Marilyn yelled to the dogs as she padded off to bed. "Time for bed. Louie! Banana! Come to bed. Goodnight, Brian. Goodnight, everybody."

Wilson paced. He went to the piano and began to play. His guests moved toward the door. From the piano, his feet shuffling in the sand, he called a perfunctory goodbye and continued to play, a melody beginning to take shape. Outside, the piano spoke from the house. Brian Wilson's guests stood for a moment, listening. As they got into their car, the melancholy piano moaned.

"Here's one that's really outasight from the fantabulous Beach Boys!" screamed a local early morning Top-40 DJ from the car radio on the way home, a little hysterical as usual, his voice drowning out the sobbing introduction to the song.

"We're sending this one out for Bob and Carol in Pomona. They've been going steady now for six months. Happy six months, kids, and dig! 'Good Vibrations!' *The Beach Boys! Outasight!*"

Nov 14
Babylon

Nov 15
Palo Alto

Nov 18
Keystone

Dec 18
San Jose
Richmond $1000

'

Wha

moon
over
lake
Michigan

Afterglow in shades of violet about to melt A ring obedient in circularity about a tree upon a lawn. Helicopters and policemen in trips of three.

It is evening now darkening into black coffee night.

No contact. It is almost as if I am already dead.

Sinking window on window eyes ⹀

The Man Who Believed in Christmas Trees

Although he was afflicted with a chronic melancholy that hung in his brain like wet laundry on a smoggy day, Franklin Cornish found it difficult to complain about his life with any great sense of righteousness. It was true that he had experienced grave unhappiness and worse pain, but he had also known times of great ecstasy. If he was not especially productive, at least his work was respected for its professional solidity. And even though he was unable to consider himself famous, an occasional compliment from a stranger would make him realize that he was not completely unknown to the public.

On the balance, then, it was not really a bad life, but balance is a concept of the reason, and reason, it seemed to Cornish, was the least likely window through which one might attempt to look at the nature of things. Righteously or unrighteously, reasonably or unreasonably, he was unhappy with the condition of the universe and, more particularly, of the world immediately outside his eyes. In fact, he was so unhappy there was not one day, sometimes not one hour, in which he did not think of suicide.

It was an obsession he tried to keep to himself, a comfortable corner to which he could retreat whenever things got particularly unpleasant, constructing in his mind various scenarios of death with appropriate solemnity, rebellious flippancy, or magnificent sentimentality. But when he came close to the action itself he found himself arrested by the insistent question, "Why am I doing this?" Unable to find any reason to continue living, he was also unable to find any reason to stop. As a result he had lived nearly half his likely term on earth without doing much of anything at all.

More and more, however, he was convincing himself that death was the answer to this impotence. One thing he was hopeful of was that it would have to be at least different from life. For when it really came down to the truth of the matter, Cornish had to admit that all he was looking for was a change. Yet all the changes he had tried so far—change of climate, change of wife, change of job, change of attitude—led him to the belief that nothing helped. He had a few well-tried emotions and was unable to find any new ones to replace them; as a result, every new situation turned out to be a repeat of the old. All that changed was the color of his car, or the furniture in his apartment, or the intensity of the way he felt about things. The feelings remained the same. If there were no new feelings to be had in life, he thought, he might as well die. This change of amplitude, up and down, was not satisfying enough.

Now, at Christmas time, he swore not to fall for the illusions of tinsel and holly, not to be aroused by the mania of gift-giving nor by the gay cards that arrived from friends all over the country. The gray winter snow cloaked him in an insulated blanket of chill that seemed to be the shroud of inexorably oncoming infinite sleep, and he was content that it should be that way, despite the revelers who seemed to be trying to convince him to interrupt his frozen dream.

Cornish and his girl friend were living in a vast, empty apartment whose undraped windows overlooked a grim vista of factories, dirty houses, littered streets, and granite skyscrapers painted on a dark sky that could have been imported from one of those English movies in which the sun never shines. He had lost his job as a commercial artist and was dead broke. The telephone had been turned off for more than two months and his usual contacts were unsympathetic to his requests for help. His only recreation was long walks through streets filled with smiling robots mechanically buying useless trash.

On almost every corner there were groves of fir trees bundled in front of delicatessens, florists' shops, hardware stores, supermarkets, and curbside trucks. They looked like the remains of some violent infection that had destroyed lovely forests, the still-living, fallen hair of beautiful women ruined by an incurable disease. Trimmed and lighted with plastic angels, aluminum foil stars, and flickering electric candles, they would glitter momentarily throughout the city like the flash fever. The wiring would fail and whole buildings would blaze in fires that would kill sleeping children. No one would feel any guilt; no one would be accused of any crime; no one would be punished; and no one would ever care what else of value had been incinerated in these insultingly accidental holiday fires. It was Christmas and no one could do anything wrong. It was a brave show against death, Cornish thought, but this time he would remember the truth.

Christmas had not always had such a special meaning for Cornish. As a child he had learned what a Christmas tree should look like in an annual ceremony in the janitor's apartment, where a lovely, conical evergreen glazed with artificial snow and dripping tinsel lighted an otherwise shabby home. As the days grew colder and colder, his childhood world would fill with these reminders placed by those who sought to bring about the coming of the spirit. Yet, as the red and green and the silver and gold began to blossom outside, none of it managed to penetrate physically into the Cornish family home.

His father never believed in Christmas, nor did his mother, and he had never discussed the matter with his brother, a student at a technical academy who took him to museums filled with electrical machinery and cutaway models of submarines controlled by buttons that made miniature lights and motors move. In fact, the topic of the trees was one of the few that was forbidden in their home by absolute silence from above.

Cornish's first contact with the spirit of the season came through relatives who lived in a nearby suburb across the river. He no longer remembered how old he was when it first happened, but it might have been when he was in the eighth grade. As a treat, his father let him stay for a few days at the home of a favorite uncle and aunt, a cheerful and modern couple.

For a variety of reasons Cornish preferred his uncle above all the other relatives, not the least of which was that he owned a four-passenger Piper Cub. The uncle also had a darkroom in which he developed his own pictures, a Packard convertible car, and a cabinet full of medals earned in competitive sports ranging from ice skating and skiing to bicycle racing and swimming.

From his uncle, Cornish learned about photography; from his aunt, he found out about antiques; and from their daughter and son, he heard, for the first time, about the meaning of the trees.

"You hang up your stocking by the chimney," the little boy told Cornish as the uncle drove the Packard through streets lined with small houses whose clustered arrangements of colored lights filled the town with picture-postcard visions. "Then Santa Claus comes down the chimney and fills it with presents."

"Not at my house," said Franklin Cornish. "We don't have any chimney." The Cornish apartment did have a white false mantel with a secret compartment in the side—presumably for a radio—and a set of andirons and ruby glass coals beneath which bulbs, flickered by rotating little fans, cast a modest, electrical version of firelight. Once, he had hung one of his socks on it, but even though he put a few pieces of candy in it himself, he never did get anything else. He began to suspect that the whole thing was just another fraud, like the Good Fairy who replaced your milk teeth with money when you put them beneath your pillow.

"What is Santa anyway, Daddy?" asked the girl, who was a couple of years older than Cornish. "Is that Santa Claus thing really true?"

"We like to think of it as the spirit of giving," said Cornish's uncle. "The spirit of children who want peace and beauty around them." That night, Cornish hung his stocking on the fireplace downstairs in his cousin's home, next to the grandfather's clock whose face showed not only the time but also the phases of the moon. The following morning, after a night of turbulently dreamy sleep on a studio couch in his aunt's sewing room, he awoke and went to his stocking. It was full.

There was lined writing paper and envelopes stamped with snowmen, green holly leaves, red berries, and a dripping lighted candle in a saucer with a handle, just like the kind Jack jumped over in Jack Be Nimble. There were also assorted candies and nuts, crayons, and a gyroscope.

On another Christmas, many years later, Cornish sat in the home of a girl whose cold loveliness triggered a flare in his viscera. He had just returned from Korea, where he had seen not war but a kind of deadly peace in which the casualties were the men who committed suicide, those who got venereal diseases, the ones whose wives and girl friends grew weary of waiting. In the arms of quick Korean whores whose short embrace yielded him only spasmodic seconds of interrupted pleasure, Cornish had longed for an American girl who would think deep thoughts. Now he was with one, her face illuminated by the

And every night that falls is winter on its way, And every winter is the time of death. City of the inland sea ═ horizons blinded ═ winds bludgeoning the shuttered windows, streets roped like the decks of a ship in stormy passage.

The angels of mercy are shut away in dungeons now.

tiny lights of the brilliantly precise tree she had decorated.

They lay on the floor facing each other, her slender hand suspended before her face in a motionless moment that was neither invitation nor refusal. I want you, Cornish wished silently, I want you more than anything in the world, which was the way he thought at the time. Her pupils opened a stop wider, the almost unnaturally full lashes forming shivering borders about her white and hazel eyes. The hand moved forward and touched his face. Later, she moaned in long and sobbing climax.

In nine months they were married. Four years later they were divorced. In the interim, there had been no tree, but branches and a soft, gentle, female tortoise-shell cat who died a few years after the divorce, a death Cornish always secretly felt was his wife's fault, though for what reason and on what basis, he could not say.

It was the third time his wife put up the branches around the gold-painted schoolroom pendulum clock that the marriage was really almost over. They were unbearably poor and trapped in misery. His father, who had once been an alcoholic and had attempted suicide on two occasions, was mired in a moody quicksand of business troubles that was slowly pulling him under. Her mother, dying for eight years of cancer of the breast, pelvis, and lungs, was becoming mentally unbalanced. They had an old car that refused to start in damp weather and needed new tires which they couldn't afford. They lived in an apartment whose walls were supposed to have been painted white but turned out dingy gray. He could not remember the last time he had had a fresh orange and he was beginning to hate sex.

"Why won't you speak to me?" His wife pleaded.

"I do speak to you."

"But that's what's wrong," she said, her voice loud and squeaky with frustration. "That's exactly what's wrong. If only you could see that. You think you're talking to me but you're not."

Cornish looked up at the fir branches with the colored cards pinned to them and wished for a new life.

The world speeded up into a dark blur through which distant lights appeared and disappeared and the telephone brought the message that his father was missing, then that he was dead, then that his wife's mother was dead. On a wet highway, at fifty miles an hour, Cornish's car skidded, jumped the divider, and hit a light pole just in time to avoid careening into the oncoming traffic.

In the mirror, he saw his bleeding mouth, the broken teeth, and the bruise that was beginning to form on his forehead. He began to weep in rage, not so much for his injuries, but for the loss of the car. Then he realized that no one would blame him for anything and he let the bystanders help him out of the wreck.

"Who got killed?" the wrecker asked.

"I was the only one in the car," Cornish answered.

"You're a lucky boy," said the other. "That's a killer if I ever saw one." Lurching grotesquely, the car was pulled off the pole, its front end dented unto a deep U embrace. A thin wash of wet was making Cornish's pants stick to his legs. When he investigated, he found bleeding bruises on both shins were the motor had jammed against them coming through the front of the car. Another inch, he thought, and he would have had no legs.

He stood on the dividing mall in the foggy rain and saw people driving to work, station wagons full of children laughing and shrieking with joy, a river of energy flowing about him, rushing and turbulent, and he knew that there was no end to it ever. And above it all, behind the chaos of the clouds, the sun in all its splendid burning torment drove forward through eternal space.

Unable to speak, Cornish stood alone among the little crowd of spectators, wreckers, and policemen and waited for them to tell him what to do, neither afraid nor joyful, but simply . . . *unafraid*. In the emergency room of the hospital he let the doctors examine him and paint him with antiseptics with the passive acceptance of a corpse, not even bothering to tell them at the end that they had somehow let a piece of broken tooth remain lodged in his lower lip, hidden in an island of drying blood.

When Cornish came home from the emergency room, his wife was still out shopping, unaware of what had happened. He lay down on the double bed in the gray light of their bedroom, staring at the square of sky projected on the ceiling in blurred, enlarged detail by the imperfect lens of the windowpane. He heard the key turn in the lock of the front door. His wife put down some bundles heavily, closed the door with a lisping click of metal against metal, and walked into the bedroom. Cornish smiled, showing his broken teeth and torn lips from which blood still oozed.

She began to laugh, gulping and grunting in some kind of bizarre hilarity. "Your mouth!" she laughed in whoops of glee. "Oh, I can't help this. God, this is horrible. Why am I laughing like this?" Each sentence was punctuated by another gasp as the laughter began to turn painful. "It's just like a Laurel and Hardy movie . . . I . . ." She sat down on the floor and looked up at him piteously. He smiled again and blew a bubble of blood at her.

"No, please, no more," she pleaded as the convulsions began again. She got on her hands and knees like a sailor trying to hold onto a pitching deck. Cornish could feel the floor twirling. They were in a ship, pitching and grabbing forward through a darkening winter storm. Cornish looked at her with the eye of a spectator at a silly movie, put his fingers into the side of his mouth, and made a gibbering putty mask of joyous greed.

"No more, please, I'm sorry. Oh God," she sobbed, "I swear I'll never do it again. I'm sorry. Oh Jesus, please stop it. It's not funny anymore. I'm really crying." She fell forward at his feet and then, her face wet and her eyes crisp and glossy and red, came up on the bed and kissed his hand. "I wished you were dead," she whispered. "I wished that you were dead." In a while, it began to snow — thick, moist snow.

For a while after that they were happy, but then the arguments began again. This time, Cornish called up a girl he had known when he was in college. After several months, his wife told him she was leaving and seemed not surprised that he told her that was fine with him. It took only a short time to divide up the furniture and find her an apartment. The night before she left, he took her in his arms, kissed her body everywhere, and that was the end of it.

For a long time after that he lived in a strange dream that he was someone else, someone else using his name and body. Very slowly, he grew used to the idea and forgot that it was a dream.

Voices that were sweet and true sing to me no more. The nurse that was my summer milk has gone to be a whore.

*E*ver since childhood, Cornish had had a dream which repeated itself over and over again through various incarnations. Invariably, he was lost in an infinitely complicated transportation system, trying to reach a destination whose name he did not know. Sometimes it was a rattling old elevated train speeding at night through decrepit slums. Cornish would get on and off at dark stations, asking directions and getting no answers, continuing through the dreary course with less and less confidence of ever finding the way, until at last he would wake up with a foul mucus of despair choking his throat.

Once, the train was a silver streamliner smoothly glistening toward a tropical city whose imminence was announced by great groves of orange trees. The train stopped and Cornish got off with other passengers to pick the golden oranges and was left alone beside the track when the streamliner without warning moved rapidly off.

In the several years following his divorce there was a time when it seemed he had almost reached his destination, but for the most part he was still traveling unknown roads at night, suffocated by an overwhelming sense of his own ignorance and stupidity. Everywhere he looked there seemed to be road maps of the soul, but they were like hieroglyphics to him, diagrams and pictures in which he could recognize a bird or a man or a house but make no other sense. The symbols were plain enough, but the meaning escaped him; yet there was the insistent compulsion to continue examining them, as though just below the surface of his life there was something terribly important he was trying to remember.

At the end of a partly cloudy year, he met a young girl who was carrying a palm frond.

"Do you belong to anyone?" he asked.

"I belong to the leaf," she answered.

He had a small house in the hills, surrounded by evergreen forests and cascades of bright blue flowers that formed dense mats of color. From his bedroom window he could see all the way across the valley to the other hill, where a white farmhouse perched out of a notch in the dark green trees. At night, there was always a lantern hanging on the farmhouse porch, one small light burning like a votive candle.

In Franklin Cornish's house there were two fireplaces, one in the living room and one in the bedroom, and when the girl with the palm frond came to live with him they seemed to spend most of their time lounging before these fires. On a night in the middle of the winter they lay naked in the firelight and looked into each other's eyes, drawing closer and closer until Cornish found himself enveloped in the astonishing detail of this one feature of her face, as if he were examining her through a microscope. In the center of her pupil, surrounded by a thousandfold lacework of color upon color, there was the reflection of his own eye, looking back at him. The vision quivered and collapsed and he stepped across the last element of space. For a long period that seemed to have nothing to do with time, he felt a yellow glowing warmth fondling a part of him whose existence he had never before suspected, much less discovered. It, too, was yellow, glowing, warm.

As winter rushed on to spring, they returned over and over again to the golden experience. It expanded out into space until it filled their entire world, which felt scrubbed and clean and polished, like the mirror of an enormous telescope burnished into a perfect, shining bowl which reflected a perfect, shining heaven. In the morning, the sun was hot, the air liquid. The forest trembled. They got into the car and drove slowly down the hill. At the bottom, Cornish turned the car in a perfect circle and drove back up again, parking beneath a drooping willow that hung over the roadway.

In bounding slow motion they walked up the hillside, passing from darkness into light, from darkness into light, and each time the light became brighter until at last they were standing before an open meadow covered with a thick frosting of tiny buttercups. Behind them was the forest; between the forest and the meadow, a road; between the road and the meadow, a line of ancient cypresses stretching left and right as far as they could see.

No longer even breathing, Cornish and his girl crossed the line of cypresses and continued on into the meadow toward a great old tree whose remarkably developed limbs dripping in midnight green formed a shadowed enclosure. In this natural room, on a floor of velvet moss, spotlighted by a cone of sunlight that dropped through the great branches, they stripped off their clothes and melted into a blaze of unspeakable grandiose delight.

This was absolute center, the meeting place of eternal question and eternal answer, pulsing over and again:

"Why?" The agonized question.

"Why not?" The most obvious answer.

It was a grand thing to watch, a neon waterfall jukebox Alpha and Omega.

When he was rich and famous and respected, a young man would ask him quite seriously and with a fetching naivete, "What is the meaning of life?"

"The squarest thing you can think of," he would answer.

Now as the brilliance faded and his identity began to return, he thought, "I guess I'd better get a job." It was time to leave. Why? Why not.

On the way out, they retraced the path of bruised and dying flowers they had crushed on the way in. At the edge of the road, they dressed quickly. The sky was filled with roiling gray clouds through which crackles of lightning flickered. By the time they reached the little house on the lower hillside, it was raining, steel nails of water that spattered on the oiled surface of the road and joined a stream rushing down to the world below bearing torn flowers, broken branches, and many tumbling pine cones. All night long the storm continued as Cornish and his girl slept in each other's arms, surrounded by shadows and firelight.

On the first day of spring, they returned to the city. A late snow, unusually thick and vigorous for this time of the year, was falling when they arrived. In the morning, the city was white and fresh, and Cornish, waking early to begin the job ahead of him, walked to his new studio through streets of snow as yet almost entirely unmarked by the traffic that would soon grind it into a dirty soup of grit and slush.

*T*hat summer there was something wrong with the sun in the city. The hotter it got the less satisfaction Cornish found in its light, which never reached the full gold he had seen in the hills.

In some similar way, the activities that has promised to be so pleasurable now turned ugly and tedious, filling him with a constant disgust at the results of his work.

Flipping back and forth between his memory and the ridiculous representations he was being paid to do, Cornish wore himself out trying to force his creations to move and glow, to raise themselves out of the indifferent mud of their clumsy beginnings.

He found that he had surrounded himself with people who knew less about the job than he did. His anger grew beyond his ability to control it, until it seemed as if his entire system was ready to scream out loud in rage at the insufferable paradox of life, at the simple-minded idiocy of everything he was doing. The world, he began to believe, was a perpetual-motion machine run on a combination of wish and pain, eating him alive as he tore pieces out of himself and fed the voracious maw.

In the middle of the summer, it all collapsed. He knew that he was approaching the end of something and searched hysterically through the books in his bedroom for any kind of clue, for anything at all to convince himself that this was not the way it had to be. Then, huddled in a corner of one room, he surrendered at last to the inevitable finale he had constructed, and let his brain fall apart around him.

The room, he saw, was a three-dimensional collage he had manufactured out of the materials in his mind, a lining, so to speak to the inside of his head, with an entrance at the door and an exit in the bathroom. Into the door came experiences from the outside, whatever the outside might be. Into the sewer, through the toilet, they went after he was finished with them. Later, converted by mysterious means into palatable new stimuli, they knocked at the door and entered this moronic machine all over again. And all he was, was the intersection of these foolish events repeated over and over again in miraculously complicated ballets that served to mark off time and space in an endlessly boring infinity of cosmic self-glorification.

His girl walked into the bedroom and smiled. To him it seemed a smile of accusation, a signal of complicity in a gigantic agreement among their several selves never to let this illusion of a planet teeming with life falter.

"What am I supposed to do?" He asked her.

"You can do anything you want," she answered. "You know that."

"How long does this last?"

"Why are you being so silly? It lasts as long as you want it to last."

"I can do anything I want?" he repeated in a child's voice. "Can I die?"

Her face turned angry and he was filled with a terrible shame. With an entire world of possibilities in front of him, he had picked the one that would jeopardize everything he had put together over so many years of groping and stumbling.

"What is this dying business?" she said. "I don't want to hear anything more about dying."

One more time back through the cycle, he thought, and then I'll do it. Just one more time.

Slowly, over the next several hours, the vision faded, but the maniacal sense of shame continued, enhanced by a dreadful foreboding that before long something terrible would happen, a punishment scaled to the measure of the sins he now knew he yearned to commit. At the summer's end, he was fired from his job, and as the leaves on the trees everywhere rushed into violent color, he saw that he was afflicted with a disease that was leading him inevitably and rapidly toward death. The name of the disease was life.

*T*he city turned cold, and Cornish and his girl walked around in it like tiny insects in a giant freezer whose walls were carved into frosty representation of buildings and streets. The clock of human activity quickened in response to the growing cold. There were harvest holidays of Thanksgiving which seemed more like ritual magic to convince the people that there was something worth giving thanks for and someone worth giving thanks to. The temperature continued to drop and Christmas decorations began to appear like prayers in shop windows everywhere. Deliverymen came to the door with food, laundry, cleaning, and other necessities, and each one had with him some piece of junk for sale — silver paper and plastic berry corsages, miniature vinyl airline bags filled with inedible candy, simulated leather manicure kits with instruments that tarnished within hours and broke within days.

Then the Christmas trees were on the streets. Cornish's neighbors placed holly and ivy wreaths upon their apartment doors. They put up trees that were doomed at the end to be thrown out like garbage or burned. This was the ultimate crime, Franklin Cornish thought — to burn these lovely trees; to cut them down, decorate them with gaudy trash, and then sacrifice them.

"That's what's going to happen to me," he told his girl, who looked at him with love and endless sympathy. "I'm going to be sacrificed to strange gods. The weather is going to get colder and colder and then I'm going to be burned alive just like those trees."

"Don't worry, darling," she said. "Everything's going to turn out all right. You'll see." In order to help out with the financial problem, she was saving the plastic wrappers in which the bread came and was planning to make them into aprons she had designed, then sell them to her friends.

"That's the answer to the plastic society," she said as she carefully opened a bag into a full sheet, folded it meticulously, and put it away in a cupboard with the others she had collected. "Take their plastic and sell it back to them! Whole families can live on the junk these people throw away."

Some days she actually had Cornish convinced that they would be able to survive on her bread-wrapper apron idea, but when she revealed the next step of the plan he pleaded with her to call the whole thing off. He could not bear the thought of her going around to the neighbors begging for bread wrappers. Nothing more was said about the matter, but Cornish watched the growing pile of gaily colored plastic sheets and suspected the worst.

The following day, he received an eviction notice in the mail. "Nothing to worry about," he told himself. "No judge would allow a person to be evicted from his apartment at Christmas time. It would destroy the whole effect of the holiday for the rest of society."

The day before Christmas, however, the situation reached the depths of desperation with the arrival of a process server with a Seventy-Two-Hour Notice of Eviction.

Cornish called his heavy guns up to the front and pulled the lanyard. Nothing happened. "I'm sorry," said the reform politician whose literature he had designed free for years. He had been able in the past to handle such crises easily enough for Cornish, but not this time. "There isn't anything I can do about it. Maybe the best thing to do would be to pay the rent."

"But I don't have any money," Cornish said. "Can't you go into court and tell the judge something that will give me a chance to breathe?"

"That's a good idea," the politician answered. "What do you think we should tell him?"

"Tell him that no right-thinking person would evict a person on Christmas day."

"But they aren't going to do it on Christmas day. This doesn't take effect until the day after Christmas. Besides, you're not a Christian. Maybe there's something else you could think of?"

They stopped to look at the trees, which leaned in taut bundles against a blue van.

"Please, Frank, can't we have a tree?"

"Never," said Cornish, "No trees of any kind. I refuse to cooperate with destructive superstition." The girl turned angrily away from him.

"That's really dumb," she said. "It's just a tradition. A charming tradition, I might add, and one that I have always enjoyed celebrating. Sometimes your Puritan neurosis gets a little boring, you know."

"Give the little lady a break," said the Christmas tree seller. "I tell you what. A nice couple like you should have a tree and

11:11ᴘᴍ the eleventh hour

Embrace Death And Be Free!

"This is ridiculous. It's totally unreasonable for anyone—Christian or not—to be thrown out of his home during the Christmas season. You have to tell that to the judge. Don't you know any judges who'll give you the benefit of the doubt? You know, as a favor?"

There was an icy silence at the other end of the phone. "I don't make deals like that," said the politician. And he hung up.

On Christmas day, Cornish and his girl walked through the streets under a covering of clouds that belonged in an Arctic cemetery. The temperature had reached zero in the early hours of the morning, and a pane of glass had fallen out of their bedroom window when Cornish tried to slam it shut against the deadly outside air. There was now a piece of cardboard taped into the hole, giving the bare room something of the look of a picture taken in a sub-standard slum dwelling. The only thing missing was a mattress on the floor.

The Christmas tree sellers were desperate. "Any tree you want, one dollar," one of them called. Each day the prices had fallen, but Cornish had so far resisted.

I am not going to stand in your way. Pick any tree you want. Fifty cents. My cost, not a penny profit. What more could a person do for you?"

"You could give it to us free," said Cornish.

"What am I, Santa Claus?"

Cornish began to walk away.

"Wait a minute," said the man. "A final offer. Twenty-five cents. That way we go 50-50. I'm going to have to burn them up anyway. For a young couple like you just starting out in life I don't mind being a sport."

"Please honey," his girl pleaded. "It really means a lot to me."

"All right," Cornish surrendered, "but I want to stipulate in advance that this is being done against my will and only because he would have to burn it anyway."

"Merry Christmas," said the Christmas tree man as Cornish handed over a quarter and picked up the smallest tree he could find.

"And a Happy New Year," said the girl.

"That's right," said the man with a great smile of victory. "That's absolutely right.

Merry Christmas and a Happy New Year."
As they walked away, Cornish was filled
with a remarkably poignant sense of having
lost some kind of very important contest.

They remembered the problem of decorations when they returned to the apartment. Not far from the building there was
a street clustered with antique shops and
they walked down to it in the hope that one
of them might have something cheap and
pretty and old that might serve to decorate
the tree.

The shops were relaxed and empty. In
several the owners sat around talking to
each other and the customers over cups of
coffee. This was the last day of their big
season. Each owner had by now either
made or not made that one sale that made
the difference between continuing in the
business another year or closing up shop,
putting some of his goods into storage,
some into his apartment, and getting a job.

In the window of the store that special-
ized in odd things from rural shops of the
Twenties, a collection of worn-out Christmas decorations gleamed out of black velvet display cases. There were scratched
silvered glass bells, sapphire crystal globes,
miniature porcelain baskets of fruit, tinsel
stars, and winged angels made of marvelously folded and pasted ruffles of lace
paper. They ranged in price from 35 cents
to a dollar. When Cornish and his girl finished making their selection, amid much
counting of money and calculation of
change to make sure they had enough, the
owner gave them a present.

"Pick out any one of them that you want.
One of the dollar ones. I want you to have
it. This is your first Christmas, isn't it?"
They took a Santa Claus in a sleigh drawn
by reindeer made of pale, delicate bisque.

From the antique dealer they learned
that downtown in the commercial used-
goods district there was a store that stocked
salvaged tree lights and other decorations.
For a few more dollars, they bought not
only several strings of match-sized lights,
but also some metallic glass globes in gold,
blue, and red. When they were finished,
Cornish was satisfied that if they were to
have to have a tree, at least it wasn't
going to look as if it belonged in a bowling
alley. And when the tree was finally
trimmed and lighted, standing on a mahog-
any table in the corner of the great front
window, he had to admit that it really made
a fine show. After dinner they turned out
the room lights and sat gazing at the trembling tree for a long time.

Late at night, Cornish was awakened by
a brilliant glow blazing through the bedroom door. Without disturbing his girl, he
managed to get out of bed and into the living room, where he half-expected to find
a fire. The tree did seem almost to be on
fire, so fiercely burning were the lights
which cast a thicket of golden shadows on
the wall. It was a living thing, growing
vigorously and defiantly out of the corner,
a definite presence that raised in Cornish
a thrill of recognition, as if he had walked
into a forgotten corner of his mind and
found something for which he had been
always searching. Here it was, still small,
but getting bigger every year, the beginning of a cosmos. The lights were the stars;
the globes were the planets; the tinsel was
rain and snow; and the tree was simply
The Tree — magical, meaningful, ultimately
powerful and everlasting, no matter how
many times it might be burned. There *was*
fire in the room, Franklin Cornish saw in
a terrible moment of primitive insight—
electrical fire, nuclear fire. The world was
made of fire and one day, he now knew,
he would wake like this in the presence of
a roaring universe.

For a moment, he stood in horror before
the burning tree and felt the taste of knowledge choking in his throat. He was a
savage starting out on an endless road
through the dark, and he was afraid.
"Peace on earth, good will to men," he
wished, whispering the words aloud, and
then, with a cringe of amused embarrassment at his ability to work himself into
these megalomaniacal states, he added,
"Sure, that's what I wish for, peace on
earth, good will to men, and a new color
television for Franklin Cornish."

The next morning, Cornish woke with the
wet laundry gone from his brain. He called
the landlord himself and got a two-week
extension of the eviction order, redesigned
his girl's bread-wrapper apron, sold the
idea to a friend in the novelty business for
five hundred dollars and got himself a full-
time job illustrating a department store
catalog. As the New Year began, he waited
confidently for the color television set to
arrive, completely sure that next year was
going to be a lot easier.

Whistle, Clock.

A sunset needs no chime
and dawn is just as prompt without
the cock. Why count these rushing
warmth away? Forget your calendar
and let your inner clock keep time.

Step on board. The ship
awaits your presence. The sky is
clear and the wind is fresh. Tonight
we voyage toward the outer fringe.
Say goodbye; turn off the phone,
you're on your way to parts unknown.

Telegram

western union

SFB0 14 450A EDT JUL 22 70 CTA0 12

CT SFA096 XST2621 JT NL PDF TDSF LAGUNITAS CALIF 21

CHRISTINE SIEGEL, DLR ONLY

CARE JENNINGS 1317 18TH ST SFRAN MS

HEAVEN HAS MANY FLAVORS. ONE DAY HAS MANY MOODS. AND FROM HEAVEN

TO HEAVEN THERE ARE MANY HELLS. SAVE THIS MESSAGE. IT MAY BE

AN IMPORTANT HISTORIC DOCUMENT

JULES

BF-1201 (R5-69)

Temple testicles and bullfrogs as big, as footballs.

pages
of
life

flickering
by
our
eyes

Conversations with Eminent Americans

The Smothers Brothers

JS: Now that you appear to have brought the CBS censors practically to their knees, can you reveal what was the most successful strategy you used in your battle for freedom of expression?

Dickie: Tantrums. Screaming and yelling. Hell, at one point we told them we were going to quit.

Tommy: We said fuck it, actually. I would go through a routine in which I would act as if I were flipping out. When I started, I would know that it was an act, but then I would really get into it and I would believe it.

I would say, "To hell with it, I'll split. I don't need this show. I don't feel good. I don't want to go through an argument and make my ulcer worse. I'll walk." I was always on the verge of walking. Every other week I was saying, "Shove the show; I don't need it. Sue me if you want, but sue me in Spain. I'm not coming back." We walked a thin line—the thin line of dropping out completely, so we got our way.

JS: It's been said that the censorship battle was really just a publicity stunt. How true is that?

Dickie: Not true at all, although it was blown out of proportion in the press. We never once asked them to cover it, but if something is newsworthy they just batter the doors down. We wanted to have a show with a point. It was never our intention to do things that were dirty. To be risqué, yes; to have a double entendre, that's groovy; but that's never the point of our show.

JS: What is the point?

Dickie: The point is to do something of importance to humanity.

JS: How did you develop this sense of social conscience?

Tommy: I started caring about a lot of things I shouldn't have cared about. I wanted people to look at me not as Tommy Smothers but as *me.* They never would. I would say something serious and they would think I was putting them on. It got to the point where I would say, "No, I'm really serious about what I'm talking about." They'd laugh: "Oh, you cut-up,

Germany

France

England

America = home of the brave!

you little thing." I got tired of it.

JS: Can you pinpoint when this began to happen?

Tommy: I had a police problem in 1964. I got beaten up and had nine stitches in the head. We were doing a concert in Elkhart, Indiana and we had a dispute with the local concessionaire over program sales. We always give the profits from this to the American Cancer Society, but he wanted 60 percent as his take. I got a girl from the Society to come over and do the selling.

After the show, he came up to me and asked for a cut. I felt he wasn't entitled to anything because he hadn't done any selling. I told him, "If you want it, you sue for it." He called the cops. They said we were all going to go down to the station to talk this over. I said there was nothing to talk over. The cop said, "You're a smartass," and words started going back and forth.

We got into the police car and then one cop said, "Get out of the car." They pulled me out and hit me with the flashlight. Kenny Fritz, our manager, went to stop them and got sapped behind the ear. They had my brother up against the car. I was a mass of blood. They took us in and kept us there for six hours. We couldn't make a single call. They took all of our money as bond for resisting arrest.

JS: What was the eventual outcome?

Tommy: Nothing ever came of it. Our attorneys said there was no chance of suing and winning because they had already filled out their lies. They kept the money and it was dropped. I became very aware then that there was a legitimate police brutality thing. I never had thought it could happen to me.

I had always considered myself a liberal, but after that all the other inequities around the world really started bothering me and pretty soon I began reflecting on-stage what I was thinking privately. Before I knew it, it was a show with meaning, absolutely the opposite of the angel show, our first series, which had nothing in it, no meaning, no comedy, nothing.

Dickie: A lot of our attitude in this show goes back to our experience with the angel show, in which we bombed. The show was bad. Professionally we were very embarrassed; not by the ratings, which were good, but because it wasn't funny. If they would let us change it to make it funny it would have been all right, but we had no

creative control. We had to be whores for the writers. In this case, the writers were whores too, so we were two sets of whores with no place to go. It was a bad year.

JS: How did this experience affect the new show?

Tommy: We swore that we weren't going to be caught up again with the old standard television people who go from disaster to disaster.

Dickie: These guys—the directors, a lot of the writers and producers—they go from bomb to bomb. This is what happens when you put creative control into the hands of businessmen. They hired a guy for the angel show who had just been on a series of two bombs. I mean *bad* shows. And he got ours. Why? Are they just trying to make the shows bad?

Tommy: It's just what happens to a lot of TV shows every year. I ended up with an ulcer and a broken marriage, both of which I attribute at least partially to the show.

JS: Yet only a few months later you were back in it again. How did that happen?

Tommy: They needed something to put in against Bonanza, because the Gary Moore Show was doing so badly. At first both of us said no, to hell with it, because I was sick at the time. Finally, I said, "Okay, let's do it, because I know we can get it over with quickly and I can split for Spain."

JS: Other performers have fought these very same battles and lost. What do you think you did that made the difference?

Tommy: We had a commodity that meant money to CBS—a hit show. What I was doing on ethics they were doing on money. I know if I did it again at the wrong time, they could say, "Go ahead, split." But it just so happened that both of our interests were going in the same area, even though they were totally different; so when I would say I was going to walk, they believed it.

No one has utilized the power that they have in television. You can do a good show —if it's a hit. Once it's a hit show, then you can do what you want, really—if you have the guts and are prepared to give it up and lose it. I was prepared to lose the show, and that made the difference.

We've talked to a lot of TV stars who just can't stand doing their own shows. They say, "They give me a crummy script," but all they do is bitch and moan about it. They don't really put it up on the line to do it or not to do it. That's what we did. And we'll continue to do that. When it comes to the point where our common aims aren't coinciding, then that's the day that they'll drop us and then we'll be out in the streets or doing something else.

JS: But what was there about you that made this one a hit?

Dickie: I think we're a product of the times. The Tidings, the Catholic newspaper, ran some articles on the show which said that it was a success because we were the voice of the young people. We don't go around saying we're the voice of anything. We just try to do what we like. It just happens that we are saying the same things that a lot of people are saying.

JS: Like what?

Tommy: Mainly those things that mark the dividing line between the young and the old, between those who want things to stay the way they are and those who want them to change. The younger generation sees the inequities clearly and wants them corrected. The older generation always say, "It isn't practical." By that, they mean we stand still.

For example, I don't think young people in control would tolerate the situation at the Department of Agriculture where there were hundreds of millions of dollars in surplus funds being returned to the Treasury instead of being released to feed people who were starving. The younger generation says, "What the hell is that? Why can't they lay that money on the poor people?" The officials answer by saying that no one is really starving, anyway, and, besides, they don't have any money to do anything about it. The younger generation says, "Why are you lying to us instead of doing something?" The older generation answers, "Now look, don't push the government around."

It isn't always politics, though, or ideas. It's also a matter of taste. The acceptance of Tiny Tim by millions of young people and the complete rejection by the older people is an example of how the orthodox and unorthodox are defined. Tiny Tim really divides it right down the center of the line.

JS: Do you think that the differences between children and their parents is fundamentally any greater in our time than in other periods of history?

Tommy: I'm not sure. It's getting harder as I get older to get inside kids' heads. Yet there's a great deal of difference. The kids are more cynical than their parents. The credibility gap isn't really a gap between the people and the government so much as it is between the old and the young. When I was growing up, our country was the best in the world as far as I was concerned. I mean there was nobody that was going to do anything better than us. Then came Sputnik. It was the biggest shock I'd ever had. I thought, "What the hell is that? That's not supposed to happen. We have more telephones, more cars, the best scientists." A crack began to appear in the national ego.

Since then the whole fabric has begun to fray. All these lies—the U-2, the Tonkin Gulf, the whole war—have destroyed our willingness to believe anything. For the ones who are younger than us, the college kids, maybe there was no willingness to believe in the first place. I mean they were brought up seeing commercials on TV that lied to them. Almost everything else that followed has been a lie also, or so it seems. The result is the government has lost the faith of a tremendous piece of the population. This is a bad thing. Dangerous situations develop and the government is powerless to do anything. The LSD story is a perfect example. When LSD first became available generally, there were people who tried to warn against it, but nobody believed them. For years the government had been screaming about how dangerous pot was, so everyone assumed that these were the same lies and exaggerations. And now, after it's all settled down, it appears that acid was almost as dangerous as they said it was—but only after a lot of people were hurt by it.

JS: The use of drugs such as marijuana seems to be one of the important dividing lines between old and young. Where do you stand on this issue?

Dickie: I don't think really well-adjusted, happy people need drugs of any kind. But let's face it, not everybody is happy and well-adjusted. If people have to use drugs, then I think marijuana is a lesser evil than alcohol.

Tommy: I would say that seventy-five percent of the people I associate with in the entertainment industry smoke grass, not constantly, but occasionally.

JS: Do you think there are any negative effects associated with the use of marijuana?

Tommy: I don't want to sound like a prude, because I still smoke, though in moderation, but I think it does reduce your ability to perform in certain ways. I mean my desk is a mess and there's little things that just don't get taken care of—the bill that doesn't get paid immediately, the letter that doesn't get answered.

JS: Do you smoke that much?

Tommy: I'm not an infrequent smoker. It's cut down, but I didn't do it purposely. There was just that awareness of things that had to be done. On the other hand there are cats I know who have, all of a sudden, begun to lay off. A friend of mine says he hasn't smoked any grass in 44 days. He feels great. He wakes up quicker and really digs the feeling. I don't know if I could do that or not, but I'd like to try it, because it might be refreshing to lay off all kinds of highs—liquor, pot, everything.

JS: What about LSD? Have you taken it?

Dickie: The performers I know have taken anywhere from two to twenty trips. I've never tried it. I'm afraid to.

JS: Why?

Dickie: I see other people who have taken it and seem to have lost almost all their aggressiveness. Maybe the world would be better off without aggressiveness, but to get anywhere and do anything you want to have this edge of it. I don't want to lose it. It's what makes me what I am. It's my personality. Aggressiveness is a very important factor.

Tommy: It takes away a little bit of that fight, that animosity thing. I've taken about five or six heavy trips, and I think I'm less effective than I was. It was the most incredibly beautiful experience I've ever had, but the residual effects have been destructive in a creative sense.

Art isn't art unless it's seen and appreciated. If you don't get to show it, it's just doodling on a wall or a monologue done in a cave, talking to yourself. But you have to fight to get something across. You have to find the platform; you have to buck the established viewpoints that won't accept what you want to say. You can't do that as well when you take acid.

JS: What makes you say that?

Tommy: I'm not guessing. I saw that

change. One trip didn't hurt and two didn't hurt, but once it got into five, six, whatever it was, I noticed things began to get through on the show that I would otherwise have fought. I'm not saying this because I saw it in someone else. I saw it in myself.

If I were to sum up what I feel it would be something like: Yes, I have taken LSD. It was an incredible experience, but I don't recommend it because it dulls the drive that makes a person live and achieve. And you've got to achieve. What is life? It's nothing. You're born and then you die. You have to do something in between. It's a working thing, an achieving thing, and that's what we're supposed to be doing.

Maybe some of those rotten criminals who step on everybody and kill the good people are the ones who need LSD in order to have a little edge taken off their insane drive. But not the soft and gentle people. They don't need it.

JS: Specifically, what are some of the things you had to cut in order to satisfy the censors?

Tommy: Unbelievably innocuous things. In one show Leigh French, who plays Goldie, was supposed to say to her husband as he came home, "I really dig you." The censor said, "That's got to come out. That's a fuck joke. Digging is a fuck joke." Leigh explained to him that it meant nothing of the kind, but he said, "Back when I was a kid, to dig meant to have sexual intercourse." This is where their mentality is. They're completely out of step with the people who are making this country happen. They're really not very bright or intellectual. They're from 1949 or 1950.

Dickie: Mason Williams, one of our writers, pointed out that you can kill on television but you can't make love. You could show this bit on television: a woman in her nightgown getting into bed; the window slowly opens; a shadow climbing in; he walks over to the bed, picks up the pillow and snuffs out her life. That's acceptable. But what if he did the same thing, only this time he picked up the pillow, shoved it under her ass and made love to her? Now he didn't kill her, he spared her life. Christ, he gave her pleasure, but it's very objectionable.

We had one skit in which Tommy played Billy the Kid. We were all bad guys and we wanted to kill him, but Belle Star stopped

us. "No, love him," she said. "He's a bad kid, yes, but it's because he's misunderstood." He was really a drag, but each time we wanted to shoot him, she wouldn't let us. Finally one guy said, "She's right. We've got to give him some love." Then he said, "Wait a minute. We're on television. We can't love. We've got to kill him." We all said, "Yeah, I guess that's right," and blasted the hell out of him. It really went across, but CBS didn't like it.

Tommy: They are constantly underestimating the intelligence of the audience. In the last show of the season, we had a line that ran, "Ronald Reagan is a well-known heterosexual." They said people would misunderstand and think we meant homosexual. One of our producers asked the censor, "What do you think heterosexual means, actually?" The guy looked very embarrassed and said, "Oh, you know, someone who goes both ways." So you see what we're dealing with here. It was the last show of the season, so I couldn't say I was going to walk. We had to compromise.

JS: What direction is the battle going to take now that it seems you've broken through some of the more obvious taboos?

Tommy: In bringing television up to date with what's going on in the country generally. Right now it's ten years behind. It's the only mass media that's that much out of step. Magazines, films, radio, music, books — everything is reflecting what's happening today except television. We're still dealing with people in continuity acceptance — which is the department that does the censoring — who are living ten years in the past.

JS: What kind of letters do you get?

Tommy: We're called Communists and, "You should be ashamed of yourself. Your father was killed in the war and you defamed and defiled his name, who died for his country." Or, "Now, it's truly the Communist Broadcasting System" — because we had Pete Seeger on the show; that's when all the vile letters came in.

Dickie: Oh, people are nuts. We tend to classify people who put us down as nuts. And most of the time we're right, judging by their letters. "You're un-American and God help our country when people like you are allowed to express their filthy, stupid ideas on the television and poison the minds of everybody." You know, that kind of shit. And it's funny that most of the praising letters — this sounds funny — are from intelligent people. At least, they sound intelligent from the way they write; and I think it must be the case because the stuff we're doing is sometimes not appealing to a person who doesn't have a brain.

JS: Do you think you ever get too far-out?

Dickie: I don't think there is any concept that is too far-out to do in television.

Tommy: There shouldn't be reverence for anything. Things that are untouchable become dead and stale. All our institutions — mom and apple pie, government and educational systems — should be put up to scrutiny, whether on television or in the other mass media.

Jack Newfield
& Paul Gorman

Gorman: Jack asked me to do this thing for his book, which I haven't been able to do, on Bobby about the night that they put the casket of Kennedy in St. Patrick's. Jack and I and Tom Hayden; Jeff Cowen walked by and some of the Kennedy staff invited us in. Tom Hayden and I and Joe Krangle, this big boss from Erie County stood by Kennedy's casket for a half hour. So Tom Hayden cried, and he was put down for crying. I did not cry.

It occurred to me then that what you got in the last eight or nine years is the first generation of people who realized that it wasn't getting better all the time in America. All of a sudden between 1958 and 1968, in that sort of period, a whole bunch of people realized that it's getting worse. It may be revolutionary, but the fact is that it is deteriorating. First of all, I think that's true and I'm curious whether you guys do. Second, I think every question you want to know has to be raised in that context.

JS: I don't see it quite that way. First of all, I only see that America becomes more and more highly conceptual. America is my mother—because my mother was born here—and Russia is my father—he was born there. And when Russia and America were allies against the Germans—the germs—the germs were out to get me and my mother and father got together and kept them off. That's the way I see America at this point. Nevertheless, when I'm out in public I have to walk around like I really believe this is America because the cop is going to hit me with the stick. But the cop is going to hit me in the head with the stick anyway because that's the way it works. Whether you're good or bad, that comes. That's his job. That's not only his job but you ask him to do it. The guy who goes into the public toilet, after all the stories about public toilets, to pick up another fag is looking to get arrested by a cop. It's as simple as that. In that case, the cops are providing a service by arresting this guy. Anyway, I got off the point. What I'm saying is that America is deteriorating. America is deteriorating in the sense that as I become more and more important to myself and more convinced of my own power and more and more convinced of the total futility of anything that we do anyway, America looks as if it is falling apart, dying. It's dying as an idea; it's dying as an authority figure and I think that's what we see. When it began for me was when the Russians beat us with Sputnik. I couldn't believe that, the Russians were this primitive race of people over in Russia, peasants; they couldn't work machinery or anything like that. And I'm sure for another generation that the same thing happened when the Japs invaded Pearl Harbor. That happens over and over again. Your authority figure is destroyed.

Newfield: For me it was when the Bay of Pigs failed, when Cuba beat John Kennedy.

JS: Really? I was expecting that. I really didn't care.

Newfield: I didn't think it would be, and then when Cuba beat off the landing I was impressed, very happy. It really was a loss of innocence for me.

JS: What I'm saying is that the loss of innocence happens to everybody. Everyone says it's television, mainly television brings the loss of innocence earlier. It's pointless to limit the kids to anything because they already know more—that's really literally true—they know more than we do. I see everything in those very personal terms.

Gorman: We're different because I feel, or I felt up until a couple months ago, I felt responsibility to make it get better all the time, or help it get better all the time. The war did that to me.

JS: Why did the war do it to you?

Gorman: It's a brutal, terrible thing that the country in which I am a citizen . . .

Newfield: The government for which you voted on a peace plank.

Gorman: . . . was murdering millions of people in the worst act in its history; and I could do something about it, at least I thought I could. I worked in the Anti-War Movement and I worked in Congress organizing seven or eight guys who would vote against war appropriations, and I wrote speeches for Gene McCarthy, and helped dump Lyndon Johnson. I thought that made a difference. It made a difference to the Vietnamese; I don't know what the fuck difference it made to America. The question is who do you think you are working for when you're working? I thought that I was working for the Vietnamese.

He not busy being born is busy recording "Blue Moon."

Richard Nixon is impotent.

Fascism will come to America wearing a wide psychedelic tie.

Fuck Rich people.

Carl Furillo was better than Gil Hodges.

Jerry Rubin is a gangster

Jack Newfield

Newfield: I think the internationalist sense is very crucial. I really don't feel any loyalty to the government. I feel a loyalty to values in my head and to the internationalists. I don't really give a shit about America.

Gorman: Yes, you do.

JS: I don't know if I do or not. I give a shit about me personally in what happens to America, but why should America survive?

Gorman: If you're asking me whether there are good things in this country worth preserving, the answer to that is yes.

JS: The Roman Empire was a great institution, the greatest government the world has ever seen and it didn't survive.

Gorman: Why should one expect it to survive is what you mean? I don't expect it to survive. I said so earlier. I don't know the pace of deterioration.

Newfield: But I also think there are things worth preserving in Cuba and Israel and . . .

JS: I think as I get older, it gets more important each year after 30—and they're right, don't trust anyone over 30—that my paranoia is that I begin to see the world as a plot against me. But it's not. I said to Pynchon one time when I really wanted to die, "There's a plot to keep me alive." "Every time you hear an ambulance siren," he said, "that's part of the plot to keep you alive." In a sense the plot is there for everybody. It's a universal plot. The secret is that it comes out any way you want it to come out.

Gorman: I don't understand that at all. I'm really stupid about all this.

JS: It's not that. It's a matter of experience. You have to be psychotic in order to experience it. The way I see the world is everything is there, you either choose death or choose life, right? If you want to choose death, there is any way of dying. If you want to choose life, there are any number of people who will help you live, no matter what situation you are in. In Bedford Stuyvesant there's a guy who is about to commit suicide, and there is probably someone in there who can help him. And yet, we all are likely to die.

Gorman: Let's talk about music.

JS: You want to change the music system? Or is the music system changing the political system? I haven't listened to music in a long time. I used to write about it, so it got boring to me. In fact, let me tell you about this. I once walked in to find Brian Wilson looking at himself on the

Ann Landers is an oracle. So is the Playboy Adviser. Every letter is individually answered. One girl wrote she was worried b Got "Spastic" when he came

moniter of the videotape machine Capitol gave him as a Christmas present. He was singing, "It's really true how nothing matters. There's no mad world and no mad hatters." Another time he had his whole family, friends and dog lined up in front of the television camera. They were all sitting there watching themselves in the monitor. Chrissy takes the microphone and says, "Ladies and Gentlemen, welcome to 'This Is Your Hangup,' starring Brian Wilson and his family and friends." It was after that he decided she was a witch and barred her from the record studio. So, why do you want to talk about music?

Gorman: As to what you would be putting in its place. I think one of the most advanced examples and the most visible is alternate culture: rock music, underground papers, free universities, electric circuits and paraphernalia are all a part. I think that is probably the cultural revolution for the more advanced. . . .

JS: Did it ever occur to you that those are all just devices to sell dope?

Gorman: So what else does music mean? So you were a big man in music? What did you learn?

Newfield: He learned that it made money for him.

Gorman: Do you believe that everything is the same? I still believe that things are different.

JS: No. I believe that the essential experiences of life are all the same and that

the in-between is all that counts. When I say in-between I mean, if you have a really good shit, that's a great experience. That's not in-between; that's an experience. If you have a really good meal, that's a great experience. If you have a really good fuck, that's a great experience. If you have a really good jerking off, that's a really great experience. If you die, that's a great experience. If you're born, that's a great experience. Writing is in-between. That's all I know about in life.

Newfield: What about dope?

JS: No, I just assume that you take dope in order to do any one of those things and enhance the experience. If you're in a good mood anything is great. The major event of life is the orgasm and, as it turns out, you find out that the orgasm at the bottom is a really dopey thing, and really very silly. And that life itself is really very silly and is really a joke. That's my vision.

Newfield: Jules, you don't really believe that you have a responsibility for anybody else's happiness, do you? The most deadend conversation I've ever heard in my life was Julie Siegel and Casey Hayden; Julie Siegel saying why he doesn't care what happens to Negroes.

JS: Did I really say that?

Newfield: Driving out to Long Island that night.

JS: I was doing that for a joke.

Newfield: I know you're perverse.

JS: Does she still remember it?

Cow people = We visited a dairy farm in Tillamook and a cheese factory. Tillamook is one of America's best cheeses, but very mild. The farmer had eyes just like his cows. His son was on his way home from Vietnam. He was worried about what the war might have done to him.

Newfield: I haven't seen her. I think you half believed it and do half believe it.

JS: I still believe it.

Newfield: But what I'm saying is that you don't have any moral feeling of obligation to act to help other people's lives.

JS: No, you're wrong about that. I'm thinking about it — whether I have any ethical feelings — and I don't think I have any. There are things that disgust me to see them, but not on an ethical basis.

Newfield: But it doesn't impose any responsibility on you to act.

JS: No.

Newfield: You just look away.

JS: I don't really feel that I can do anything for people's lives.

Gorman: You mean you would if you could, but you can't so you don't.

JS: No, I feel that I do whenever I can. Like writing an article for Playboy, as far as I'm concerned, is my contribution. When you read the story in the New American Review — I don't even know if you'll like it — but that was my contribution this year. I got $500 for the thing. That's like doing it free.

Newfield: But that's not politics.

JS: But I'm not interested in politics except as an observer.

Newfield: That's not the point. The point is you don't feel the responsibility to act to make other people happy.

JS: I do feel the responsibility to act to make Jerry Kretchmer more happy.

Newfield: He's a friend.

JS: I feel responsible to act to make you more happy.

Newfield: But to make strangers' lives better?

JS: If I happen to meet them on the street at the moment, yes. If I'm in a coffee shop and the waitress looks unhappy . . .

Gorman: Philanthropy is not politics.

JS: What I'm talking about is this. As far as I can see, all I can do is to attempt to make that a way of life, at the moment — for myself, at that moment — because there really is no future and that's really the truth; and I don't know that this building is not going to fall in, it could cave in on us right now, and then what the hell was the point of being good?

Gorman: That's a conversation stopper.

Newfield: Why don't we talk about the newspapers in America? I think the New York Times and Time Magazine tell less truth than the Village Voice.

JS: I think almost anybody we know would agree with that.

Newfield: I don't think the 6,000,000 readers of Playboy will accept that as a given.

JS: I think they would say that Playboy tells more truth than the New York Times does, and they'd be right.

Newfield: But Playboy doesn't try to tell the truth about important things.

JS: Yes, it does. It tries its best to do it. It's just that it is very difficult for it to do it.

Newfield: When did they talk about poverty, or the assassinations. What has

Playboy ever done about the Vietnam war? Aside from the one article by John Kenneth Galbraith.

JS: They also did an interview with William Coffin. They also did an interview with Spock. Playboy has done more and better stuff in those areas than Esquire. You didn't read it, but that doesn't mean they didn't have it. What I'm saying about Playboy is that the magazine is one of the most important publications in the country on a very dumb level; it's not the Village Voice. It's like the East Village Other, a lot better really. But you can't poo-poo the magazine.

It's a lot better than Life. It's very clumsy; it's Chicago; it's Midwest. It looks like the inside of an airline or something like that. But nonetheless the direction is absolutely right. They're trying their best.

Gorman: It challenges people, challenges values without asking people to change their lives. In that sense it is a counter-revolutionary . . .

Newfield: It has plagiarized the style of dissent, grafted on upward mobility and tits. . . .

JS: You just don't understand it.

Newfield: Hi-fi's. . . .

JS: Playboy is a magazine which is essentially involved in two things, right? One is sex and the other is masturbation and the psychiatrist would say to you that there is no difference between the two.

Gorman: What's the difference in the magazine?

JS: One is never mentioned and one is always mentioned.

Gorman: Well, the two are the same in the magazine.

JS: The pictures of the girls is the masturbation. The sex is all the articles like the Playboy Forum, The Playboy Advisor, things like that—How To Make It With Girls, What Not To Be Afraid Of, you know, you're not going to go insane, you're not going to get hair on your hands. But in those terms, that's what the magazine is really interested in. Those are the things that Hefner wants to do, wants to be permitted to do personally.

Newfield: He wants to sell sex with repression.

JS: No, he doesn't want to sell sex with repression; he wants to eliminate repression from sex. What you don't see is that as repressed as Playboy looks . . .

Newfield: Why do all the playmates have to look like virgins?

JS: Well, they don't look like virgins to me. They all look like they're made out of pneumatic plastic. But that's what he likes, personally. That's what Hugh Hefner likes. That's what he likes girls to look like. To him, sex without repression has only reached the level of that playgirl. You know, a nice, clean girl—a clean, bright girl—by bright I mean bright looking. Our idea of a good looking girl would be ugly to him and would be ugly in most of the country. And the fact that he's gone that far is a tremendous achievement. All you have to do is look at the magazines from 20 years ago and what they thought was sexy. I went up to 42nd Street to see *The Night They Raided Minsky's* and the guy I was with says, "You have to go in and look at the magazines." So we all went in. And there spread out all over the place were these pictures. It wasn't shocking but astonishing. But they were the kind that you got out of your father's drawer printed in Havana. And they're openly displayed—and every variety. They had teen nudes, black stockings, bosoms, behinds, all that kind of stuff. And that could not have happened without Playboy.

Gorman: It's a very heavy point.

JS: It's a very heavy point because it's more important than the war in Vietnam.

Gorman: The difference is crystallized.

Newfield: Julie Siegel goes to Vietnamese refugee camp and sells dirty pictures. Forget about your napalm face.

JS: What I'm saying is that at the bottom that's what they're fighting about.

Newfield: Do you think people's lives have been liberated by reading Playboy? Do they have better sex or more frequent sex?

JS: Yes. Definitely. There's no doubt about it. People use these things. They clip things and show it to each other. It comes up in conversation. Including Republicans, Democrats, all walks of life, men, women, children. Anyway, what do you want instead of Playboy?

Newfield: Live girls.

JS: What's standing in the way of you getting them? The way the system is now? I mean does the New Left have any sexual position?

Newfield: Prone.

John Sinclair

I was like the first one on my block to get arrested for dope, you know, in Detroit.

When did that happen?

Sixty-four.

That was early.

I was dealin' grass in the neighborhood. That's why I got to know most of the people. Our program was rock and roll, dope, and fucking in the street.

That's my program, too.

Yeah. And dope—a lot of people try to play down dope and say it isn't political—but I know, man, that whole community in Detroit was based on dope, man. The one thing that everybody had in common was that they all got high. It was so great that everybody had to get into it.

But not that many people knew about it; distribution, advertising and the whole media thing was not in effect.

So what I started doing in '64 in the summer was all these people that I was meeting and getting high with, we started talking about organizing a community, say call it an artists' workshop. We had musicians, poets, but we were defining ourselves as artists, you know, it wasn't like a painter's thing. It was an artists', with an apostrophe after the s, because we were defining ourselves very clearly as artists, rather than just being people who were doing it for a job.

Where was this?

In Detroit, in '64. No scene there at all. No scene that you could recognize or relate to. I was there three months before I ever saw the freaks. And that was at a showing of underground films at the Art Institute and I went there and all of a sudden here were all these freaks man, all these beatniks. And I was walking around every day going to school, going to graduate school, with a full beard and a head of hair.

Then a beard was the thing.

Yeah, a full beard, head of hair, denim work shirt, brown corduroy jacket, levis and sandals, a book bag. I mean, I had a costume down perfect because that's what I wanted to be. That's what I wanted to be, man, I wanted to identify myself so clearly that anybody else who was like that could know that that's what I was. It took like two or three months before I even saw the freaks. I was getting discouraged. After I met just a few people here and there I saw these people and I just flipped out— Wow, this is it! I'll bet all these people get high, you know. And then I eventually met them all through dealing grass.

I remember when I went to the Peace March in '67. I never went to those things, I still don't like them, but anyway I went to it high and I walked up towards Central Park and then suddenly there were these two hundred thousand people I knew that I could get high with. There were that many of us, and I had thought up until then that it was just a few guys.

'Cause you didn't have any media, you know.

You didn't have any connections.

We didn't know what the fuck we were doing. Like we started, man, there were 16 people. Called a meeting of the people and 16 people showed up. We talked about it and said okay let's do this and everybody put up $5 and we went out and rented a house. We knew we had to have a physical facility because if you're going to say you're something then you have got to have some place where people can come and meet you and see what you're doing. So we got a house, artists' workshop. Right in the neighborhood.

The interesting thing about it is that you had no guidelines at all.

None.

You just did it naturally.

Well, we had our fantasy. See we read all these—by that time we were deep into the avant garde—all the poetry magazines, all the avant garde jazz musicians and we were just into all of that and propagating it. We had this fantasy that New York, man, was just Mecca. There was all these people there who created all this great stuff and they all knew each other and it was all one big community of people working together. Like you'd read in a magazine, like you'd read in Kultur.

But they were all in competition with each other. It just blew my mind. I was completely disillusioned, man. It was like the musicians, the jazz composers guild, man, I thought, wow man, these are the greatest fuckin' minds in the world and they've all got together man, they've got their own place, and they're going to have their own record company, and do everything right. Find out later they all hate each other, they're all bickerin' with each other.

And we also found out the people in New York were always afraid somebody else was trying to burn them because there was always some money involved. No money involved in ours man, nobody ever got paid. Everything we did was free. People supported themselves.

And after the first time the band came to New York, we were supposed to go back home and never be heard from again. But this time we just came out with twice as much stuff, phew. Everything was cool. We related to the people, man, and they know that all that stuff is bullshit, even what they thought.

It was a community dance this time, man. All the people from the radical community were there and especially people who we had all the trouble with in December, you know, because they misinterpreted what we were doing.

Well, what were the criticisms?

Well, okay, The Motherfuckers were having a big battle with Graham over the use of the building.

Yeah, right, they wanted to use it one day.

The week before, see, we had come here especially from Boston. We came down here to play free Wednesday night for the Motherfuckers. Because we wanted to show them here we were coming from our community up there. We wanted to show them we wanted to form an alliance. So we did that. We found out at that time that their community wasn't anything like our community, you know. It was much more negativistic, much more destructive, because of the geography and everything, the East Side. So we had this killer positive show and they couldn't really relate to it, you know, but they could relate to us being there. But they weren't quite sure because there wasn't like the kind of music that they could relate. If it would have been folk rock or something like that they could have related to it right away, you know. But you know, I mean just something, if it would have been like the Fugs, or Country Joe and the Fish . . .

If it was a category that they knew about.

Yeah, something that they could relate to. We came in there playing maniac rock and roll, leaping around and bright costumes and shit. Everybody is in there with army clothes, walking around like that and they just couldn't equate us with "revolution."

So that was the state. And then we come in and give the free concert. The way we looked at it they were trying to put on free concerts every week, have a free thing there, well we ripped the record company off for a free concert for everybody. Graham couldn't throw anybody out or anything. The record company rented the hall for the night and put on a free concert.

Who paid for it?

Elektra paid for it, you know. We set it up. Yeah. December, the day after Christmas. And to us that was the way that you go about getting a free concert.

Right.

To me use doesn't necessarily mean ripping it down, you know what I mean.

That's right, that's right. This is the whole argument that I had. You can co-opt the institutions.

Right. You know. We just made this deal with Atlantic, man, for a bunch of money and they gave us everything we wanted.

They don't give a fuck as long as they get their end. That's all and that's fair enough. They're not essentially evil of themselves. They're evil if they use for evil purposes. And I'm not even sure there is any—

Right, right, right. Evil is not an operative term I don't think. Or good, you know except in this is good stuff, you know I mean that sure felt good, you know. Yeah, okay. There's right and wrong I think. Right meaning what works and wrong meaning what don't work. But I mean if you're gonna deal with reality you gotta deal with reality the way things are and not your illusions, which are real again in another sense, but it ain't the kind of reality that you've gotta work with. You've got to find out what's going on and deal with that, rather than trying to force your terms on the world. That's the folly of the fuckin' white man. They're doomed by it. It just isn't reality. It just doesn't work. This shit doesn't work.

Getting back to the thing about the Motherfuckers and the Fillmore, what they felt is that he won't give us the place. We're in here tonight, if we don't get an agreement from him tonight, ya know, then we'll never get the place, ya know. Essentially, it was just a desperation position, man. Ben Morea said, "If we leave this building tonight, man don't you see, we won't ever be able to come back in." I really related to that.

And it was just like, "Well, what are we going to do, we got to do somethin'. You know," they said, "rip the place up. You guys get behind it, man," they said. "You just give the word, man, and we'll destroy this place." Fuck that shit, man, that ain't what we were there for, ya know. We went through a whole thing, man to get this fucking concert, ya know and uh that ain't what we were there for. And they got pissed off ya know. But we wanted to make it very clear that we weren't part of that. The band hates politics, they can't relate to it at all, ya know. It doesn't have nothin' to do with anything that they got on their minds, ya know. Because they meet those people and they're all uptight and they're out and they write all this stuff, ya know. They ain't havin' a good time.

So we went on stage man and J.C. and Tyner Vos said well, we're here to play rock and roll and have a good time, you know we ain't here for politics. All these people in there, they said, "Whoa, jesus christ. How could they be revolutionaries and say something like that. It's a hype. They're just using the revolution, they're co-opting it, you know. Trying to use the underground press."

What we finally had to get across to them what we're dealing with now, is that we are the underground press, ya know. I was writing for underground papers before any of these other ones existed, ya know. And still do.

Well what do they think they're trying to do?

Well, they're just desperate. I mean I'm just saying that was a desperation measure. Most of those moves are made out of desperation.

So you think that people have just lost so much that they can't—

Oh, no, they're trying to organize the community. They want the things that we want. They want the things everybody wants but they're in the middle of the Lower East Side and it's a fucking hell hole, man. You know, I mean it's bad for somebody that's living over here, you know, or on 20th Street, but I mean, coming from Ann Arbor, man, which is paradise. The band calls it the rock and roll sanctuary of the world. You come to the Lower East Side and it's just like going to hell. Man, like you just lost. You know and there you are. They can't even find a place to put on a free

dance. Ya know, and that's their culture, man. I mean they're revolutionary dudes, man, the Motherfuckers. And their documents, those are some of the most brilliant things that have come out of the whole movement. They've written statements in there, man, about revolutionary culture that have just completely blown me away. I just loved them, great influences.

I mean they just can't because of where they are and the things that they have to deal with in day to day terms, the people they deal with who are the down and out street people, the old winos and bums and the runaway kids and speed freaks and junkies, ya know. The most desperate people in the world, man, are all those people, and they actually deal with them, and they have to be more concerned with where is this old bum going to get fifty cents for his next jar of wine and where are these kids going to stay the night where the police won't be able to catch them and I mean they don't have—they feel they ain't got nothin' to say to Playboy. They're not interested in talking about their ideas and shit. They ain't got no ideas. They just live their thing. You know, they live their culture. And the statements they make are so great, phew.

Why do they seem to feel called upon to do it?

Well, they just are, you know. I mean they have a holy purpose. They're just inspired like any other. You know they're acid head freak visionaries, in a sense. I mean not to make that sound cheap or anything. They're activists. They're out there in the streets doing it. And they know what they're doing and they know why they're doing it and they don't care about relating to somebody else, because they still have got to get that shit together right there. And that's absolutely right.

Most groups and movements or whatever that have come up have just been like super eager to get stuff in the press since a lot of people involved in them are on ego trips . . .

Yeah, right, they want to be celebrities.

If you asked me what I'd like to do, man, when all this shit is over, man, I'd just like to be in Ann Arbor and play with my kids, ya know, listen to records and get high, and fuck and like that, and talk to my friends, go walkin' around town all the time. That's what I like to do.

Luna

Kosmic Kapers. We pay only for publishable material, sir. This is bullshit. Go back to your place and correct your sins. Kafka was a realist. I am a Wise guy shitting in the stream of consciousness.

Well, why aren't you doing it?

Well, because I mean there's all this other possibility and shit to do, ya know. I mean, because all it comes down to man, you'd be out walking around the street and some kid comes up and tells you the police broke his door down yesterday and took him away, ya know, and his buddy's still in jail on $5000 bond man. They gotta get the money up, ya know. Undercover agents, ya know. You can't be free unless everybody's free, man.

Now I feel man that, ya know, that people can be free. 'Cause of the technology. Purely and simply—you get down to paleo-cybernetics; the idea of that is to be able to establish a term through the use of cyber-nation, a living term on the planet that would be like that that existed in paleolithic times. Paleocybernetic culture. And maintain too. The time when you go back to the first people on the planet, they had a whole planet. They didn't even have to build houses, they lived in caves. And there was enough. And then it came to a point where there were more people on the planet than there was room to live in caves,

so somebody had to start staking off this area, I mean, as there got to be more people. Once there's not enough for everybody, then everybody has to make sure that he gets enough for himself. And you never know when it's enough, either. But 1929 showed them—the guys who had the most money of all, you know, were the most to go right down the barrel. You could never get enough as long as everybody doesn't have enough. As much as you got somebody's going to try and take it away from you. I haven't even read Marx or nothing like that, or Engels. But I just think—I just try and figure it out, take everything back down.

It goes back to if there ain't enough for everybody then all this other stuff developed.

Now you make enough for everybody—if you can make enough of all this shit, to keep everybody from just gettin' up in the morning going to these jobs and stuff, you can easily do it the other way. Just isn't any question it could be done. We got to do it, that's all. We got to do it.

Abbie Hoffman

God, your wife is really pretty. Will you get jealous if I flirt with her?

Oh no. Are you kidding? That's what it's all about.

You can flirt with my wife. Screw her, I don't care. Non-possession.

I once asked Danny Hutton in a moment of euphoria, "Can I fuck June?" He said "No."

That was his wife?

His girlfriend — the girl he was living with. And I said, "Well, I guess I should have asked her, not you."

Well, if you can you should ask.

Yes.

Like one of my best friends, I really like his wife, but I wouldn't sleep with her unless he slept with my wife. I wouldn't feel it was like . . .

Fair.

When are you going to turn the tape recorder on?

It is on. It's been on all the time.

Oh.

How do you feel when you get arrested? I mean, exactly, when they say, "Okay, this is it."

Well, it depends. They usually don't say; they usually start swinging.

At some point you know that you are going to be arrested, right? You know that you have to go to jail and have a trial . . .

No, it doesn't work that way now. You know, since — it used to work that way when we were into non-violent protests, you know pacifism as a tactical approach — say when I was involved in the Civil Rights movement. You sit down in the street, start singing "We Shall Overcome" and the police come and you know you're going to get arrested and you're all prepared for that psychologically, and you're carried off, and you go limp and all that. But it's not that way now. Since some of us have long hair and high visibility, you know, and because our way of life is an affront to the forces of law and order, we can get arrested at any minute of the day.

As a matter of fact, that is what happened to me. A week ago I was on trial for participating in the Columbia demonstrations, even though at the time I was at a radio station 50 blocks away. I was on recess downstairs in the courtroom and there was a Black Panther rally outside, you see. I couldn't participate in that because I had my own trial inside. I was in a phone booth making a call when the cops like decided to clear the whole lobby and pulled me out of the phone booth and hit me right off with a club. I turned around and said, "Hey, I'm not part of the demonstration. I'm on trial here; I'm going to my trial." He hit me again and I proceeded to do my karate demonstration and sent three of them to the hospital and I'm charged with felonious assault and five other charges and was held on $2,500 bail, beaten up in the station and, you know, that's average. That's an average week. I was arrested for not appearing at my trial even though I was in jail at the time. Try to work through that. But going to prison itself is very difficult. They know that because out of 40 arrests I've had like three convictions, two of which are on appeal and one of which I served no time on.

But I understand the way that the system uses the courts. See, for example, one arrest I had when I went back to Chicago to stand trial they took me off the plane, took me right out of the plane and accused me of trying to sneak into Chicago and skip my trial, even though I was coming with my lawyer. I was held in the airport and searched and they found a knife on me, a pocket knife that I bought right around the corner here, legal and everything in every city in the country. They charged me with carrying a concealed weapon. When they released me, the FBI arrested me for crimes aboard an aircraft, for carrying a switch blade — the papers identified it as a switch blade. But it wasn't a switch blade, that's irrelevant. The FBI knows it wasn't a switch blade but they wanted to arrest me because, you see, that arrest allowed the federal government to confine me to the district of Chicago and the district of Manhattan. I was, in effect, under house arrest and I was prevented from like going to Europe, which I wanted to do at the time.

Why were you going to Europe?

I was going to Prague. I was on my way to Prague. We had been invited by some Czechoslovakian poets and writers, but the government didn't want us to like move around in international stuff so this was their way of doing it.

Now, I had to make four appearances, you see, with my lawyer in Chicago before the case even came to trial. And I had to remain in Manhattan; I couldn't leave. In fact, the only time I slipped out was to go to Boston to see two of my kids — my only two kids — and I was immediately picked up by the FBI and had to fly right back to Chicago and attend a hearing as to why I left Manhattan. This was even when they knew that they were going to drop the charges when it came to trial. They knew it wasn't a switch blade; they knew it wasn't illegal; they knew they were going to drop the charges. But you see that cost $600 or $700 — all that flight stuff, and a lot of time, and going to courts and sitting there all day.

Where does the money come from to pay for all this?

I have no idea where it comes from; it comes, though. We steal it. We steal some, we print some, we learn to survive. We live down here in the Lower East Side and know how to survive because we live in a jungle, so we know how to exist. I don't have a bank account; I don't know how I exist — but we get the money. We cheat, we lie, we steal, I don't know — we get it.

What do you want out of all this?

Out of all what? You mean the big vision? Well, the big vision is freedom — a society of the free where everything is free. America, the land of the free. That's what my old man told me at an early age, free means you don't pay. I think that was the vision of the founders of this country that you produce a society in which the technology, and the goods and services that came out of the society were available to whoever wants them, counting me . . . free of charge, free.

How do you arrange the traffic problem?

Well, we certainly could do better than the society is doing now. Those kinds of problems: who is going to collect garbage, who is going to do the traffic and all that— you mean who is going to do the work, isn't that what you're asking?

I mean, literally, suppose that everybody decides that they want to use the telephone system. You know it happens; the telephone just stops, it doesn't work.

I think that what these types of questions are geared to is a picture of a society with scarcity, a society built on economic scarcity. Our vision is that the future is going to be a society of abundance. That's a very important distinction. Therefore, these questions are very immaterial. It's like say 50 years ago you were talking about going to San Francisco, you would say, "How can you talk about going to San Francisco, that would take like seven or eight days. What are we talking about?" How can you talk about communicating with them and living in community with San Francisco? And now we talk about it quite easily, we just get on our horizontal elevators called airplanes and we're there in two hours.

Who would create the technology to do all this?

People who enjoy creating technology. That's their thing, you know, people like that. You start with the view that man is basically productive and creative, and if he is given more and more freedom this productivity and creativity come to the surface. It should never be defined as work. This is your religious life. This is your play area. This is your love life. This is your family. It's like fragments. This fragmented existence is necessary in a capitalistic society because then you can have all the consumers out there and you can cater directly to them — this is for the women, this is for the young people, this is for the workers, this is for the blacks, you know? But in a revolution there is just people and that concept of work is meaningless. You work, play and have your religion and they are all the same. Once you have capitalism and you have this concept of work, there's clean work and dirty work, right? As to a question like who is going to pick up the garbage — you never ask like who is going to want to be a doctor? That's clean work in this society. You don't ask that because there would be people who would dig that. But I know that people like dig everything in a revolution, they would dig all that. You would dig picking up garbage. I was a psychologist; I was in group therapy and there was a shoe salesman that I remember who said, "I hate my work, I hate this, I hate this, I hate my boss, I hate everything about my job." But after a couple of months and we plowed through all that shit, it turned out that the guy really dug what he was doing. He liked the whole game of like trying on different pairs of shoes on ladies, looking up their dresses and everything.

When people exist in a healthy society, they dig what they are doing. I don't know if that's like clear, but it's very important.

And you say you aim towards a society where everything is going to be free. I say you *aim* to that. That's what they are doing in Cuba. Castro says the goal of the Cuban revolution is the abolition of money and they get a surplus of goods and they immediately make it free to the people. Phone calls are free in Cuba now; they have the Isle of Youth, formerly the Isle of Pine, where like 20,000 young people live in a pay toilets. That's our program.

Do you think there is any danger, in the course of bringing this about or in attempting to bring this about that you might just create another elite class?

Could you explain that? I don't know what you mean.

The history of the revolution so far has been invariably there is a new bureaucracy created and a new elite created who then become the exploiters.

Well, that might happen. I've been wrong for the last year and a half ever since

abbie hoffman said, "in the new society there shall be only one law—it is forbidden to forbid." even he's far away from that goal. witness his putdown of the rev. dr. leary who has been writing about his prison experience with his usual pollyanna positive thinking smile. politicians are politicians. even the anarchists are on a power trip.

total moneyless, free society. I'm not saying they don't like play very hard—I hesitate to use the other four letter word because that's a dirty four letter word.

What do you mean?

Work. So, I don't know what to call it but let's say they live, that's a good four letter word. They live very high and with a very strong commitment. But cutting corn is not separate from dancing in the streets, there's not that separation. And there isn't for us living down here. There's no difference. We're trying to levitate the Pentagon 300 feet in the air, you know. And we'll meditate at the Pentagon. Where do you go to church? I go to church at the Pentagon.

That's a classic thing to do. That's where a lot of meditation goes on.

Inside and out. So the question of who is going to do the work is, I don't know, a misleading question. There's going to be no work. We are going to aim towards full unemployment—that's our goal—full unemployment. We offer everything, whatever the people want, eternal life to free

Lyndon Johnson pulled out and we didn't get a permit to have a festival of life in Chicago ten miles away from the convention. I've been wrong every single time. I'm not very good at predicting the future but that might happen. The only thing that I would say that it might not happen in this country is simply because it's a very rich country and we're talking about an attack on the government that is chiefly responsible for everything that is going on in the world that is bad. Once you have to talk about the world without the United States of America government, that's a very different kind of world.

You're talking about a world without government.

No. I don't know. It certainly can be conceived of as some form of United Nations that makes some kind of sense. What I see in this country in 40 or 50 years, you know, when the revolution has finally succeeded— and I think it will succeed or there won't be any country—we'll have this free society and what I see is a lot of different tribes around the country—I just use that word because I don't know a better one—maybe community is a better one.

It's anarchy. Anarchy is—I view it as mass experimentation with different life styles. I don't view it as chaos. This a commonly held view. I don't view it as chaos. On top of this you still would have a highly centralized government, but you see the government's role would be like highways, keeping the grass clean, and so on. And people where they live would have much more power to determine those decisions that directly affected their lives. Like people who worked in their community called a factory would all participate. It wouldn't be an institution, it would be a community and in a community all people would participate. If you have a skill, if you're better at something else, you would like naturally want to use that skill. If your skill was like preparing books, you know, to help keep those machines running, or repairing those machines, it would be natural that that skill would be used. If I lived in Cuba today, because I do believe in that government and the vision of those people, I would commit myself to that revolution in any way that they saw necessary in any skill that I had.

Specifically, if you could do anything that you wanted to do now . . .

I would wreck the government—this government. That's what I'm doing right now. I like it, that's why it's for the hell of it.

Let's say that the government is wrecked; there is no more government. What would you then do?

I would be a poet.

Why would you do that?

I am. I am doing that now. I am a poem. What do you mean poet? I live a life of poetry.

———

Do you like getting hit on the head?

No. Of course I don't like it. Who likes getting hit on the head?

Well, Hemingway did.

Well, Hemingway is a schmuck. He killed himself.

Do you think you might do that?

No.

Why not?

Because I'm not into that trip.

Do you think you might put yourself into a position where somebody might kill you?

I run risks of that, sure. I recognize those risks. But, see, that's relatively unessential because my view of the alternatives for like young white kids, of which I am one, is: 1) sitting at a desk in some office in a very punky position with very starched clothes being in the whole value system which I view as death—die in that kind of death, or 2) die in the streets for what you believe in. Those are the only two kinds of alternatives I see in this country. I choose the second one and I don't even consider that death. I consider that form of death—of dying for what you believe in—just another form of life. And I have like no fear of that death. I haven't worked out the prison thing in my head as well as I've worked out the death thing. The prison thing is a much more difficult trip, for me anyway, maybe not for someone else.

Why?

Just like still being alive and knowing that there was like a struggle going on outside and you were penned up in a cage and prevented from participating in that struggle. Like that. And because of my temperament; I like to jump around, I like freedom, and I like moving around. Being confined would be very difficult for me. It would be very depressing. I've gotten enough of a taste of jail to know that it can be a very demoralizing experience—dehumanizing and demoralizing and it could—I could lose my sense of humor. I'll still be funny after I'm dead, still have a sense of humor.

The point is that prison is a state that you know about, death is a state that you don't know about.

I prefer death to prison. I think I've gotten it in my head where I can do like a year, a year and a half, but other than that, no. They would have to take me with guns.

They might not put you in prison at all. They might put you in the Esalen Institute.

Well, that's prison. Prison is every kind of institution in society. They could put me in a factory; they could put me in a school and that would be prison too. Wouldn't that be a terrible fate? Being sentenced to go to college . . .

———

What kind of gun is that?

Pellet gun. It's not even loaded. I was just making a movie with it. I have a real gun. It's not here though.

How did you get into this racket?

Guns?

No, this whole revolution racket.

Well, it's a long process. Like I was in the Civil Rights movement. I've been around since about 1960.

Did you go to the South?

I was there in 1964, 1965, 1966.

How many months did you spend in Mississippi?

Well, two months. I was in Americus, Georgia, Alabama. I was three weeks in Atlantic City for the Mississippi Freedom Democratic challenge. But essentially during that time I was in New England organizing the SNCC groups and getting ministers to support the actions in the South and stuff like that. I was vice-chairman of the Massachusetts CORE.

I was also involved in my two political campaigns there: Stuart Hughes in 1962 and Adams in 1965, anti-war campaigns.

What made you give up psychology for a larger group therapy system?

It was the experience of working in a mental hospital. Seeing the way the people come in and the way the whole institution was organized and how it wasn't relating to the needs of those people. What it wanted to do was get a good record, so you were encouraged to get people out in 30 days so that you would have a nice turnover rate. They were no better off than when they came in and the hospitals failed to mention that they kept coming back repeatedly. And you were throwing them back into a society that wasn't helping them, leading them towards help. For example, there was a black man with an IQ like 138, and he had feelings of persecution. He said that he liked it in the mental hospital because he could like dance with white girls, nobody bitched, nobody yelled. And he didn't like it out there, there were people trying to get him and they were mostly white. He went off. He was certainly a lulu. He had a thing

about people constantly trying to poison
him. He was ill but his basic complaints
were justified.

*I've had those same complaints myself. I
can't object to someone having them and
they're usually true in one way or another.*

So I started to think there might be something to do out there and when I was a
graduate student at Berkeley I participated
in the Caryl Chessman demonstration and
the anti-HUAC demonstrations. I just like
went to look and see what it was. I sort of
like didn't believe it. I've always been like
kind of naive. You know, I said, "Oh, I
don't believe it. They're driving us out of
the park? They want us to go downtown in
Chicago? Why won't they let us stay in the
park? What are they, dumb or something?"

I think the thing in Atlantic City had a
big effect on me. Up to then it was totally
a moral struggle. I believed the blacks were
being mistreated and that it could be corrected within the system and that if we
brought this case to the Democratic party
and said, "Look, there are racists running
the state of Mississippi and they won't let
blacks participate and they ought to be allowed to vote and be represented, that once
we did that—and especially since we had
so much support from Northern congress-
men who gave us money and everything,
we were sure we were going to win. When
we didn't, then we started to recognize
things like power and how that is being
distributed and moralities—you know, like
everybody's moral, everybody has moralities. Much more militant methods were
needed, methods that were going to be outside the political system.

*Why did you feel that it was your mission
to do this?*

I feel it's the mission of everybody. Why
am I doing it? Because I wasn't enjoying
my life. I had another life at this time. In
1964 and 1965 I lived in a white suburb in
an $18,000 home. I was making $15,000 a
year working for a drug company, only
four hours a week too. I spent the rest of the
time working in the ghetto and I had two
kids and everything.

Then in summer 1965, during that period
I was working for a thing called Poor People's Corporation which was an attempt to
set up craft programs in Mississippi, co-
operatives. The blacks owned it. It was
called Liberty House, too. I was like sales
coordinator, you know, I would run around

New England while I was doing this drug
thing. I would go to one drug store and run
around to all the other stores trying to get
them to buy these goods.

I went with SNCC and PPC; together we
had a booth at the Newport Folk Festival
in the summer of 1965 and Stokley was
there, Cleve Sellers, about ten guys from
the national office of SNCC. They were
there to get folk singers to do tours and
benefits for them. We were sitting around
the booth at about 1 AM and just down the
way about ten booths we saw about 15 cops
who had been drinking a lot, drunk as a
bitch, yelling and screaming. They said,
"There are the black power guys." So they
came and started to club the shit out of
us and I got beat up pretty bad that time.
It was really wierd. They drove us down
this fuckin' dirt road and it was pretty dark,
about 2 AM and they just kept clubbing us.
I had some grass and I was trying to ditch
it. I didn't give a shit. Hit all you want,
just don't search me.

So, then after we reached the stadium
officials and told them, they were very furious and everything so we wanted to go back
and check on the booth and someone else
said they wanted to get to their car. So we
rode up this dirt road with them and there
were like 50 cops guarding the road and
they wouldn't let us through. Finally an
official got us through and the booth had
been ripped apart, all the bags and everything. I think it was like that incident that
I felt that I was going to go total. I wasn't
happy in my marriage with my wife so I
gave her everything, the house. I said "You
can have the house, kids, all the money;
I'm just like going." I came here to live on
the Lower East Side. I was living in a place
for $40 a month rent. I was the only one
who spoke English in the whole building.
Then I came to start Liberty House in the
West Village to serve as an outlet for these
goods. So I started it and a couple of people came by and gave me a little bread—not
much. It was like down on a shoestring. I
made a little to survive. Now this year I'm
going to make $100,000.

How?

The book is doing very well. I get $1,000
to speak at a college, $400 or $500 an article. I don't know. It just all comes. I don't
do like TV. I won't go on TV unless I get
paid—talk show. Dope shit I'm in—everything.

2:47 A.M insanity

mad scene

this is really peculiar, isn't it?

It will all be so amusing when I look back on it some happy day hence

of course, it has happened before and I have come out of it =u=

please don't laugh

I am in pain and it's not funny!

today's : fantasy

Getting paid for writing in my book =

3:24am

will power is not my main gift.

3:25 a m

≡ⅢⅢZIP!≡Ⅲ≡

STOP LAUGHing

3:26am

Caption in September 1971 PLAYBOY: "Le Cyprès et l'arbre en Fleurs, painted by Vincent van Gogh at the height of his artistic abilities, while he was in a mental hospital ...."

Three forty-eight and weird

days
of
awe

now the days of
awe are upon us
when the solitary
tree waits for the
wind and every man
faces the harvest of
his acts = who will
save you when the
earth trembles and
the sky is filled with
poison rain? = con-
sider the message
of the sand, children
of the sea and wonder
where the green has
gone = and will it
come again? = and will
you see it come again?

The Black Panthers

When Huey P. Newton and Bobby Seale founded the Black Panther Party in 1966, it is possible that they could have fantasized a future in which Huey would go to jail for killing an Oakland police officer, that the Panthers would eventually be a nationwide organization, that there would be 40 chapters by 1969, that they would publish a weekly 24-page tabloid newspaper with a claimed circulation of 100,000. Maybe they would not have been surprised to look into a crystal ball and see Eldridge Cleaver's name on the best-seller list as the author of *Soul On Ice* and, simultaneously, on the ballot as a candidate for President of the United States.

Perhaps they would not have been filled with disbelief at the prediction that in July, 1969, the Black Panthers would sponsor the National Conference for a United Front Against Fascism and that it would be covered by reporters from the national media and the cameras of major television stations. Maybe they could have accepted all of this as the inevitable working of destiny. After all, how many political parties start with more than two men sitting down and writing a manifesto? It is an act that requires megalomaniacal self-faith.

It does not seem likely, however, that they would have taken with anything like full faith the word of even the most authoritative prophet if he told them that at this conference a white boy born in Winston-Salem, N.C., would stand on the platform wearing a beret with a confederate flag enamel pin and deliver a short speech in a hillbilly accent expressing the solidarity of a group called the Young Patriots with the Black Panthers.

"We can take it," said the Young Patriot, who called himself Preacher Man. "We can take anything the pigs hand out. Jesus took it. He said, 'Put that fucking nail right there, because that nail is the people's nail.' But we're finished with that. We aren't taking it any more."

The Young Patriots are one of the white organizations allied with the Black Panthers. In Detroit, there is the White Panther Party, which has a ten-point program modelled on the Black Panthers' ten-point platform. In the Chinatowns of San Francisco, Los Angeles and New York there are Red Guard organizations which are in contact with local Panther chapters. In Chicago, the Young Patriots were joined by the

Young Lords, Puerto Rican youths, at a press conference with the Black Panthers.

On a Sunday morning following the Preacher Man's speech, two of the Young Patriots and a Black Panther from Chicago who called himself Poison told me about their lives.

"I came from the South, from Winston-Salem, North Carolina, where cigarettes are made," said Preacher Man. "There are no unions down there. Some people haven't even heard of a union. My mother's been working in a mill for years and she still don't make hardly $1.65 an hour. My whole family's come out of the South and now they're working in a system which allows for no freedom to form their own lives.

"I was in Chicago for two years before I related what was happening in Uptown to what was happening in the South—feudalism and brutality against the lives of the people. It's the same kind of reality you find on the West Side of Chicago, on the South Side of Chicago, in Detroit.

"It might be that the Patriots are the ones who can really lay down some stuff that seem to come directly out of the pages of Faulkner, inherited from some Snopes who never made it to Mississippi. His partner was Bobby Joe, a 20-year-old with curly black hair and a paper-white Hogarth face. His voice was shy and whispering and very Southern.

"My family comes from Georgia," he said. "When people ran out of work in the South we came up to Chicago. Uptown is one of the big places for people who come up. It's a transient area. People don't stay too long. A lot of them are in the factories doing assembly line work. That kind of work don't pay much for the common things a family needs. They never have anything to show for it. After 20 years they still have the same problem they had when they started out."

Bobby Joe dropped out of school after eighth grade. "I didn't dig the schools," he explained. "I didn't get along with the teachers. I couldn't relate to what they was teaching. I hustled—pool, faggots, rolling people. Then I got political through JOIN—

students who came to Chicago from Berkeley.

"They talked a lot of good stuff about how the people have to get together because the system is oppressing them. I dug what they said, because it's true.

"I felt that one of the main groups that had to be organized was the young hustling dudes on the street."

The Young Patriots publish Rising Up Angry, a monthly tabloid. They say they have been feeding some 40 to 50 persons a week and they hope to set up a free health clinic. They have been aided by some small businessmen and churches, but they have been turned away by the usual charitable agencies.

"We saw that the service agencies get a lot of money and pay a lot of people to do paperwork, but they don't get the job done," Preacher Man said. "They've got some leftover capitalism they're trying to fry up again and serve to the people."

Like the Panthers, the Young Patriots see the police as the enemy. "We say it's not safe to walk the streets of Uptown because of the pigs," Preacher Man explained. "On their cars there are signs that say 'We serve and protect.' That's right. They serve the oppressed people of the community with subpoenas and search warrants and they protect the property owners.

"There's a new authority emerging—the authority of the people to design their own lives."

Poison, 19 and a field lieutenant in the Black Panther Chicago chapter, was slender, self-confident and cool. He told how he had intervened in a rumble between white and black students at a Chicago high school.

"They was standing there facing each other in two mobs acting like they really wanted to get it on," he said. "It had been going on for three days when I got there and the pigs was just waiting and watching for them to give them an excuse to break their heads. I stood out in the center and told them they were doing what the pigs wanted them to do.

"I turned to one side and said, 'All right now, whoever wants to fight come on out here and let's get it on.' No one hurried out, so I turned to the other side and said the same thing. They wasn't running out to me either. I said, 'Since nobody wants to get his head busted, why don't we all just go on into the auditorium and talk this thing out.'

"They liked that a lot. The pigs started to get that disappointed look. My idea was to call off all classes and get everybody together talking to each other, but the principal wouldn't let me in the school.

"I left and they went right back to it. Then the pigs got their chance to do their thing. It wasn't necessary for it to come out that way."

Poison described the feelings that brought him to the Panthers. "At a young age, I saw these cats shooting pool, getting high. I saw they don't have no jobs, they don't have nothing, and I started wondering, 'Why?' I said, 'I don't want to be like this.' I don't know if I'll ever get to be what I want, but I'd like to see my children do what I wanted to do, or do what they really want to do.

"I was in Greensboro where the sit-ins first started. I got sick seeing those sit-ins. I got tired of marching. I got tired of asking. All through my life I've known that the best way to get something was to take it. The Black Panther Party was the only organization that was actually taking what they wanted. When they formed the Black Panther Party for the city of Chicago, I joined.

"I read about Huey P. Newton, how he stood up in the face of all these pigs and said that he had his gun and they had their guns and they could start right there getting it on. I realized that I had to stand up for my manhood and the only way to do it was to establish a means of communication with the opposition.

"The only means of communication I could have with the opposition was to carry my gun with me, because they had guns. I already had guns because I used to go hunting and I knew how to use them.

"I used to think it was a race struggle, but from listening to Malcolm X and just adding things up I realized that it was a class struggle. I saw rich black people in my community who had stores and who robbed me and robbed my people and I realized then that it was a class struggle.

"That was what the Black Panther Party was talking about. The Illinois chapter, when they first started off, tended slightly toward overtones of racism. This had to be expected. You don't wake up the morning after you're born and be 21. The news

media is what has really fucked things up. When people start realizing what actually is to the news media of the establishment then their false ideas will just fall away."

Poison was asked if he thought the Black Panthers wanted to be policemen once community control of the police was accomplished. "Lots of people don't understand what community control means. It means giving the people a voice. Right now they have no voice because it is a centralist form of government. Community control of the police doesn't mean that the community would take over the present pig department. It means that the people will have people from within that community policing that community.

"If one of these police would commit a crime against the people, he would have to come home at night. It's a hard thing to go home if you've committed a crime against your own people. Before you commit that crime, you begin to think.

"It's got to be a better thing, the community supervising what goes down. The answer to your question is that it would not be up to the Black Panthers. It would be up to the community. If the people desire the Black Panther Party to police their community, we will."

*S*unday night, the Black Panthers laid out the details of their plan in a slide presentation. They proposed that Oakland be divided into two departments. Each department would have five neighborhood divisions with boundaries drawn according to ethnic and racial population patterns. The people of each division would elect 15 councilmen and the commissioner would be responsible for all policy matters within his own neighborhood, including hiring and firing of officers, training them and arming them. There would be a central facility for the entire city of Oakland, but its services would be available on a voluntary rather than mandatory basis.

Bobby Seale explained that what the Panthers sought was to establish at least one model of an operating police department controlled by a community so that the nation could see that the concept was not only workable but desirable. In each city where there were National Committees to Combat Fascism, there would be a petition circulated calling for a referendum on the proposal. The United Front and the Panthers would supply legal and technical advice through a committee of attorneys. If necessary, experts from the national office would be flown out for on-the-spot consultations. A voter registration drive would be carried on as part of the petition effort.

The final question in the audience participation period that followed the presentation came from a New York girl who wanted to know what would happen if the community control plan was voted into law and the police refused to disarm.

Although obviously exhausted, Seale grabbed the question with ferocious enthusiasm. "If they are not going to give up their jobs," he said, "that means that the fascists are not going to give up control of the state and that means, baby, we got open, righteous revolution. The people that voted are going to move to what the revolutionaries told them. They're going to move to getting guns and keeping guns in their homes and defending themselves from those fascists."

One important question still had not been asked, but the conference was at an end. What would the Panthers propose to do with all the unemployed policemen in the event of the enactment of their community control plan? It was time to get close to Bobby Seale and see what he had to say about the treatment of enemies. A Panther platform official directed the request for an appointment with Bobby Seale to Field Marshal D.C.

D.C., an enormous man with tawny skin, a helmet of wooly black hair in a natural cut and an Oriental goatee, was standing near an exit politely listening to James Kimmel, the delegate from the Kingdom of Heaven. Kimmel, a former employee of the Atomic Energy Commission who had once had a Q security clearance, was now receiving $86 a month home relief. He had been fired from his job as a high school teacher in Novato, Calif., after being arrested on marijuana charges.

James Kimmel was wearing a flowered shirt and striped bell bottoms. From a leather string around his neck there depended a leather peace symbol five inches in diameter. His blonde hair was ten inches long and bound at the forehead Indian-wise by a string of iridescent beads. His beard was thin and scraggly. He had left his wife to marry a girl who had almost been Play-

The Black Panthers sometimes live in abandoned buildings, of which there are 110,000 in New York alone. They do not recognize the authority of the City of New York. In their districts, the landlords who have abandoned their property have ratified in retreat the defeat of American government in the ghetto. The rebels talk about liberated territory. Some people think this is delusional. Yet the abandoned buildings are liberated territory. It remains for someone very clever and very strong to take over the property, make an armistice with the former owner, if that is thought necessary, and renovate the structure. As long as the force of central law does not extend homogeneously throughout every nook and cranny it is possible to be free in America. The ghetto is the new frontier, not space. The outlaws in their hideouts are becoming so numerous that they recognize themselves as constituting a society. The Black Panthers, The Young Lords, The Blackstone Rangers, The White Panthers, The Red Guards, The Young Patriots are the government which have seized power, the governments of the outlaws. The Mafia, it is interesting to note, started out in much the same way in Sicily. The United States of America, it is interesting to note, did too. Just because people defend their homes with guns does not mean they are evil — unless government by force is itself evil per se.

Self-governed people need no government. Individual restraint is the safest form of control. It is probably also the most efficient. You can't run away from yourself. Those who won't govern themselves will be governed by others.

mate of the Month in the days when Playboy paid a $300 model fee for its centerfold.
The marriage ceremony, which took place
without the benefit of a prior divorce, had
been reported in a recent issue of Time—
possibly because everyone present was
nude.

"I'm against guns," Kimmel was telling
D.C. "The universe gives you back exactly
what you put into it. Trying to fight violence with violence only creates more bad
karma. Peace is not possible when people
are putting out hostile vibrations.

"I've got something better to offer you,
brother. I want the Black Panthers to enter
into the Kingdom of Heaven. It's yours for
the asking. Just say the word and I'll lead
you right in through the cosmic gates.

"You can walk into the Kingdom of Heaven; you can dance in; you can fly in. But
you can't shoot your way in. You've got to
give up guns. Do you dig what I mean?
They're just primitive weapons compared
to what I can give you. I can show you how
to make an atomic bomb. Are you ready for
that?"

D.C. told Kimmel to put his proposal in
writing and send it to the national office,
smiled warmly and turned to the next problem. Chairman Seale did not have time for
a personal interview, but later in the week,
after the business of the conference was
finished, he said, it might be possible to
arrange something.

"All the brothers are in from chapters all
over the country," he explained. "We're all
tied up in meetings. Call the national office
in Berkeley later on and speak to the Officer
of the Day." Smiling the same warm smile
he had used on Kimmel, the big man opened the exit door and loped casually away.
In the auditorium, the closing benedictions
were over. In the parking lot outside the
hall, people were hitching rides home.
None of them seemed to be having any
trouble.

*T*he National Headquarters
of the Black Panther Party turned out to be
one of those two-story California bunga-
lows pretending to be Swiss chalets that
line the streets of communities throughout
the state, randomly mixed among Spanish
Mission cottages, miniature Romanesque
confections and the other architectural an-
omalies evidently inspired by the movies of

Walt Disney. In California there are few
homes, but plenty of stage sets.

Inside the house at 3106 Shattuck Avenue, there was a maple-stained knotty
pine waiting room in which worn furniture
was arranged without any evidence of the
aid of an interior decorator. Literature and
posters were piled everywhere. On the wall
behind the desk of the Officer of the Day,
who was a young woman, there was a giant
photograph of Joseph Stalin. On the cor-
nering wall hung a slate. Among the messages chalked on it were:

*No Panther will carry a piece without
authorization.*

Eat breakfast before reporting for duty.

*Do not throw trash in the street or in the
people's yards.*

It is not necessary to go into the details
of the next 20 minutes in which the Officer
of the Day did her best to locate someone
who could handle the appointment set up
by telephone the day before. It is sufficient
to say that the Revolution showed itself to
be just as bureaucratically unglued as any
agency of the Establishment at its worst.
Just as the entire project was about to be
abandoned, D.C. walked in, smiling
warmly.

In the absence of Brother Seale, who was
upstairs in a meeting, D.C. volunteered to
be interviewed. When the meeting was
finished, he said, he would see what he
could do about getting some of the Chairman's time. Meanwhile, he began with an
analysis of the Panther's chief enemies
outside the police—Ron Karenga's US
organization, a faction of the ultra-African
cultural nationalist movement held responsible by the Panthers for the murder of two
party members in what seems to have been
a dispute over a $20,000 job as chairman of
the UCLA black studies program; and Progressive Labor, a super-leftist group which
tried to take over SDS earlier in the year.

"A cultural nationalist is a pork chop,"
D.C. said. "That's a part of a pig. Their
support comes mainly from people like
Rockefeller, Yorty, Reagan. It's in the
interest of the power structure to propagate
the idea that it's a race struggle rather than
a class struggle. As long as they can keep
people divided into ethnic groups, the
masses are not going to join together to
form a united front against the exploiter
who is oppressing everyone.

"PL is probably a CIA front. They con-

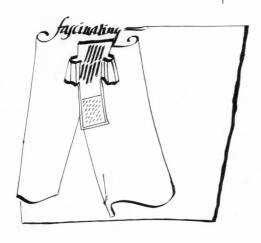

fascinating

Yes, we have a need for a coven of loyal witches

demn all liberation movements in the world. They say the primary contradiction in the world today is between United States imperialism and Soviet revisionism. In the current issue of their magazine they say that we spout Marxist phrases but that our real thing is to go out and kill all whites.

"In actuality, all you have to do is check our program and practice since the party started and you see that everything in the United States was going toward a race conflict of black against white and it was the Panther Party that came along and said, 'No, there's another way,' and formed an alliance with the Peace and Freedom Party.

"We're out to change this system, smash it, destroy it—this bourgeois capitalism, dictatorship of the minority—and replace it with a government of the people, by the people and for the people. We know that it can't be done through parliamentary procedures, through the election box. It has to be smashed, overthrown, and it's going to take violence to do that.

"Our job is not to start the war. We'd do a little bit of damage, but we'd be wiped out. Our job is to educate the people. That's the role of the vanguard—to educate the people through example, through literature and through activities. One of our most successful efforts is the Breakfast for Children program, which started in January with 20 children. Now we are feeding close to 50,000 per week all across the country.

"We all support ourselves by selling those newspapers. Circulation is up to nearly 100,000. Every branch supports itself this way. We don't keep records of how many members we have. I didn't bother to even check how many votes our candidates got in the elections. We weren't concerned about winning. We were concerned about using electoral politics as a forum to get our ideas across.

"One of the things we say is 'Defend Yourself.' People have picked up on that. We can read in the papers that the unorganized masses are beginning more and more to defend themselves.

"One of the main problems is that people recognize fascism three or four thousand miles away in other countries and fail to see it under their own noses. They tend to identify it by the clothes that it wears and fail to recognize it when it dons new clothes. They expect to see a megalomaniac with a little moustache riding a horse down Telegraph Avenue, or storm troopers running around with knee boots and swastikas.

"It has been called police brutality. It's a matter of educating people to the fact that yes, it's brutal, but the term for it is fascism. Black people already know, because they've lived under fascist terror ever since we've been in this country. Fascism is the police running amok in the black community.

"Is the treatment of our political prisoners any different from the way Mussolini treated his enemies? About 50 of our people are in jail in this country. Many of them are in solitary confinement for no reason other than being Black Panthers. We have thousands of cases pending."

D.C. sketched how he had come to his beliefs: "I was born in a little old country town in Missouri. My father was an automobile mechanic. I went to college for two and a half years. I'm married, 33 years old, two children — boys, 11 and 5.

"A year ago, I was a production manager in a graphic arts firm. I'd been there ten years. I quit in May, 1968 and started working full time for the party. I was struggling with the idea of quitting for about a year. I had joined CORE in 1963, but I only stayed in it for three months. I didn't know what to do, but I knew that wasn't it. At the time, I thought that was all wasted energy. I feel now that all of those organizations were necessary steps to get us to where we are now.

"The job helped radicalize me more than anything else. I was in the position where I had to extract the most production out of the people for the least amount of money. We had conversations and meetings about how we were supposed to concentrate on holding back on salaries.

"Those contradictions were too much for me. I couldn't handle it. I began to develop a more revolutionary perspective. Without having read much, without knowing much theory, I was still stumbling in the dark.

"Then one day I saw a picture on the front page of the San Francisco Chronicle of niggers with guns in the state capitol in Sacramento. I knew right then where it was at."

Into the waiting room, scowling, with a newspaper clipping in his hand, walked Bobby Seale. It was a story about Eldridge Cleaver in Algeria. Seale handed it to D.C. and walked away. The interview was over. D.C. went upstairs. Outside the house, Bobby Seale stood talking with Bob Avakian of SDS, kicking his feet sullenly against the curb as Avakian engaged him in a long largely theoretical discussion of the worker-student alliance.

"If you want to really help me," Seale interrupted after some fifteen minutes, "tell me how we can get 15,000 people here in October. Even 10,000 will blow their minds."

Seale went back upstairs and word came down to the waiting room that he was tied up again. There would be no time for any questions.

Suddenly, Seale was in the waiting room again. "All right, let's get it on," he announced and wearily sat down on the plastic couch. His anthracite face with a small black beard was quick with impatience. The slender body was slouched low in an attitude of taut indifference. He spoke in a soft voice that had a rasp of speed somewhere deep down. It was the voice of an intelligent man forced to recite the same story over and over again without showing anger. His answers were abrupt, offering no more information than was directly required. The whole thing was over in a few minutes.

"What are we going to do with the unemployed cops?" he said in a tone of disbelief. "What have they done for the black people who have been unemployed all their lives? If we had a socialistic state and real socialistic education, maybe we could pay them to go to school to learn how to be human. If they want to be fascists and beat and murder and brutalize people and wish masochistically for concentration camps then the people are going to have to get rid of them and let them know that if they attack us we're going to defend ourselves."

Why had he used the word masochist rather than sadist? The answer came with a flash of a smile: "Oh, excuse me. That's right, I meant to say sadistically. I always mix up Masoch and DeSade. Maybe it's because they're both white." The conversation continued uneasily, covering ground already familiar. After a moment of silence in which he rubbed his eyes and stretched back, Seale answered the last question, already rising to leave.

"How come they haven't killed me? I don't know. I'm not worried about it. If you worry about what's going to happen to you, you never can accomplish anything. If I catch them trying to kill me, I hope I can take the pigs with me." With a brief goodbye, he was gone. From upstairs the tape recording of his voice speaking at the conference was loud and sharp. It had been playing all along.

*T*here are no meaningless gestures, Penelope Gilliat wrote in one of her New Yorker short stories. A gesture, by definition, has meaning — certainly to its author, if not to the observer. There is no way to know enough about what happened at the National Conference for a United Front Against Fascism to say exactly what it meant. The event was a gesture with a different meaning to each participant. Yet it does seem that some moments are more significant than others. Even so, the interpretation is always totally subjective.

As each delegate entered the hall and presented the registration documents for which a $6 fee had been charged, there was one last rite of initiation: a thorough and methodical body search. Every person was frisked for weapons—all 3,500 delegates—not once, but several times. Any person who passed through the door at any time during the conference was examined, even if only returning from a few minute breather outside. Male Panthers searched male delegates. Female Panthers searched female delegates.

"There are a lot of excitable people here," said one Panther officer. "We just want to make sure that no one has the capability of doing any damage to anyone else." On the stage or in front of it, two Panthers scanned the crowd impassively as each speaker made his moment. At each exit there was a Black Panther watching with grave patience, offering no conversation that was out of their line of duty, not even to the pretty girls who frequently tried to break their armor.

There were some people who refused to allow themselves to be searched. They were not allowed into the conference. It is easy to speculate what they thought of the security measures. Perhaps the word fascism entered their minds. Others submitted to the search, but rather unwillingly. There was something going on inside that they wanted to be a part of. If this was the price of admission, then they just had to pay it.

Many of the people laughed and joked as they were searched. A sexual banter began to develop in tentative counterpoint to the heavy business of the meeting. Most delegates, however, said nothing and showed nothing as the hands explored their bodies. Their thoughts were their own. It was a new experience to be touched by a black person. To each, that experience will have had some private and possibly inexpressible meaning. In the end, though, it does seem possible that this particular moment was the most important of all. Black people were touching white people.

Cannabis flowers =

Guada-
lahara

Panama
Red

Michoacan

Guerrero

Oaxaca

Guadalahara

Panama
Red

Michoacan

Zacatecas

Yucatan

ayarit

Anger

Are you really interested in the story of
Chrissie and the prowler? I don't like to
repeat myself, but that one is worth getting
into again, if you are willing to grope
through some necessary background information which may not seem quite pertinent
at first. Be patient if I seem to ramble; it
is all leading to an ending you will enjoy.

I want to tell you about anger. I usually
become most angry when I consider myself
the victim of injustice. For example, take
the case of the phone call from my mother's
friend Rose Meshnick. She is one of the
best friends our family has ever had. I know
that I ought to treat her with forgiving kind-
ness even when she is being awful. At her
worst, which is really not very bad at all,
she is a lot better than most of the people
I have to tolerate in getting through an ordinary day in the real world.

She and her husband, Sam, a trucker
who has the jaw-slung smile of Stewart
Granger, have never been just lip-service
friends to us. They are the real thing. They
always were. When my father was in the
tombs on a knifing charge, they were the
ones who came up with $10,000 in securi-
ties for the bail bond. While Sam had done
well in the stock market over the years, he
has not done well enough to casually risk
that kind of money. The Meshnicks are not
extravagant people, but they made the
bond for us with no fuss or fanfare, as
though making a five dollar loan, or picking up the check in the Young China Restaurant on 170th Street in the Bronx.

The Meshnicks still live in the Bronx,
but on the Grand Concourse now. That's
the Park Avenue of the Bronx. In the old
days, they lived on Walton Avenue, near
Mount Eden, in a dark old apartment
building that had a tiny elevator, room
enough for one woman and a baby car-
riage. We lived on Walton Avenue too, a
few blocks away. There were no trees on
Walton Avenue, but it was clean and the
apartments were big and cheap. When my
father killed himself and my mother moved
to Los Angeles to live with my brother, who
had just completed his internship in a hospital in Long Beach, the rent on our five-
room flat was only $76.

We had lived in those rooms for twenty-
one years, moving there from Brooklyn in
September, 1939. When the lease came up
for renewal the first time, in 1941, my
father told the owner we were waiting for

purple prose. Sunday
28 March 1971
rainy day = green trees

empty houses = pleasant scenes
29 March 1971. Waiting,

51   1   The Creative

The Arousing

a place on the Grand Concourse. To in-
duce us to stay, the landlord reduced the
rent three dollars a month and installed
a new kitchen sink. Then came World War
II and the housing shortage. We never did
make it to the Grand Concourse.

Eventually, I wound up in a brownstone
in Brooklyn Heights and my mother in a
motel-modern building with a swimming
pool in Beverly Hills. In retrospect the
Grand Concourse looks shabby, but at one
time it was as high as we could think. At
the time the Meshnicks produced my
father's bail bond, they were still living on
Walton Avenue, which gives you an idea of

how big a gesture it must have been. This
was only one of their kindnesses. The
others were more subtle, but equally gen-
erous. The sum would be a very great debt
if Sam and Rose were the kind to measure
those things.

As any reasonable person will agree, I
had no business getting angry at Rose
Meshnick, then, even if she was out of order
in her phone call. It's my burden to be
unable to handle injustice, however, and
she was incredibly unjust. At least I
thought so, although perhaps I was being
hypersensitive. I could also argue that I
had a right to be hypersensitive. She was

striking a hot sore which had begun to erupt several months earlier when Rose had called to tell me that my mother's first husband, Gray, was about to leave for California, where he intended to visit his son, the doctor, and his former wife, neither of whom had seen or heard from him in some forty years.

"It's their business, Rose," I had told her.

"You have to call them and tell them," she insisted. "You're mother is a very delicate person. Who knows what the shock could do." She pleaded with me forcefully to warn my mother and brother. Now, I am a strong person, but I am never going to be a match for a fiftyish lady who used to change my diapers and was now speaking to me with the full authority of her years and the special power of her intimate status in the extended family. Who am I to test will and wisdom with matriarchs? After a struggle, I agreed to call Gray and see how serious his plans were.

"I don't want to go where I'm not wanted, you understand," he told me, "but I think a father has a right to see his own son. The mother, she didn't want me to mix in, so I stayed away out of respect for her feelings, but now I think I got a right to see my own son. After all, how much longer have I got? If he don't want to see me, which I can't believe, I'm not going to force myself on no one. I got pride, too, you know. But I don't believe that a son will refuse to see his own father." His voice was hoarse, but strong, with a trace of accent that was mostly old-time New York plus a distinct Eastern European undertone. It was the kind of voice I had once been accustomed to obey.

"Maybe the mother, she turned him against me," Gray continued. "That could be. You hear about such things. I don't think that she would do that, but a person has got to be a realist in situations where people are concerned. I always been a realist. That's why I am not worried that my son wouldn't want to see his father. He don't know it, she don't know it, but I watched over them all these years. I knew whatever they did. I knew when she sent him to Europe. I knew when he became a doctor. I was always there ready to spring forward in case she should need me.

"So now I'm retired, you know what I mean, taking it easy. Thank God, I got my health. Still, like I said, I'm a realist. At my age you don't fool yourself. You count the years. Usually I go to Florida, Miami, for a few months. Every year I like to go to Florida. I got a few dollars. I can afford it. This year I decided I'll go to California to see my son, how he's doing."

I told Gray that I would deliver his message and call him back with an answer. Then I got Rose Meshnick on the phone again. "He won't go if he thinks he's going to be unwelcome," I said. "I'm going to wait a while and then tell him that I spoke to them and that they would prefer not to see him." If I were a more cunning strategist, I might have just gone ahead with that plan without seeking Rose's agreement, but I was afraid to take the chance that she might talk about the situation to my mother and unknowingly reveal my duplicity. In any case, I was not unsure of the right move. It was possible that Rose Meshnick's perspective was more accurate than mine.

"Who are you to make that decision for them?" she said. "How do you know? Maybe they want to see him. You can't take it on yourself to predict what's right for another person. And suppose he goes ahead and barges in on them anyway, which he could easily do. He's a very stubborn man. Besides, he's not completely in the wrong you know. After all, he is a father. A father shouldn't be ignored. Forty years is a long time, but he is still a father.

"Listen to me," said Rose Meshnick in the indomitable tones of a line of women accustomed to ruling men since the days when Deborah was a judge over Israel. "Listen to me. I know your mother. She has never been a well girl. She don't need the shock she would get if he turned up at her door. You better call her right now so she should be able to prepare herself."

I went ahead and did as I was told. My mother was 'not happy to hear the news. "If he was always waiting ready to help out, how come he never sent a check?" she asked. "After forty years, when other people did all the work and the boy is a success, he first remembers that he is a father. I'm not saying I wanted to hear from him. After the divorce I told him, 'Gray, a boy can't have two fathers.' I was a baby myself. I was still in high school when I got married. When your brother was teething I was cutting my first wisdom teeth. I used to rub the paregoric on his gums and then rub it on my own. But look how smart I was. I told him that a boy can't have two fathers and he listened to me and stayed away. But if he was so anxious to be a father, he could have sent a check. He was watching over us? Then he must have known what desperate times we went through. Now that the job is done, he wants the reward. Some beauty."

"I don't need him here," my mother said. "What your brother decides is another story."

I telephoned my brother. "I don't even know him," he said. "He'll be just another

keep you company," I told her. "Don't go into the hospital. Don't take shock treatment. I'll be there in four weeks." There was something very pleasurable in countermanding the doctor's orders. Having been quite insane occasionally in my own life I was not as worried about the illness as he was. My brother, the sanest person I have ever known, was understandably impressed by the gravity of symptoms that were totally beyond his own experience. Also, being a much nicer person than I am, and a far more devoted son, he was genuinely wor-

Philosophy is the mind's chewing gum

old guy to me. Tell him that you couldn't reach me, that I was on a trip and you'll get back to him if I want to see him when I return, but make sure he understands that it is not very likely that I will be interested." I relayed the story to Gray and that was the end of the problem for a while.

Opening a door closed for forty years stirs dangerous dust, poisoned memories better left untouched. My mother had been the victim over the years of a recurrent emotional disorder which had been relatively controlled for quite some time, although it had once required hospitalization. A couple of months later, my brother called me from California with the news that she was sick again. "I may have to put her in the hospital," he said. "She may need shock treatment. How soon can you be here?" I was in the middle of a project I couldn't leave for at least four weeks. In the meantime, my wife, Chrissie, would go to California to be a companion to my mother. If the situation was really desperate I would drop my work and come out too. After finishing the conversation with my brother, I phoned my mother.

"How are you feeling," I asked.

"Not a hundred per cent, darling," she answered, whining weakly.

"Chrissie will be there in two days to

ried. I was too annoyed to be worried. How could my mother do this to me when I was in the middle of such important work?

"And Mother," I continued in a voice of pure command I had never before been able to manage to anyone, much less to her, "when I get there, I expect you to be well— or you'll first see some real insanity."

"Are you threatening me?" she answered, giving up the whine abruptly for a quite rational tone of irritated disbelief.

"Yes, I'm threatening you. If you aren't better by this time I arrive, I am going to go completely nuts and we can both go to the hospital together. You're not the only one who's been sick, you know."

"What a son of a bitch you are," my mother said, amazed at my cruelty, but recognizing, I think, the absolute honesty of what I was doing. Reality was cutting through to her. When I hung up the phone, I laughed loudly for a while, quite satisfied with myself. In four weeks, I had Chrissie meet me in San Francisco, where I had business to do. From there I had another telephone conversation with my mother, again treating her brutally each time she reverted to the emotional illness role.

"How long are you going to treat me like this?" she asked.

"Until you stop acting sick," I answered.

I have no opinion about the rightness or wrongness of what I did. As I have explained, I have been insane and seen that right and wrong can become meaningless concepts. Perhaps I still am insane. If so, I am hardly required to be reasonable to my mother when it is about all I can do to be reasonable to my business associates. She above all who know me ought to be capable of understanding how difficult it is for an insane person to be reasonable when in the grip of madness. Whatever the answer, by the time I got to Los Angeles she had almost completely recovered and we had a good time together.

In the telling, this all sounds cold and heartless, but it was not while it was going on. An account of various personal telephone calls, like an epistolatory novel or memoir, may not be the most accurate method of reporting emotion, but I don't know any other way to describe what happened. The first time my mother became ill, I was 14 years old. For years I had been awakened in terror by her nightmare screams. All my life I would suffer from nightmares myself. At times, my days would begin to resemble those dreams. When I finally broke, it was a relief to see horror clearly. I will not try to describe what I saw. That kind of poetry is beyond me. I will tell you only that when my mother began the cycle again, I was brought to see my own memory of a misery that went back to primeval fears, ancient rituals of dread.

I left my mother in good health and came back to Brooklyn Heights with my wife. A few days ago, Rose Meshnick called.

"How's your mother?" she asked.

"She's much better."

"You know, that business with Gray was very bad for her. You should have listened to me."

"What do you mean, Rose?"

"I told you not to tell her about him."

I do not remember exactly what I said to her. My wife took the phone away from me. Later, she said, "Rose kept saying, 'You're husband sure is a nervous person. What did I say that made him so angry?' What did she say to you? You were *unbelievable*."

As I told you, injustice makes me angry.

You have to keep that in mind if you are really to understand the significance of the story of Chrissie and the prowler. If there is any softness in me, it is because of her. She is one of those perfect blonde girls you find mostly in California, which is where I met her. She was a hippie and a flower child before any of that had a name. Thirteen years younger than I, Chrissie was still in high school and living at home when I found her. She had an allowance of a dollar a week. We quickly became lovers. I found her almost completely innocent of any notions of reality, untouched, trembling fearfully on the brink of surprise.

"I would have done it before but I didn't know what to do," she told me. "The boys I went with always used to ask me permission. I didn't know what they were talking about. If they had just gone ahead, I probably would have been too surprised to stop them. I thought they liked me because they could talk with me about Martin Buber and Herman Hesse and stuff like that. I didn't know they just wanted to fuck me."

Her home was in San Marino. Mine was in Laurel Canyon. It was an hour and a half drive back and forth. The only answer was for her to move in with me. We went out to San Marino to tell her mother about our plans. Her mother refused to believe any of it. She asked me about my background. Where did my parents come from? My father was born in Russia, I explained; my mother in the United States, her father in Poland.

"A noble people, the Poles," said Chrissie's mother quite seriously. The following evening she came to dinner at my mother's apartment and met my brother. We all told her that it was perfectly reasonable for her daughter to live in sin with an older man.

"Virginia," my mother said emphatically, "would it be better for them to marry now and be divorced a year from now?" In the face of this kind of argument and others I have forgotten, Virginia made the best of it and allowed her little girl to move out of the house. For a long time, though, she pretended to believe that we were living in separate bedrooms at my mother's apartment, refusing to know that I had my own place.

"Your mother is such a darling person," she told me, "taking care of Chrissie like that. I don't know how I would ever be able to be as kind as her. How does she ever put up with giving up her privacy?" It did not seem right, somehow, to contradict the fantasy. Before long, anyway, Chrissie and I were on our way to New York. A day or so before we left, we had lunch with her father, an aircraft executive with pale, shining eyes. He had left Virginia and four children some years earlier for a lady of about the same age but more pliable temperament who had five children of her own. With nine children to worry about, he reduced the demands on his role by adopting an intelligent and good-natured permissiveness.

"The only thing that worries me about your arrangement is what might happen if it doesn't work out," he said. "You can't just take her to New York and kick her out when you get tired of each other, you know." I promised faithfully that if Chrissie and I should separate I would not leave her financially destitute. The rest of the meal was spent in animated conversation about rock and roll music, politics, science and psychology. As we parted, he took his daughter by the shoulders and shook her vigorously in deepest affection.

*A*rriving in Greenwich Village, where I had an apartment in an ugly, ·massive building with a doorman and a view, Chrissie was stunned. She had expected to find a little country village. Instead there was this enormous city within a city. When summer came, she went to school at the Art Students League and drew black chalk sketches on rough newsprint, perfectly captured nudes presented with a strength and authority that made manifest the depths of perception I had only glimpsed in her before. At Paraphernalia, she bought a fragment of a frock made out of the cotton knit more usually found in winter underwear, which, in fact, it did resemble. She wore the dress one night in the heat of August with no brassiere or stockings, but with a big blue felt hat. On Eighth Street, people stopped and stared. She was nearly naked, too beautiful to bear, as self-possessed and unselfconscious as a child walking on a deserted beach. It hurt to look at her.

I am not going to make you suffer through the tedious details of the bad period that followed. At the end of the year we were evicted from the apartment. We returned to California, where I slipped and fell running after my mother's white Persian cat and broke my hip. As I lay there, my mother burst into tears and said, "Darling, this is all for the best. I was praying for you to get some kind of break." As it turned out, she was right. Six months later, Chrissie and I, married now, went back to New York. For the first time in my life, I was happy.

We found an apartment in an old brownstone town house in the museum village of Brooklyn Heights. We moved in immediately, although our only possessions were a convertible sofa lent to us by friends, and a color television set my brother had bought for us while I lay recovering in California. It was early autumn. As night fell, a horse and wagon creaked and clopped down the street outside our windows, the driver speaking to the horse loudly in its own language. I made a fire in the living room fireplace. Smoke filled the room. The damper was closed and the handle that operated it was missing. We opened the windows wide and fled. When we came back into the house hours later, the smoke smell was still strong, so we left the living room windows open and went to bed. Sea noises from the harbor lulled us to sleep.

Late at night, I woke suddenly. Someone was in the house. I slipped out of bed and stood by the bedroom door, which opened onto a small foyer and entranceway. A man was standing at the open front door.

"Who is it?" I called.

"It's me, Al," was the answer.

"You've got the wrong apartment, buddy," I said.

"Excuse me," the intruder replied and was gone. I thought I remembered locking the door before we went to bed, but evidently I had not. I locked it carefully now and bolted it and returned to the bedroom. My heartbeat, which had pounded up to the panic rate, slowed and I fell asleep again.

Again I woke up. Someone was in the apartment. Naked and very calm I slithered out to the front door. A small man with dark hair, wearing a cheap windbreaker and Chino pants was fumbling at the door, trying to unlock it. I realized that he had come in through the open window and was now trying to get out the front door, but couldn't manage the lock.

"Just unlock this fucking door and let

NOON

chrissie said, "I am writing a list of basic questions that have to be explored and answered."

The Heat   uh-oh. what did she mean by that?

me out," he whispered. In my family, we have never been very much afraid of thieves. My father, after all, had done time for armed robbery and so had my mother's older brother. One of the favorite stories was about another brother of hers, my Uncle Menashe, who had been sitting in the kitchen during the Depression and observed a burglar on the fire escape. Uncle Menashe went to the window and let the man in, made him a cup of coffee and sent him on his way out through the front door.

"There are only poor people living in this house," Uncle Menashe told the burglar. "Don't rob here. Go where there are rich people."

I have never been the peaceful person that my Uncle Menashe was. I was furious that prowlers should enter the apartment where I had embarked on a career of happiness and sanity. I opened the door for the thief, snapping the lock angrily. He hesitated in the hall light for a moment.

"Come on, beat it," I barked at him.

"Hey, don't talk to me that way," he said. He was a little man, a nasty piece of rat. I think he was annoyed that I refused to treat him with the proper respect a householder is traditionally supposed to show a thief. It did not occur to me to be afraid of someone so small and furtive.

"Look, man," I said, "don't stand there arguing with me. Just get out of here."

"Give me some money," he demanded.

"I don't have any money," I told him impatiently. "I don't have anything at all. The apartment is empty, as you can see for yourself."

"You've got a television set. I'm taking your television set."

"You are not taking my television set. It is the only thing in the world that I own. This is completely ridiculous. Look at me, you idiot. I'm standing here naked in the doorway arguing with you. My wife is in the bedroom listening to all this and she is probably going to get hysterical and stick her head out the window and scream for the cops. Do you know what a terrible hassle that's going to be?"

"I've got a knife," he said, pulling out a linoleum cutter with a shiny hooked blade. I was filled with a terrible rage at the insane logic of a world in which a person without possessions should stand in fear of damage to his most intimate flesh from someone who was too stupid to give up and go away. "She screams and I stab you," the prowler threatened.

"You are not going to stab me."

"Yes I am unless you give me that television set." The set was in the living room on the packing case in which it had arrived from Los Angeles. On the floor next to it was the heavy iron crowbar I had used to open the case. I could let him take the television, I thought, then break his skull from behind with one blow of the bar as he carried the set out. If I did that, however, he would drop the set and it would undoubtedly be damaged.

"Please go away and let me go back to sleep," I said. "You are not going to stab me for a television set that you're going to sell for thirty-five dollars." The bedroom door opened and Chrissie came out.

"Get out of here, you creep," she shouted at him. "Go rob rich people. Go rob the people upstairs. They've got plenty of stuff. Go rob people on Columbia Heights." The thief threw up his hands as she ran at him brandishing a heavy volume with which she hammered at his head. He kicked her in the thigh and punched me in the head, just below the ear and ran backwards down the hall like a crab and disappeared. The book in Chrissie's hands was *On Thermonuclear War,* by Herman Kahn.

"That's probably the first time anyone has ever actually used the book for defense," I said, taking it from her and kissing her. We went back into the bedroom after locking the front door and closing and locking the living-room windows. For a while we lay awake talking about the incident.

"I just couldn't stand it that you were being so nice and peaceful and that bastard was going to stab you," she said. "It was so . . . it was so . . . unjust."

"I know exactly what you mean," I answered. There was a bruise on her thigh and I felt a pain in my head. The whole situation was totally unjust. I felt cheated.

Not only had I been protected by a woman, but also I had allowed her to be hurt, a failure to defend. At the same time, I had failed to get rid of the intruder with the same graceful softness my Uncle Menashe had established as the model of behavior. I was clumsy. I had allowed my anger to interfere with my efficiency. Had I not barked indignantly at the prowler, he would probably have been happy to slip away. Instead, I offended his dignity and forced him to defend his masculinity.

Chrissie turned over and slept. I lay awake stoking my anger. I pictured the iron bar descending into the crook's skull, squashing it heavily. For the sake of a lousy television set I had thrown away the opportunity to kill a man, to purge my anger, to defend my home, to do an evil deed and get away with it. How many more chances would I get to play God again? Not many. Unable to sleep, I rose and went into the living room. I opened the street window wide and looked down the brown intaglio row of brownstones and the leaning trees. An oil truck, lights flashing red, grumbled past, followed by a bread delivery truck. In the room I noticed that the television set was unplugged and the antenna stowed. The prowler had come in through the window and unhooked the TV, then gone to the door to open it so that he could get out easily while carrying the television. I wondered if he had realized that it was a color model. Would that have made a difference in the outcome?

I picked up the crowbar and hefted it. As I had guessed, the bar was a good weapon. It swung easily, almost as if it had been weighted for killing rather than opening crates. In a dark corner of the room, I sat on my haunches with the bar across my knees. For a long time I waited there, but no one came in through the open window. At last, as grey dawn began to pearl into the high-ceilinged room, reason returned. It was highly improbable to have two prowlers in one night. There was no point in hoping for a third. Besides, it was getting too light. I got up, stretched my legs and went back into the bedroom, crawling sleepily under the covers and reaching for Chrissie's bare, hot body. Instantly aroused, she turned to me with a soft, excited cry that burned away all thoughts of anger in a blaze of terrifying love.

Onward → North

Migrating masses wandering
across deserts
of industrial waste ── slow
thoughts of pale mornings,
frowning gray light, aluminum
foil sun.

City burning with anodized
lust, envisions gilded and
burnished buttery metallic temples
on a dry, windy plain, moderne
domes at evening golden mushrooms
promising more colors from the
womb of night.

Love letter to an ordinary world.

Where are you today, reader?
Looking into a strangely beautiful
time=warped mirror. Connecting
thread tingling gently from head to
head. Once were. Upon a time.
Remember when. Backward running
river. Mask of used to be so long, long
long ago.

rushing clocks in
an old castle, white
faced maiden, young
breasts, faded purple velvet
gown, candles and guitar

thick yellow rope
of shining hair,
fire and fur

blaz

West of Eden

Modern civilization stoops to a low profile outside of Taos, N.M. In good weather an ordinary sedan can take you to Indian pueblos unchanged in a thousand years. More recent settlements of young Americans who have elected to drop out of the affluent society are usually more primitive than the pueblos and harder to find, tucked away on dirt roads beyond the easy reach of interfering authority.

One day last summer at Morning Star, a communal colony hidden in the lower reaches of the Sangre de Cristo Mountains, it was possible to believe that the calendar had been entirely erased. The time machine here is tuned permanently to pioneer days, but this was a scene out of history's earliest morning.

Stripped naked in the afternoon heat, a dozen long-haired, bearded boys and girls were furiously working adobe, their bare, brown young bodies glazed with mud and sweat. Out on a raw, open, high tract covered with coarse, brown grass and stunted clumps of aromatic pinon trees, they looked like aborigines, savages, primitive peoples in a documentary about New Guinea.

In this area of New Mexico, the sky is like the open sea. You can see the weather forming a long way off. In one section of the enormous sky, turbulent gray clouds were sputtering dark veils of rain and bright hairline crackles of lightning. The storm had been hovering down near Taos all morning. Now it seemed to be moving up.

The young workers were paying the storm no particular attention. They were packing earth, water and straw into simple wooden forms to make adobe blocks. In the lower fields, thousands of sun-dried bricks were stacked neatly among the canvas teepees in which most of the members of the commune were living. Many more bricks were needed. Summer was nearly over. In these mountains, snow begins to fall early in October.

Life was not easy at Morning Star. There was no electricity, no well. Even the water for the adobe had to be trucked up from New Buffalo, a commune out on the other side of the paved highway that ran through Arroyo Hondo. Morning Star shared a cornfield with neighboring Reality Construction Company, hard-nosed Marxists who had greeted reporters with shotguns. "If you don't work, you don't eat," was the rule at Reality Construction.

Fruit and vegetables often came up from the orchards and gardens of Five Star, a collective farm located near a natural hot spring in the sage desert south of Taos. All along the road to Five Star the desert was littered with trash. The farm was dusty and stony. Some of the people were living in crude dugouts roofed over with tarpaper. There was plenty of food. Five Star had planted more than it could harvest. Some of the crop had begun to rot in the fields.

Morning Star was more picturesque. About twenty yards down from the work site, a crumbling old adobe house was flanked by a couple of ancient trucks leaning anachronistically against mud walls. A tom turkey wandered out of a clot of trees and strutted past naked babies playing in the dust. A cast-iron wood-burning stove stood out in the open, its sheet-metal chimney wobbling in the wind. Over a campfire, water boiled in a 55-gallon steel drum. A naked girl with the wiry black hair and lean, tawny body of a squaw was chatting idly with two hugely pregnant girls in faded cotton dresses lounging on the torn cushions of the former rear seat of a car.

In a couple of years, Morning Star might be as prosperous as New Buffalo, where one large adobe house was already occupied and two others were under construction, walls finished, fireplaces installed and roofing with pine poles begun. New Buffalo had seen its share of troubles, but there seemed to be money available to the commune. There was a tool shed filled with power equipment, a new yellow tractor, a Mercedes Benz sedan. In the small rooms of the adobe house, sheepskin rugs covered the raw earth floors. The Governor of New Mexico had visited New Buffalo and been impressed.

There was no telephone at New Buffalo, but there was electricity and water, even a washing machine. The food was tasty and substantial, including not only the usual beans and rice, but also homemade jams and cookies. The kitchen was filthy, though, and filled with flies. Young women, naked to the waist, were shucking corn back of the cook house. They saved the best ears for seed and dried the rest on the roof. Even the big yellow worms were kept and fed to the chickens. "We have something very important here," one girl said. "We believe in God."

If New Buffalo was medieval, Morning Star was neolithic — freakier, somewhat desperate, not very talkative, much more dramatic. People might freeze to death in those teepees come winter. There was a sense of presence.

From around the back of the house, a bearded blonde boy in hitch-up jeans guided a mule-drawn buckboard to a halt. Wordlessly, he stopped and embraced a tall, slender girl who was wearing a long gingham granny dress and headkerchief.

For a long time they held each other — a tiny, fragile tableau of human need set in the overpoweringly grand theater of the Sangre de Cristo mountains and the trembling storm-cloud heaven.

The sky blackened. Rain fell. Lightning chattered angrily. The boy and girl bounced apart to arms' length, still holding hands. The storm delivered its full load. Heads thrown back to the sky, mouths open and laughing, they gamboled in the downpour.

Up on the adobe ground, the naked workers continued uninterrupted by the rain. The hot cast-iron stove sizzled. The campfire smoked and steamed. In the open doorway of the house, one of the pregnant girls stood staring across the wide plateau to tree-covered mountains beyond where the sky was a crisp, transparent cobalt blue. At twilight, her labor would begin. Attended only by her friends, she would give birth at dawn. After a day's rest, she would return to work in the fields, carrying her infant on her back in a cloth sling, pausing occasionally to give the baby her breast while the work of survival went on all around her, serenely confident that when winter arrived Morning Star would be ready.

*J*ames Marcus Ayers of Denver, Colo., called himself a "tripper drifter." He had been hitchhiking for months throughout the Southwest and seen many communes. Now, on his way back to Taos, headed toward home and civilization, wrapped in a striped wool poncho and carrying an Indian charm made of horsehair and hawk feathers, he was still trying to make sense of what he had seen.

"It's hard to understand why people would want to give up everything that has

gone before," he said. "Why suffer if you don't have to?"

For the past few years, American parents have been trying to answer the same question. As the decade of the Sixties ended, it seemed as if more and more young people were rejecting the fruits of urban capitalism, in a rush to rural communalism.

In doing so, they were following an old tradition. America was settled by people very much like the kids with long hair in the communal colonies of the Southwest. It is no accident that Massachusetts and Pennsylvania call themselves Commonwealths. Our history is filled with utopian experiments—Oneida, Amana, New Harmony, Brook Farm. A few survived. Most failed. Yet the urge to create new societies continued.

The modern history of communalism started with the French Revolution of 1789. The communes of Paris were the city's smallest political subdivisions, roughly the equivalent of today's neighborhood political clubs. When the government fell, they elected a committee called the Commune to run Paris. It lasted until 1794. The Commune was revived for a few months in 1871 after the evacuation of Paris by Prussian troops, then suppressed.

The word itself comes from the Old French *communer*, to share. The root is the Latin *munis*, gift or civic duty. This, in turn, appears to be derived from the San-

skrit *maya*, magical power. Ultimately, then, commune means shared power. From the same sources we get community, communism, communicate and Communion, a sharing with God.

Commune is closely related to common, as in the Boston Common, a municipal park that was once a sheep meadow belonging to the settlement as a whole. This is the central idea in communalism—the elimination of individual, exclusive ownership of property.

Communalism and communism once meant pretty much the same thing. Today, the communist is usually thought of as a central planner and theoretician, a politician. The communalist is an activist, less interested in the business of deciding how to share, but vitally involved in promoting the experience of sharing.

Newsweek once called 1969 "The Year of the Commune" and guessed that there might be as many as 500 communes in America, with a total membership of 10,000 persons. The Modern Utopian, a magazine published by the Alternatives Foundation, Berkeley, Calif., printed an alphabetical listing of 120 active communes. It began with the Ahimsa Community of Parsons, Kansas ("Buddhist, eight adults, no new members wanted") and ended with the Yellow Submarine Commune, 2449 Floral Hill, Eugene, Oregon.

Three communes were based on one

best-selling novel, *The Harrad Experiment.* In Ann Arbor, Mich., there was one commune living in four houses supported by three rock groups. This was Trans-Love-Energy, home of the White Panther Party and the MC5. It had been organized by John Sinclair, now serving a ten year prison sentence for giving two marijuana cigarettes to undercover narcotics agents.

In Brooklyn, N.Y., a real estate firm called The Apartment Key advertised house rentals "suitable for communes." In Menlo Park, Calif., the Portola Institute, a hip think tank, had created the Whole Earth Truck Store, a kind of travelling Sears for rural collectives.

It turned out that there were communes all over America — urban, rural, suburban and semi-rural. Some banned drugs. Others gave LSD free to all members and visitors. Many were little more than crash pads, but some were as comfortable as any good fraternity house. And, in a way, that was what most of them resembled — coed fraternities where the parties smelled of grass instead of beer. Yet, at the bottom, it seemed as if something important and serious might be going on.

To the adult experts one thing was very clear: The communal living thing was real. It might be dangerous. The communes had something to do with drugs and revolution. There were warnings.

"More and more of our children will move into psychedelic communes unless society tries to understand the stresses that alienated them in the first place," said Dr. David E. Smith, director of the Haight-Ashbury Medical Clinic.

What were those stresses? What was that alienation all about? Why were the children of America rejecting everything their parents had tried to give them? Why did everything go wrong, just as it seemed to be going right?

*T*he 1960s opened with a burst of laughter. John F. Kennedy was making jokes in the White House. Jolly old Pope John XXIII was breaking them up in the Vatican. Nikita Khruschev was banging his shoe in the United Nations.

The laughter was cut off by rifle bullets. The nation became expert at staging state funerals. We wallowed in the gloom of imperial responsibility.

In the depths of our bereavement, we attempted to energize ourselves out of misery the way we had energized ourselves out of the Depression. We went to war. This time, we lost. The game was ugly and boring. Parents were sending their boys to die in Asia for no reason that anyone could fathom, especially the young. They asked questions and we lied to them and to each other. The children began shouting dirty words — dope, sex, love — and, receiving no response, began to run about wildly in a mad hysteria cued on the side of tears by Bob Dylan and on the side of laughter by the Beatles, while Timothy Leary, high on acid, proclaimed the glorious pleasure of the dirtiest word of them all — death. It seemed that America was dying. A mad wake was in progress for a corpse that refused to submit to the oncoming night, flailing with the blind power of a cold Golem and striking down doctors and next of kin alike.

While some of the young tried to save themselves by fighting the manic national parent directly, others ran and hid. Orphans of affluence, they knew almost nothing about survival. To most of them, money was something that came out of a wallet; food was found in refrigerators, and work was a tedious magic that Daddy did to make the house machine keep buzzing. The techniques of manipulating the industrial society to produce the necessities of life were as incomprehensible to them as the techniques of growing food might be to monkeys. Scrounging in the rich garbage of the American dream, they returned, in effect, to man's original state. They became hunters and food gatherers.

Because they were still children, kept that way by a society that prolongs adolescence longer than any other, they turned life on the street into a game. Lonely runaways met other lonely runaways. They rediscovered the joys of companionship. Vagabonds released from the prison supervision of upper middle - class family routine in which every activity is scheduled and checked, they found freedom to do as they pleased. They smoked marijuana, took any pill that anyone offered, made love to each other. They did not go to school and they did not receive grades. They dressed themselves in any old crazy costumes and made every day Halloween.

Finally, they began to explore one of the

dirtiest words of them all: communism. There was a great sharing. In the general euphoria of this communion of the children, even grown-ups could smile and take a flower. It was a charming relief from the grim news that relentlessly pumped through the adult communications network. It was 1967 and the Summer of Love was at hand, transforming the foul tenements of San Francisco's Haight-Ashbury and New York's Lower East Side into the temples of what was to be a new society in which money and profits would not exist.

No one wanted to believe that it all had the sad beauty of the games children played at the entrance to the gas chamber. No one wanted to believe that the lovely girl with the strange stare and the soft voice and the woven crown of flowers in her hair was really Ophelia. No one wanted to believe that those were funeral flowers. No one wanted to believe that death could be so satisfying.

At the Monterey Pop Festival in July, 1967, Augustus Stanley Owsley, the Henry Ford of LSD, walked through the multitudes giving acid away by the handful. The performers were so wiped out by the effects of Owsley's philanthropy that some of them were finding it difficult to get on stage. The management barred him from the backstage area and pleaded with him to stop turning on entertainers. Doc Stanley then focussed his attention on the stagehands, grips, drivers and other support personnel.

Grass was smoked openly throughout the crowd. At one point during the three-day festival, a uniformed motorcycle policeman in shiny black boots and leather trim was observed skipping joyously down a path carrying in front of him in his extended hands his helmet. It was filled with tiny flowers.

At the end of the affair, the Monterey police, who had been allegedly guaranteed $70,000 for providing off-duty officers as a traffic and security force, reportedly accepted only $40,000. The job hadn't been worth more, they explained.

During the next month, it was rumored that Owsley and Leary planned to lead teams of hippies giving away handsful of LSD and STP on street corners everywhere. Owsley's Monterey Purple began appearing throughout the hip community. For many people, it turned out to be the worst psychedelic bummer in history. It was said that the pill contained strychnine. Everyone survived this pill, but some of those who took STP did not. The word was out that the Beatles and Donovan were giving up hallucinogenic drugs.

In August, Bob Dylan broke his neck in a motorcycle accident. In September, Groovey, a pleasant mental defective, and his girl friend, Linda Fitzpatrick, the daughter of a well-to-do Connecticut exurbanite, were murdered in the cellar of an East Village tenement where they had hoped to score some acid.

The Summer of Love was over and the Winter of Speed was beginning. Hip was buried in a mock funeral on Haight Street. Long-haired dealers with guns were running the scene now. The original hippies who had not disappeared into the desert when the teenyboppers arrived were looking for safe holes to hide in. Shivering was epidemic.

Many of the casualties of this dream that failed fled into the Indian country. A defeated people, they went to the Indians to learn how to live off the land. They saw no other way to survive.

*E*ver since the beginning of the psychedelic revolution in the late Sixties, there has been an intensive fascination with the Indian roots of the American experience among the turned-on young. A cynic might suggest that this was only a more pretentious version of an old game— cowboys and Indians. A student of cultural and literary history would see it as an inevitable symptom of a Romantic revival, a return to the Noble Savage as the model of the ideal life style. A pharmacologically astute analyst could see an obvious connection between the American Indian use of peyote and other hallucinogens and the hippies dependence upon these same drugs.

The most significant perspective might be this: The young may reject their parents, but they are still afraid of the dark. They need experts to teach them how to live in the raw. The Indians are experts. They have been out there in the wild a long time, existing quite well without the benefits of industrial civilization.

The Taos Pueblo was already old when the Spanish conquistador Francisco Vasquez de Coronado came to New Mexico

seeking the mythical golden cities of Ci-
bola. Today, the Indians of the pueblo
live much as they did then, practising only
so much Catholicism as they have found
necessary to varnish their ancient rituals in
order to satisfy the priests who accompanied the soldiers.

Among the 1400 occupants of the adobe
pueblo, there are a few who earn extra
money by selling hand-worked silver and
bead trinkets to the tourists, but the pueblo
as a whole shares the fees charged for permission to park automobiles on the reservation and the right to take pictures. With the
exception of personal possessions, such as
clothing and jewelry, the Indians have
never accepted modern concepts of individual ownership of land or improvements.
The reservation and the buildings belong
ultimately and obviously not to any person
or family, not even in any important way
to the pueblo itself, but only to the universal
life force from which the present generation
derives the benefits of existence and holds
its gifts in trust for generations yet unborn.

The Indians of the Taos Pueblo share
with the inhabitants of the other pueblo
tribes of New Mexico and Arizona — Tiwa,
Hopi, Zuni — a cultural ethic which anthro-
pologist Ruth Benedict called Appollonian,
idealizing peace and order and seeking to
eliminate the aggressive expression of
individual ego drives in order to achieve
and maintain union with nature. Although
they willingly subordinate themselves to
the group spirit in a surrender of personal
self-determination that might seem humili-
ating to Americans who have been brought
up to believe in the creation and protection
of a unique, precious identity as the only
appropriate satisfaction in the life struggle,
the Indians of the pueblos do not recognize
in any real way the validity of master-slave
transactions.

The Taosenos, especially, have refused
to accept, in principle, the authority of any
government to direct their lives as a moral,
ethical or natural right. Out of a desire for
peace and in the face of superior force, they
have accommodated themselves to succes-
sive Spanish, Mexican and American colo-
nial presences. During the past four hundred years they have successfully — if
temporarily — revolted against each of their
conquerors whenever the external rule began to interfere with the basic experiences
of the way of life of the Taos Pueblo.

Recently, the Taos Pueblo appeared to be
on the verge of winning another important
battle against outside influence. For as long
as they can remember, the Taosenos have
used the waters of their sacred Blue Lake
high in the Sangre de Cristo Mountains as
a holy shrine upon whose purity, they believe, depends the effectiveness of religious
rituals at the center of their faith.

The lake is inside the boundaries of Car-
son National Forest and, under the admin-
istration of the United States National Park
Service, has been open to recreational use.
The Taos Indians have claimed that the
Blue Lake and its surrounding forest are
being polluted and spoiled by outsiders. If
this goes on, they have warned, the shrine
will be permanently defiled and the survival of life in the Taos area endangered
when the ceremonials which have, for thousands of years, insured the fertility of the
region fail.

A court fight to return the lake and forest
to the exclusive use of the Indians of the
Taos Pueblo has not worked. At the end of
the summer of 1969, however, the United
States House of Representatives passed a
bill that would make the Blue Lake and
some 50,000 surrounding acres part of the
Taos Pueblo Reservation. Now the Taosenos are waiting for the Senate and the
President to make the bill a law. They are
confident of eventual success, not because
they believe they are entitled to any right of
ownership or title in the land and the water,
but because they believe the natural consciousness which transcends all governments and all men seeks more responsible
stewards for an important piece of life's
collective property that has been abused by
those hands into which it was given in trust.

*T*he young Americans liv-
ing in the communal groups that have begun
to dot northern New Mexico with canvas
teepees, old school busses decorated in the
psychedelic style, tents, trailers and new
adobe huts often say that the Indians were
the original hippies.

Morning Star in New Mexico is the off-
shoot of an earlier commune with the same
name set up on a 31-acre ranch in Santa
Rosa, Calif., by Lou Gottlieb, formerly of
the Limelighters folksinging group.

When Gottlieb began the venture in 1965,
he thought it would be a start toward the

formation of what he called the Alternate Society, the opposite of the Great Society, an answer to the problems of the "age of cybernation, economic abundance and technological unemployability."

Gottlieb's experiment fragmented under the pressure of local hostility. Some of the people went to New Mexico and tried to create a new Morning Star that would succeed.

Other longhairs began arriving in New Mexico as early as 1967. Within two years they had spent more than $500,000 on land. In Taos, there was a general store run by longhairs on what appeared to be a low-profit basis. A hippie automobile repair shop was accepting payment from those who could afford it and allowing others to use its facilities free. A free medical clinic was in operation.

If a totally moneyless society was undoubtedly a long way off, still there was evidence of a budding Alternate Society. The runaways were learning how to take care of their own. Yet they were hardly welcome among the local people, who were afraid of drugs and disease. There were two cases of bubonic plague in the hippie colony in Placitas. During the Thirties, plague had ripped through northern New Mexico. No one wanted to see it return.

There was also something less rational, the kind of intangible prejudice that greets any minority group. A discussion overheard in the Kiva Coffee Shop of the Kachina Lodge in Taos was typical.

It was going on at a corner table among two real Americans in short-sleeved shirts and a middle-aged man whose orange shirt and leather string tie were evidently supposed to suggest solidarity with Western tradition.

"Them hippies are trying to take over, but they don't want to work," said one of the white shirts.

"Oh, they'll work all right," the Wild Westerner said. "You just got to give them the kind of work they like. Executive work, that's what they like. Of course, there's not much of that around, is there?"

"Haw haw!" they laughed, pounding the table and stamping their feet. "You hit the nail right on the head," said one. "They gonna be executives with the telephone company or nothing. They ain't lazy. They just particular. Haw hee haw!"

About thirty miles south of the Kiva Cof-

fee Shop of the Kachina Lodge, the 50 current members of the Hog Farm, a travelling circus of a commune which had just spent the last 18 months moving like gypsies from town to town in three large gaily painted busses and a motley caravan of other motor vehicles, were sitting in front of the Road Hog, their oldest and favorite bus, discussing plans to build a real kiva in which they could live comfortably during the winter.

A kiva is ordinarily understood to be a ceremonial building, traditionally circular and consisting mainly of a large round hole dug into the ground, walled about with adobe and roofed with pine poles called vegas. It is one of the oldest forms of shelter known to man. The pueblo Indians no longer live in kivas, but they use them

for sacred rites. In many languages the word for temple is the same as the word for house. So important a breakthrough in human development as housing is thus understandably memorialized in religious ritual.

The Hog Farm was among the most recent communes to settle in the New Mexico area, but one of the oldest groups in the psychedelic movement, a wild seed that sprung from novelist Ken Kesey's Merry Pranksters. Kesey, not long released from jail after serving six months for possession of marijuana, was living on a ranch outside Eugene, Oregon.

"Ken told me that it's a place to die, not a place to live," former Prankster Hugh Romney announced to the group after the work meeting was finished. "He said, 'I am building a graveyard.' He doesn't want anyone coming up there."

In the colorful world of the super hip underground scene, it is not likely that there are many men more colorful than Hugh Romney, who used to walk around Manhattan wearing an orange nylon jump suit and a sweat-stained cowboy hat with a steer horn projecting horizontally from the crown. He lost his front teeth somewhere and has never found time to replace them. Richard Avedon was on his way out to New Mexico to photograph Romney for the Museum of Modern Art. "If I ever get my front teeth back, I'm dynamite," Romney said.

The Hog Farm got its name when Romney and his wife Bonnie Jean began living with a couple of friends on a pig farm in the San Fernando Valley, Calif., rent free in return for feeding the forty pigs every day.

Romney, formerly a psychologist at California State University, maneuvered the rapidly growing group all across the country putting on concerts and light shows. In an article in The Realist he described the Hog Farm as "an expanded family, a mobile hallucination, a sociological experiment, an army of clowns." Among its members is a 400-pound female pig named Pigasus which ran for President in 1968. More recently, Pigasus was bred to a local stud. One of the Hog Farm's most precious possessions is a photograph of Pigasus getting it on with her swain.

The Hog Farm came out of the underground into the national media in August, 1969 as a result of its services at the Woodstock Music Festival. The Hog Farmers ran the freak-out tent, where victims of bad drug trips were brought down. The Hog Farm was credited with major responsibility in keeping the peace when some 500,000 fans arrived for an outdoor show on a farm in Bethel, N.Y. where no more than 100,000 were expected. Hog Farmers also provided similar services at the Dallas Music Festival. A psychiatrist who observed in the freak-out tent was amazed at the skill with which bum trippers were calmed.

Asked for his professional opinion on Hog Farm techniques, he replied, "How can I comment on what they're doing? I'm here to learn."

Not everyone was quite as impressed with the Hog Farm's total performance at Woodstock.

"I didn't like the way they treated their women," complained Jim Fouratt, a former house freak at Columbia Records and a founding member of Gay Liberation Front. "I thought it was ugly the way a guy would just grab a naked girl, throw her to the ground and get his rocks off."

In New Mexico, three or four boys and girls would crowd into a tiny pup tent "sweat lodge" heated sauna-style with hot stones, then dance out into the open to plunge into the cold waters of a big pond.

At one point, Lou Todd, the commissioner of Vehicles, one of the original Hog Farmers, was walking around crying, "Let's have an orgy," but he was unable to get anything going.

During a conversation about sex in communes, one visitor said, "My wife spent

Hugh Romney [yes I know he wants to be called Wavy Gravy — which is what we are, protoplasm being very wavy gravy = but you know me, I'm still calling that colored fellow Cassius Clay] said, "Jules, man has disrupted the balance of the universe and we must set it right."

two months in a commune in San Francisco and never got fucked."

"It is very easy to spend two months in a commune without getting fucked," a girl replied. Another said, "Well, winter is coming soon, the cold will bring everyone together again."

Sexual freedom is part of the Hog Farm ethic — so much so that one person's venereal infection can zip through the commune faster than a short circuit in a high tension line. In Hugh Romney's room there is what must be the world's largest bottle of tetracycline capsules, a broad-mouthed jar the size of a carboy. Tetracycline is an antibiotic used for a broad spectrum of gram negative bacterial infections, a category including many of the diseases of love. The drug is frequently used as a follow-up to penicillin. The inference here may be unfair, of course. Maybe the Hog Farmers suffer from carbuncles or something equally innocent. If so, the commune will undoubtedly take the cruel accusation in good sport.

The Hog Farm, unlike many of the communes in New Mexico, has a ribald sense of humor and refuses to take itself seriously. Romney, in particular, has the almost mystical genius to make fun of life without offending anyone's belief in the dignity of human existence.

"The Tibetan National Anthem is 'Shaboom, shaboom, life is just a dream," he said. Earlier in the day, he had been informed that Red Dog, the Money Commissioner for the Hog Farm, had lost the commune's entire bankroll of $900, leaving them without funds for food while they waited for a $6500 check to arrive from the promoters of the Woodstock Festival.

Commissioners volunteer for their jobs. They continue in them as long as they find the work satisfying. A commissioner who is not performing well quickly loses a taste for the position. He is constantly in direct contact with the people he serves. Their feelings are not likely to be hidden from him. Honesty is a fetish at the Hog Farm.

In addition to the more predictable commissions — sanitation, work, housing and so on — there is a full-time Dope Commissioner who forages for drugs. On this day, the Dope Commissioner was in Denver. When he returned with a shopping bag full of grass there was a great communal smoke-in. Dozens of Hog Farmers rolled joints in mass production, while others lighted up.

"Hugh," says I, I says to him "Don't worry about that; it will set us right." That's what I says to him — and it will, yes it will.

Soon there was a joint in every hand. Musicians got their instruments and the mountain air was filled with rock music and the herbal smell of burning grass. In addition to the communal smoking, there were invitation-only sessions later on. When it comes to dope, the Hog Farm has not reached pure socialism. There are always private stashes, not only as a hedge against scarcity, but also, frequently, because of the somewhat limited availability of really high class product. There is a widespread feeling that publicly-distributed grass is rarely as good as private stock. If the Hog Farm is any guide, there will probably be a black market in bootleg marijuana even after the weed is legalized. It is human nature to mistrust officially-sanctioned pleasure.

Despite the loss of the bankroll, the kitchen crew was trying to figure out an evening meal. Feeding is the responsibility of a volunteer called the Dance Mistress, who plans the menu and supervises the cooking. It looked as if the commune was going to get something like rice and beans.

Fortunately, a reporter and a photographer from a national magazine showed up with enough expense account money to feed the entire commune for a couple of days. The magazine men bought meat for the evening meal, not realizing that many of the Hog Farmers were devout vegetarians.

The following morning all the vegetarians agreed that the night had been filled with bad dreams, screaming and widespread bum trips as a result of the meat-eating. The more probable cause of the excitement was a girl who freaked out in a high fever resulting from what appeared to be pneumonia. In the early hours of morning she was taken to the hospital at Embudo. While being examined by the doctor on duty, she asked dreamily, "Doctor, how much does an angel weigh?"

"How should I know?" the physician replied.

"You ought to," the girl said. "There's one sitting on your shoulder."

In the ordinary course of a day, crises such as this are a routine part of the Hog Farm adventure. In fact, they provide one of the more significant attractions of communal life for Hugh Romney.

"If you're married and you have a kid," he said, "maybe something important will happen once every six months. The baby will step on a nail. Your wife will damage the car. Here something is happening every minute. Every day you get the opportunity to make significant decisions."

Communal living allows people to work out hang-ups acquired in the course of growing up in the nuclear family. A man like Hugh Romney has the satisfaction of playing parent over and over again. The more dependent members get to be children as much as they please, until tired of the role. Each person can act out his own fantasy in a highly permissive setting in which the demands of reality are minimal.

The rewards are not limited to transference, role-playing and fantasy-achievement. Psychology aside, just being in the country is a source of pleasure.

"Living close to nature is tremendously sensual and erotic," said Dr. Timothy Leary, the Norman Vincent Peale of acid. He was having Sunday brunch at the Black Rabbit Inn in Los Angeles, a little piece of Big Sur created on Melrose Ave. by Billy James, Doris Day's press agent.

Radiating a halo of positive energy, the one-time psychedelic candidate for governor of California had come in from a farming commune in the nearby San Bernardino Mountains.

"You are getting back to your animal nature," he said. "There's no question that electricity cuts down sexual activity. If a couple sits around watching TV they are less likely to be aroused to an erotic state than if they were watching a campfire.

"Do you remember what happened after the Northeast power blackout? Nine months later there was a sharp rise in births. Couples were deprived of distractions and had to fall back on their own resources."

No one at the table told Dr. Leary that the blackout birth rate story was a myth officially denied by the Department of Health of the City of New York. It seemed impolite to interrupt a sermon with facts.

"Many city people feel that going to the country is somehow uncomfortable," he went on, "as though you're giving up sensuality in the sense of hot showers. The truth is the closer you get to nature the hornier you get."

Timothy Leary did not agree that the

Summer of Love had been a disaster. "I saw the Haight Ashbury as a free university," he said, "where thousands and thousands of young people who would have drifted to Las Vegas and become call girls were exposed instead to many holy traditions and met many holy people. Like any large university, some of them used it and some didn't.

"There was nothing tragic about the Haight-Ashbury. To me, it's dumb to go there and say, 'There's the hippie movement for you—speedfreaks hustling tourists.' Junkies have always been killing each other in the slums of big cities. It has nothing to do with the hippie movement.

"I live in a straight LSD commune," he said. "We all take LSD once a week, but there's no big thing about it. Sometimes you'll see a person who's on an LSD trip and you won't know what he's doing, because he's milking the cows, weeding the gardens.

"The problem with the acid head is that he takes LSD and discovers that he's God, which means that he controls his own nervous system and creates his own reality. Then he wanders around saying, 'I'm God!' Really experienced acid people don't have to go around saying that. They simply live it out.

"I think that a lot of the communes, particularly the more publicized, are really open mental hospitals," he said. "Of course, I think that a housing tract is a mental hospital, too. The really successful communes are the ones you never hear about.

"Many of the people living in communes have failed somehow to harness their energies. There is a certain kind of man who feels called upon to help them, a nurturant male, some sort of psychiatric Jewish mother," Leary observed.

What did Dr. Timothy Leary's mother think about what he was doing? Dr. Leary giggled. There was something very unhappy and nervous about that giggle.

"She wanted me to be a Harvard professor," Timothy Leary said, speaking very fast, his voice high-pitched. "And a doctor. And there I was at Harvard with a PhD. It seemed as if all her dreams were coming true. And . . . then . . . it . . . all fell apart." The giggle squeaked in this throat. He stopped speaking for a moment.

"She doesn't understand," Leary continued quietly. "She knows I'm making waves and that pleases her. But she doesn't understand."

If Timothy Leary's mother fails to understand what has happened to her son, how must the parents of less successful soldiers of the psychedelic revolution feel? Into whose hands have they delivered their children? Charles Manson's?

When Life ran a cover story on communal living, the pictures combined the rugged poetic patina of Marlboro Country with the romantic sentimentality of Bible illustrations. In reality, many of the communes were physically little better than prison camps. If the government had forced hippies to live in them, the Red Cross would have complained. Yet they were much better than our mental hospitals, reform schools, orphanages and jails.

At the energy centers of the communalist movement are social workers without portfolio, unable to accept the stupid brutalities of official charity and unwilling to ignore the victims of America's continuing urban disaster. There is a war going on between our cities and our people. The communes are emergency wards and rest homes for the casualties.

This aspect is most obvious in Synanon and Daytop, but it is visible also in groups operating without any formal philosophy or mission. Last summer, 15-25 persons were fed and housed daily in Lagunitas, Calif., by an outfit called Young Ideas which seems to have started out as a business but evolved into a commune.

The driving force here was Jim Brewster, 32, an Army helicopter pilot who was shot down four times in Vietnam and discharged for the good of the service under less than honorable conditions. Young Ideas was headquartered in a big old Chinese-style roadhouse owned by the Lotus Fortune Cookie Company. The building was evidently once a restaurant. One of its huge kitchen ranges was fitted with woks, broad, sloped-sided pans used in Chinese cooking.

The pagoda flourishes of the house curled against great redwood trees. The property bordered on a state park. There was a small creek running in and out of the trees to a deep pond. In the summer, the pond was thick with kids, many of them naked. Highway workers, linemen and other utilities service people sometimes ate lunch on the roadside up above and watched the show.

*We are
all here in school unlearning conventional science. Giving up toys
is the hardest part of the trip
home to that old beginning. Who
are you, out there, peering at my
exposed nerves? There has to be
unconditional trust between us. This
is not a novel, but a sacramental
testimony of a time and space, as
faithful as gospel.*

Someone once asked, "Do you have communal sex?" The answer was, "How can we avoid it? There are no walls."

There was only one bathroom. Efficient use required a suspension of the rules of privacy. A boy would be taking a bath. Sherri would come in to wash her face. Nancy would sit on the pot.

Very tall and blonde, Nancy had a voluptuous figure which she exhibited as often as possible. She seemed to have a profound sexual itch that she was unable to relieve for very long.

"Nancy's on a heavy fuck trip," said Brewster. A drop-out from Brigham Young University, she seemed to be determined to act out some idealized standards of free love. She had one steady lover and lots of in-betweens. When Nancy was getting to know a new lover, her moans and cries filled the house at all hours. When she was looking for satisfaction, it was impossible to ignore her constant display of flesh. Getting caught with her in the narrow kitchen was an exercise in grope therapy. She hit mercilessly with her breasts, her behind, her thighs. Sometimes she was only play-

ing. Too quick or crude a response could cause her to act suddenly offended.

"You're crazy! You're crazy!" she would shriek, running away in a funny goosey sway that was not very sexy at all.

"Love is the form of communication I know best," Nancy explained. "When I'm having trouble with someone, I find that the best way to work it through is to ball him. It clears the obstacles fast. I don't think people really know each other until they've balled."

The other people attempted to maintain at least the appearance of monogamy. There were flirtations that cut across the lines, but, as in conventional society, they were usually well-hidden despite the close quarters.

For privacy you had to go outside.

In July and August, Jim Brewster and his girl, Sherri Wik, slept out in the open in a big fourposter bed planted on the hillside like an advertisement for antique furniture. Next to the bed there was an old oak nightchest with a white china pitcher of wildflowers.

Young Ideas was in the business of odd

6 am

Brewster and I are going out to the Sacramento Valley today to look for a hobo jungle for a story for True. There is no hot water this morning. I am the only person in America who would worry about not being clean enough to go to a hobo jungle.

jobs—gardening, home repairs, house painting. The workers and their girls and wives lived in the Chinese House. They were paid two dollars an hour, of which one dollar was deducted for room and board. Young Ideas charged its customers four dollars an hour. No great profits accumulated. Once, when there was no money, Brewster pawned his Rolex gold wristwatch for $175 and bought food. Individuals who had outside incomes were expected to pay their way. At peak population it cost upwards of $1500 a month to keep the place alive. During one four week period last summer, no one who came to the Chinese House was refused food or temporary shelter.

Among the long-term residents were a few teenagers. One sixteen-year-old girl had apparently been abandoned by her parents. There were two married couples in their early twenties, two adult single girls and five single men. One man was in his fifties. He had done five years penal servitude. A couple of the others had done time too, mainly for petty offenses. Sherri's daughter Santee, a two-year-old, was the only child. On weekends there might be as many as ten visitors eating and sleeping there.

Each of these people had a highly personal notion of what Young Ideas might be. A girl who wrote free-lance advertising copy for an agency in San Francisco knew she was living in a commune. So did Bill Aquarius, the young poet. Steve Scorpio, nineteen, always referred to the group as The Family. You could hear the capital letters. It is hard to know what most of the others thought. Many were spaced out inside their heads far beyond this kind of conceptual communication.

Brewster and Sherri were the dominant figures. They had started the whole thing. They paid the rent and the bills and dealt with the outside authority. They were the adults. The others, for the most part, were children who would grow up and move on. Jim and Sherri and the baby would remain. Everything else was subject to reinterpretation.

If there was any unifying philosophy at the Chinese House, it was not more than this: no violence. There was the unques-

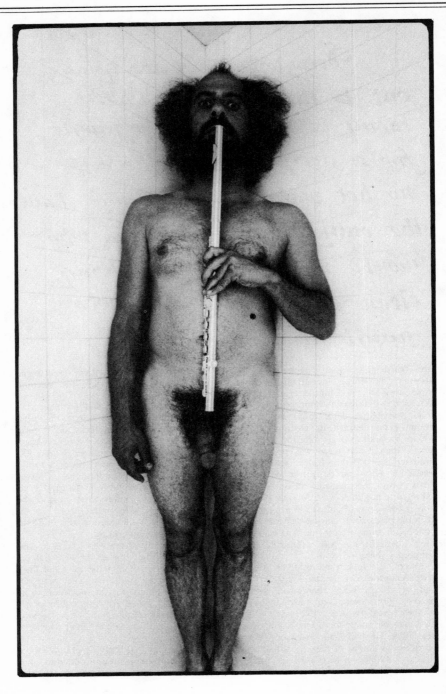

tioning belief that no situation could possibly require force. It was an unspoken but absolute denial of the existence of incurable evil.

Bill Aquarius chose for a while to live in an abandoned metal water tower in the woods. He shared it with a scorpion. He refused to entertain a visitor's suggestion that he kill it.

"That's not necessary," he said. "The scorpion and I have to learn how to live together. If it gets used to me and I get used to it, then we can get into each other's thing and understand each other."

Guy, a big, young Georgian who commuted between the Chinese House and his apartment in San Francisco, was a recent convert to pacificism. At one time, he had carried a pistol. For a while, Guy had been obsessed with the fate of the American Indian. Wearing feathers, buckskins and beads, a hunting knife at his waist, he had sermonized the patrons of the cheap bars of San Francisco's Tenderloin, pounding a Bible and commanding sinners to repent and do something about their Indian brothers.

"I don't think I was quite rational then," he admitted, "but, you know, I converted some of them. It didn't take permanently, of course, but I did get a few righteously hooked."

Like most of the people who lived in the Chinese House, Guy kept his hair short and wore ordinary heavy-duty work clothes. In a frayed straw hat, Li'l Abner boots, plaid cotton shirt and blue denim hammer jeans, he was Mr. Hick. Beneath the get-up there was a very complicated, subtle and indivi-

abalone had the fresh essence of the open sea, a very special experience.

Guy found a runaway Siberian Malemute in the woods and brought it back to the house. The dog was a wild brute with thick fangs made for grinding bones. There were three other dogs living at the house: a russet Weimaraner named Janice, a heavy-boned black Labrador called Barney, and Lilith, an elegantly successful product of the mating of a male coyote and a female Alsatian. They were beautiful hounds, constantly posing, waiting for Andrew Wyeth to paint their portraits.

Lilith and Janice were Brewster's dogs. Janice had taken acid once. Her eyes still seemed to burn with what she had seen. Lilith was feline and tawny, more cat than dog. She had a serious case of the hots for Brewster. He would sometimes take her in his arms and embrace her, rolling on the floor, kissing her mouth and making love noises in her ear, feeling her up shamelessly.

"She's a *chick*," Brewster explained as he got up from a heavy make-out session with Lilith. The dog lay on her back, her legs spread, pumping her sex in pleading passion, her dignity totally forgotten. "Holy *shit*, Lilith!" Brewster howled, "give us some *slack*!" For the rest of the month, Santee imitated Jim's vehement plea. "Gimmee *slack*!" she would shout in her high baby voice, cracking the last word like the tail of a whip.

When the Siberian arrived, Janice was in heat. The big dog immediately claimed her as his own. He was a jealous lover, suspicious of the easy immorality of com-

"I am in the city, and when I am in the city I sometimes play my flute," Ron Thal wrote from Glendale

dual intellect. A skindiver, he seemed to be searching in the dark, cold waters off Pt. Reyes Peninsula with a singleness of purpose for a satisfaction that had eluded him on land. In the course of his search, he amused himself by hunting abalone, which he brought back to the kitchen at Young Ideas. Restaurant abalone usually tastes like fishy eggplant. The life is too long gone by the time it reaches the plate. Guy's

munal life. Whenever Barney approached Janice for a friendly sniff, the new dog attacked with the blunt fury of a wolf. Guy was warned that the Siberian was dangerous.

"That dog is a good dog," he argued. "Just don't mess around in his thing with Janice and he'll be peaceful as a pup." Visiting dogs who showed up at the Chinese House for the usual light socializing were immediately driven out by the Siberian male, who walked around in a stiff-legged patrol, growling deep down in his chest every once in a while. Sometimes he would stand next to Janice in dumb adoration, lost in a love trance.

Several times a day the house was in uproar, dogs whirling and roaring. One of the men trying to separate them was bitten about the chest and arm by the Siberian. While the victim was being taken to the emergency room at Marin General Hospital, the new dog growled at Brewster.

Quick and big, Brewster is a perfect mesomorph with the round, thick muscles of a boxer. In eight years in the service, he had worked his way up to master sergeant before becoming an officer and a helicopter pilot. At the time of his discharge, which had something to do with an AWOL charge and a lot more to do with the black market, he was a captain. On the biceps of his right arm there was a fat white scar from a shrapnel wound.

Brewster had neatly trimmed hair. He was wearing striped white and blue pants and a Phi Mu sorority tee shirt, one of a collection which included an official Mickey Mouse Club tee shirt and another emblazoned with the slogan of Olympia Beer: "It's the water!" It showed a cascading mountain stream just like the illustration on the Olympia label. Into this stream a little boy was urinating.

Jim Brewster wore costumes, not clothing. They were subtle costumes, selected to enhance roles, rather than merely to adorn. It seemed sometimes that he could remember which role he was playing at the moment only by looking in the mirror. In a tan poplin bush jacket, he was a young field executive in the construction business. A football jersey turned him into an All-American college jock. When he went to court to explain how he had managed to accumulate $1200 worth of traffic citations, he wore a navy blazer with brass buttons, a peach-striped white button-down oxford shirt and cream white flannel pants.

"Your honor," he testified crisply, looking the judge straight in the eye, "I don't know exactly how it happened myself. My marriage was breaking up and I was living alone. I was going through a great deal of emotional confusion."

"You say you were not living at home?" the judge asked. "Where were you living?"

"I moved around a lot."

"Did your wife forward the citations?" the judge questioned.

"I guess not, your honor," said Jim Brewster, picking up his cue, "but I know that's no excuse." The boyish sincerity of his *mea culpa* was laid on with a fine sense of drama. He was the most clean-cut person in the courtroom. You could tell that he was a stable young householder who had gotten

mixed up and had now put himself back together again. Go and sin no more was the verdict.

"Sometimes I think I ought to just go ahead and become an actor," Brewster confided later. "That's all I do is play all these different roles."

In any case, Jim Brewster was not about to take any crude shit from a hound. He leaped for the dog, grabbing it by the collar with the evident intention of throwing it out of the house. The dog snapped, its solid jaws hardly seeming to move. Brewster jumped back, blood dripping from his forearm. The Siberian ran out of the house. For the next day the doors were kept locked while attempts were made to convince Guy that the dog had to go.

"That dog doesn't bother anyone unless

you get on his case," said Guy. "You'll notice that he hasn't attacked one person first. You just got to give him time to settle himself. You got to *understand* him." The following day, Guy was bitten. Still the dog remained. Janice looked embarrassed. *"I know he's a gangster,"* she seemed to be saying with her liquid, human eyes, *"but I can't help myself—I love him."*

That afternoon Guy took the Siberian to Rancho Olompali, a big spread near Novato. As many as two hundred persons had once lived there communally, supported by a millionaire who had taken LSD and gone all the way on a Jesus trip. A fire had gutted the main house. The columned ruins were Grecian. They stood unrepaired, a bombed-out myth. Two children had drowned in the swimming pool. There was a new fence around it, but the water was green with slime, effluent from the bowels of the Minotaur.

There were ovens at Olompali in which 900 loaves of bread had been baked every day and given away. A wedding had been performed with bride, groom, preacher and guests all naked. Before the tragedies, the people at Olompali had considered themselves gods, conduits to Earth for immense energies from mystical sources. The millionaire's family committed him to an institution. Now there were only a few scavengers left on the estate.

A bearded boy brought corn, squash and tomatoes out of the Olompali vegetable garden and laid it at the feet of the visitors from the Chinese House. They ate the young corn raw. It was sweet and tender, but the kernels were misshapen and irregular from inconsistent watering. The squash and tomatoes were just coming ripe. The visitors filled shopping baskets with the vegetables.

A little billy goat walked up to the Siberian dog. The massive jaws flicked once. The kid fell dead without a sound. Guy was stunned. He took the dog into his pick-up truck and left. He did not come back to the Chinese House for several days. When he did the Siberian was not with him.

"I suddenly realized—*that could have been the baby,*" Guy confessed.

"Right! Finally!" Brewster shouted in his electrical vibrato. His voice was cheerfully cynical, almost pleased to express the I-told-you-so, but weary of pushing, filled with grim undertone.

"Happiness is unheard of unless advertised on television," Jim Brewster wrote later on in his trip book. A trip book is a kind of journal or diary, a shorthand record of a person's psychedelic trips, an attempt to retain the fleeting experience. Many are filled with drawings and notes from friends. The best time to keep your trip book up to date is when you are on acid or speed or just plain grass. Few people seem to make entries when straight. The preferred instrument for writing is a felt-tipped pen, which glides smoothly, producing a bold line filled with character and color.

Many people like rice paper tablets with rough, hand-made colored paper covers, the kind you can buy in any Japanese notion store. Brewster's book was an ordinary gray sales-expense ledger that cost 69¢. It was filled with block writing. Many words were misspelled and the grammar was shaky. Redeeming these faults were lines that revealed a very private Jim Brewster in moments approaching poetry. They were an explanation of the riddle of what a cashiered Army captain who looked like an astronaut was doing running a psychedelic communal-living experiment.

Here are a few excerpts:
Countless nows ago a shadow went undetected.
Final figures do not matter; each individual has his own timekeeper.
God has become a household word instead of a good father.
As the years roll by, what happens to the minutes?
Clear light! Pulsing plasma echoes through the iceberg. Bravo, Mingo, you've succeeded again!
"I want to be a me when I grow up"
"That's absurd. You've got to be like us."
The past tense of me is you.
The constant river changes. When will we catch up?
Electric dust settles on my outer crust.
Cancel my subscription to the world.

In more linear moments, Jim Brewster confessed to a sense of mission which seemed to make him feel anxious and uncomfortable. He liked taking care of people who weren't making it on their own. He liked watching the movie that was performed every day in the living room of the Chinese House: thick yellow sunlight filling the open door; Santee playing in the dust motes, her face smeared with chocolate; Lilith rising gracefully in liquid shivers to exit on the run; a naked girl prancing lightly down the steps to stand and chat before the bathroom door; blonde Vicki in her blue shift bringing fresh baked pies out of the kitchen oven; Harvey Mandel's burnt sienna sleepy music pouring through the room; and Sherri, dark-haired Sherri of the slender legs, walking across the shadows and the light, only her cryptic smile announcing that she knew he saw her dancing to the beat.

He did not know, did not like to think about, how they got here, where they were going. "I don't know how it happened," he answered once. "I don't know why I'm doing this. I just deal with whatever is in front of my nose at the moment." Another time he said, "I came back from Vietnam with a duffle bag full of grass and got into the acid scene. I spent two years hallucinating at the Avalon. I heard all these assholes jacking themselves off verbally about The Movement. When I couldn't take it any more, I decided to see what I could do that was better."

Finally, he came up with this answer: "I believe that the system is falling apart. I am attempting to arrange for my own survival when it gets into the heavy scenes." In his tone of voice there seemed to be the unspoken implication that if it came to revolution and civil war, he would not have to assemble soldiers. All he would have to do is issue weapons. It was not a pleasant vision. The death trip held no romance for the former gunship pilot.

At the end of 1969, the Chinese House was almost empty. After Christmas, the remaining few were sent away. Jim Brewster was tired of playing social worker. "I guess it failed because of overindulgence," said Fred, a young acid head botanist who had helped out with the gardening. A few days later, Sherri and Jim were alone with Santee in the big house. It looked as if Young Ideas was finished as a communal experience. Brewster was calling up friends with theatrical connections. He was going to become an actor. Or, he and Sherri were going to move north, way up the coast. They would find a big old comfortable house and turn it into a country inn. They would charge cash in advance.

By the time January was over, though, there were five souls living at the Chinese House — Wolf, an old-timer, Pamela, a newcomer, and Sherri and Jim and the baby. After a long rainy spell, the forest was green and fresh. Sherri and Jim came in and the telephone was ringing. It was a friend, one who had returned to the city and was now sorry to have left the house near Muir Woods.

"What are we doing?" said Brewster. "We just came in from walking in the hills in the most gorgeous golden sunset. And now I'm standing at the living room window watching salmon leap in the creek.

"You wish you were here? Well, come on out, brother. We got a groovy trip going. What color do you want us to paint your room?"

*P*erhaps to the person in the city the question still remained. "Why give up all that has gone before?" The answer is existential. A rural commune is a base camp on the edge of time, a platform for mounting expeditions into the raw and original moments of existence.

Sometimes it is impossible to achieve the peak of awareness without surrendering the tools of civilization. It becomes necessary to get out of the automobile and walk into the elemental wilderness beyond the road. In order to be reborn, you have to strip off the protective clothing — both symbolic and real — and leave the path for the depths of the forest, assuming as part of the adventure the possibility of getting lost.

From the Young Ideas, there was one expedition that began to approach this kind of experience. On the beach at Point Reyes, a national seashore on the Pacific Ocean where a primeval wind roars constantly, Jim Brewster stood with a small group of people who had forgotten each others' names and called to a seal swimming about twenty yards off shore.

"Tse-tse," Brewster howled in an outrageously playful baby talk. "Come on, tsetse." For some long period that no one wanted to measure, the big man spoke to the seal in noises that really did sound like seal talk. The seal poked its head up out of the water, scanned the humans curiously and moved a few yards closer in. At this point where the three phases of earth, air and sea met, intelligent animals from to-

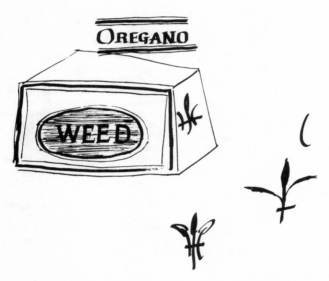

KEEP SMILING

tally foreign worlds were in contact, recognizing each other as strange but living inhabitants of the same universe.

The sun was setting. It was growing too cold to enjoy the game. On the way back, one person looked at the scene and said in a voice quivering on the point of ecstasy, "It's so beautiful—and it's not symbolic of anything!" When the long climb up through high seaside grass was nearly completed and the road was almost in sight, the flashing beacon light on the RCA Communications Center appeared in the rapidly darkening sky, a message from America calling its straying children home from their play on the shores of eternity.

*O*n a Sunday in September the Hog farm was scheduled to give a benefit concert in the Greer Garson Theatre in Sante Fe for Embudo Hospital. Four Hog Farmers awoke well before dawn in order to reach a hot spring in the mountains near Los Alamos by sunrise. There were two couples and two babies.

As the sky began to brighten, they passed

the big butte which housed the pueblo near which the Hog Farm had originally located, before being ejected by the governor of the pueblo when the Hog Farmers had grown too numerous for the Indians' comfort.

The road climbed up out of the desert through enormous finger-shaped eroded cliffs that looked like the rocky, sea-worn bluffs at Point Reyes. Next came pine-covered mountains. High in the mountains, a car came around a long curve and broke out into the open. On the right, a meadow as big as Manhattan Island extended like some cosmic football field. It was a place for 500-foot-high gods to hold decathlons, a pasture for Apollo's cattle, a vista that called for words like majestic and grand. The total physical beauty of the view brought tears.

Several miles further, the car stopped at an unmarked gravel parking area by the roadside. The Hog Farmers walked down a steep hillside and across a stream bridged by fallen logs, then up through the woods about a quarter-mile to a natural pool into which streaming water flowed from a crack in the rock. On the rocks were the remains of candles lighted by people who had used the pool at night.

Everyone undressed and got into the hot water. From a sitting position it was possible to see the entire valley. Before long, a couple of Indian forest rangers appeared and chatted jovially with the naked Hog Farmers.

"This spring is a sacred Indian spring," the older of the two foresters explained. "You come in this spring and it will cure all sicknesses, leaving you refreshed and healthy. People come from all over to bathe in this water. It cures the arthritis, the rheumatism, the aches and pains. These waters purify and sanctify the soul."

"Do you bathe in this spring?" someone asked.

"No," the Indian replied. "I'm too busy. I got to keep this place clean." While he talked, the forester and his partner carefully picked up debris left by previous bathers. The older man held up a piece of glass. "See, this is what I am afraid of."

"Don't you have a day off?"

"My wife, she got all kinds of work for me on my day off. I got my gardening."

"This is your garden," one bather said in the traditionally pontifical and symbolic rhetoric used for conversing with Indians.

The gray-haired forester looked at him blankly, then understood that he meant the forest.

"Oh, no," he said, "I got a vegetable garden. I grow melons. Well, we got to go now. Good luck to you."

When the foresters left, the Hog Farmers carried out a relaxing exercise. Two people, one holding the feet, the other the hands, gently rocked a third person in the water slowly and rhythmically. The muscles of the body relaxed, the breath diminished and the soul entered the timeless void. One by one they served each other. The babies dozed on the rocks. Young acid heads who had been camping overnight on the mountain above the spring came down to bathe. An astonishingly beautiful blonde eight-year-old girl stripped and got into the hot spring, paddling up to each man and looking him deeply in the eyes with a frank stare of love while her mother sat on a rock and watched.

After washing, with Dr. Bonner's Bio-Degradable Liquid Soap and drinking the waters pouring out of the rock, the Hog Farmers dressed and walked slowly back to the car, stopping to drink of an icy spring on the way. When they reached the parking area, the campers were there too, passing a bottle of wine and eating cheese.

Someone brought out a loaf of dense bread baked in the Hog Farm kitchen for the trip to Santa Fe. There was also a jar of home-grown peach preserves made by a girl named Jane at New Buffalo. The food was shared. One of the campers brought out a guitar and played with professional polish. Otherwise the meal was taken almost in silence. It was not necessary to point out that this was Sunday and this meal was communion. On the way back down, a sudden rain fell briefly and stopped, leaving the air moist and sweet.

That night in Santa Fe, the Hog Farm collected $780 for Embudo Hospital, a way of returning the kindness shown toward sick hippies. After the light show and the concert were finished, the entire commune walked solemnly through the center aisle and on out into the lobby, arm-in-arm, hand-in-hand singing, "All we are saying, is give peace a chance."

Over and over again they sang that refrain until it echoed in the brain like an insistent hypnotic prayer: "All we are saying, is give peace a chance."

slender —————————————————— frail

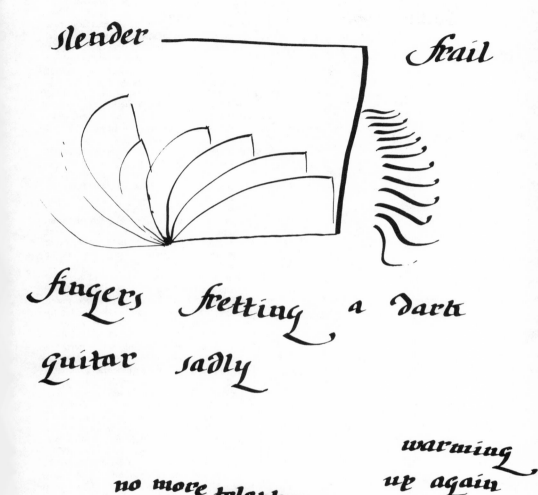

fingers fretting a dark

guitar sadly

warming

no more telephones up again

drowsy golden afternoon music

The Evergreen Home

More than almost anything else, Noble Benson wanted something real. His life had lately become a fantasy he found difficult to accept as anything more than a vivid movie. He seemed to be a spectator in a theater in which he always turned out to be the chief actor. Now he was becoming a kind of hood usually played by Humphrey Bogart. The role, so far, was a success, but it was not quite comfortable. Perhaps it was a reversion to type. His father had done time. Was Benson imitating him? It was not anything his father would have liked.

When Noble Benson met Elizabeth Small he had already almost convinced himself that he had to get out of the business. It was not fear or disgust or any other dramatic emotion, although there were many moments of fear and many moments of disgust. He had learned to accept fear as a necessary condition early in the game. With experience in the feeling, Benson even found real benefits in being afraid. It kept him alert, releasing adrenalin energy that crackled throughout his muscles, tuning body and brain into a state of unification surpassed only in the act of love. At the peak, he was beginning to discover, all human weakness faded and a higher, purer, richer fire blazed triumphantly. In this ultimate flame the childhood of existence was cremated, fueling the endlessly clear light.

Although Benson had never been infected with the ordinary religious diseases, he thought of this experience as a holy ecstasy. When he was coming out of it, the language of the visionary scriptures seemed so appropriate, concrete and precise in metaphor, voice and scale that he wanted to laugh with pleasure. He was the butt of a wonderful joke in which the most preposterously poetic and grandiose ravings of Biblical mysticism turned out to be merely understated testimony of sober witnesses to a reality that skipped and bounced and jogged effortlessly in and out of every descriptive net.

Noble Benson was big and fast and he liked to fight with his hands. It was a trait he shared with his old man. His father, a pick and shovel laborer who knew little more formal English than was required to read the Daily News and Daily Mirror, had gotten the family through the Depression working for a German who owned an ancient dump truck, a coal-fired asphalt furnace and a small steamroller. The steam-

sunday
sept 27, 1970
Indian Summer

a door in the
woods

if I forget thee o Babylon
city of deserts

roller was originally the property of the
Army Corps of Engineers, which had purchased it used in Cherbourg in 1917 and
brought it all the way back across the Atlantic at the end of the Great War, selling
it absent-mindedly for scrap. It was a fee-
ble collection of equipment, antique and
cranky, constantly dying of old age, but,
continually resurrected by Werner Stock's
self-taught mechanical magic, it was the
sole support of the German and his wife.
When Thomas Benson was released from
the Elmira Correctional Institute after
serving five years of a three to five sentence for aggravated assault, Werner Stock
was standing at the prison gate, looking for
a helper. This was 1932 and ten million men
were on the streets, but none of them were
hungry enough for the German.

Of the four men let out that day, Thomas
Benson was the only one that Stock judged
capable of becoming the first hired employee of the Stock Asphalt Paving & Construction Co., W. Stock, Prop., Est. 1901.
One man, in any case, was not interested,
although it is doubtful that he would have
been seriously considered. Charlie Cohen
had well-dressed friends waiting for him
in a big Franklin touring car. Even at the
depth of the worst financial collapse in
American history, there was well-paid work
waiting for the man the tabloids had called
Duke of Death. He came to trial for the
killing of a 12-year-old girl who was picking
up two quarts of local hootch when the
buckshot blew Marvin Menashe Beitel's
face across the bakery counter. The Grand
Jury returned no indictment in the Beitel
killing, but the girl could not be ignored.
Cohen was found guilty of first degree
manslaughter.

"I wanted to let him off," one juror told
newspaper reporters, "but I was per-
suaded by the others that an example had
to be made in order to protect innocent bystanders, that if we was too easy it would
be encouraging lack of respect for the
safety of honest citizens. That made a lot
of sense to me, so I voted guilty, although
I don't really believe the man was responsible. It was an accident, the way I see it.
If a policeman did the same thing in appre-
hending a criminal, you fellows know better than anyone how it would be hushed
up with money and jobs and whatever.

"If you ask my opinion, Charlie Cohen
is just a policeman without the uniform or

badge. You got to have people like that.
You don't have to like them, but you got to
have them. You want the hootch, don't
you? We all like a nip, isn't that right?
There isn't a person with any sense who
will tell you that you're a criminal if you
buy a bottle. If it's such a crime, how come
you don't hear no one asking to put the
parents on trial for sending a 12-year-old
little girl to a hootch shop?

"You fellows are a lot smarter than I am,
so maybe you can show me where I'm in the
wrong on this. All I know is that the people
want their nip even if it is against the law.
So there's other people willing to stick out
their necks to make a dollar and sell it to
them. So they have their own problems
amongst themselves like in any business.
So they can't hire a judge and a jury and
police officers and penitentiaries to settle
it for them.

"It ain't an honest world, boys. It never
was and it never will be. You got to hold the
people to their word at the point of a gun.
You got to have enforcement."

When Charlie Cohen was found dead in
the high weeds of a vacant lot in Sunnyside,
Queens, the newspaper clippings in the
morgue file given to the wire service man
who was writing the story included these
remarks in several versions. The reporter
reconstructed the full quotation as accu-
rately and completely as the sources allowed and used it to end his piece. It appeared
in the same Evergreen newspaper in which
Werner Stock was running a daily class-
ified advertisement written for him by the
assistant managing editor and carried for
thirty days at no charge as payment in kind
for repairs made to the street in front of the
managing editor's house.

Thomas Benson, who had a powerful
leaning toward the old magic of omens and
signs, showed the coincidence to Werner. It
seemed to him an oracle of imminent success. Just as his life had turned into a new
direction on the steps of the prison even as
he was enviously watching Charlie Cohen,
who had been a big man even in the can,
embrace his prosperous friends and step
into the expensive motor car that would take
him to a destiny that any worldly person
would have agreed had to be a lot better
than Thomas Benson's, so now the appearance of the report of the gangster's fate in
the same issue of the newspaper in which
the first advertisement of the Stock & Ben-

son Asphalt Paving & Street Construction Co., W. Stock, Pres., saw light was divine confirmation of his own visions.

"That's a sign, Werner," he said after reading the story haltingly aloud. They were drinking coffee out of thick white china mugs in the tiny kitchen of the Stock house. The cottage had been built by the railroad, one of a dozen identical yellow clapboard three-roomers lined up facing a rusting single track. Stock had worked for the line from the day he had arrived in Evergreen, N.Y. directly from the Castle Gardens immigration station in New York. The Great War had just ended and maintenance gangs were out on the line around the clock. When the Market crashed and the circulation of the nation began to fail, he was a foreman and this company house was one of the perquisites of his rank. Traffic on the line slowed and then stopped entirely. The company went into receivership. The trustees examined the tree of steel the tracks formed and began pruning dead limbs. The Evergreen section was abandoned early. Werner Stock was not surprised when he was asked to leave the little yellow house. He and his wife were the last occupants left in the row, the other houses boarded up and already peeling.

A railroad, even a little nothing of a second-rate railroad like this one which had built a line into Evergreen, is a valuable property that needs to be taken care of in death as well as in life. The German had watched the houses begin to peel and seen the rest of the line begin to deteriorate and had understood that it was not necessary for this to happen, that it made no sense to allow the structure to rot. A leaking roof in a company house was the beginning of its destruction, an entry for the inexorable forces of nature. Fix that leak and the house would last a hundred years. Even a cemetary needs a caretaker, he knew. Now that everyone else was gone, he could be the caretaker of this small, dead section of a system in which life circulated elsewhere, however feebly. If the cost were cheap enough it would be only good husbandry for the trustees to save the property against a future day.

Werner Stock put on his black suit and, using an outdated pass which no one bothered to challenge, took the train to the head office in Buffalo. In his pocket he had four dollars and a soft leather case contain-

ing two dozen brand new calling cards on which in ink that was still wet was a printed message that represented his entire hope for the future: "Stock Railroad Maintainance Co., Est. 1901, Head Office: Evergreen N.Y., W. Stock. Prop." He presented this card at the front desk and waited for two hours. Finally, he was shown into a small, neat office with a curtainless window that faced a blank brick wall. On the plain wooden desk, there was a telephone, a brown paper blotter and an ornately sculptured brass inkwell and pen set. Behind the desk sat a man he judged to be his own age, immaculately dressed in a pearl gray flannel suit and vest, wearing rimless glasses that made him look foxy and precise. On the office wall, hung a framed aerial photograph of the Evergreen station showing the entire section of right of way on which Stock had worked. Squinting, he could make out the 12 company houses, picking out his own at the head of the row.

So this was the big boss. The German recognized him now as the man who had come out once a year to inspect the section. In this small, spare office, so insignificant and poverty-stricken compared to the palatial suites he had seen on the way in, the big boss did not look quite so big as he had in Evergreen. Without waiting for an invitation, Werner sat down and began to speak in slow, heavily-accented but easily understandable English. When he was finished, the railroad executive asked him a few questions, spoke on the telephone and got up to go to another office, leaving the German to wait.

"You've got a deal, Stock," he said when he returned. The Stock Railroad Maintainance Company would undertake the upkeep of the Evergreen station and properties using its own labor but drawing equipment as necessary from the line's toolhouse and local yard. In the event any work required additional help, application was to be made to the head office. In return, Stock would be allowed to live in the company house he was now occupying as long as the agreement continued. A secretary was summoned and the contract was typed. Werner signed his name in a spidery, slow hand.

They shook hands and the German turned to go, trying to remain dignified and businesslike even though he wanted to sing.

"Oh, Stock, there's just one question I have," the executive said, calling him back.

"Your calling card says 'Established 1901.' How can that be? I thought you were working for us all this time."

"I worked for you, but I was working for myself. Do you understand? Every man is working for himself. Even when he works for the boss. He works for the food. The food goes into his own mouth. He is working to feed himself."

"Very true. Very interesting. But what about the date? How did you pick that date, 1901? You must have been an infant in 1901."

"I was born in 1901," Stock answered. "I have been working for myself from the first day I was born. It is work even to suck at the mother's breast. Nothing comes without work. Life is work." The two men smiled gravely at each other. In the executive's eyes, Stock saw for the first time a certain recognition. During the years ahead, the recognition would grow more and more profound until finally, when they were both old men, the American would find himself treating this common laborer with a deference and respect that he could never explain, not to himself, not to anyone. In Werner Stock's presence, he was no longer a big boss. He was small and weak and living in endless darkness. His office got bigger and bigger and the photograph was replaced by a succession of maps on which his area of responsibility grew greater and greater. He would employ bank presidents the way other men employed clerks. His name would be whispered in foreign capitals. He would understand that he was significant, that everything he had done was important.

"Sure, boss," Werner Stock would say and smile gravely, and for a moment all his constructions would collapse into a small, plain office with a window facing a brick wall and he would remember again that all he was boss of was himself. It did not seem like much to be boss over at all.

*B*y the time he found Thomas Benson on the steps of the Evergreen Prison, Stock had managed to nurse a little life out of the dying property he had taken under his control. The railroad work paid little cash but it gave him a place to eat and live and sleep. It was too much for one person to do, really, if it were to be done the way it ought, but he knew that he was not required to do very much at all. There were no inspections, no priorities, no specifications from the head office. Occasionally, a letter would arrive asking him to look after some small item a citizen had called to the company's attention. When he discovered major work, he would requisition help and the head office would always send him someone. For the most part, he was master of the domain and his main responsibility was simply to be there to respond when a message came from Buffalo.

In the economic disorganization of the Depression, the town, like the railroad, began to die. There was no money to pay for repairs. At the end of the first winter, holes began to appear in the street where ice and snow had worked the paving loose. The townspeople knew that it was pointless to complain. In the poor neighborhoods, there was hardly any traffic anyway. The streets could rot back into their original state and no one would really care. It was enough trouble to find food to eat, to keep a roof over the family's head, to manage clothing and shoes. After these things were taken care of, the condition of the street was of no consequence. Whole sections of town faded and softened and began to disintegrate.

The better people ignored all the broken streets but the ones in front of their houses. Many of them had automobiles. They required smooth roadways. Offended that holes should appear in their streets and remain unrepaired, they complained to the Department of Public Works and wondered what they ought to do about the answers they received. There was no money to buy materials, they were told. The equipment was broken down and could not be replaced. There were no funds for luxuries such as fixing streets.

Werner Stock, who had the railroad equipment at his disposal, went from house to house offering to fix streets and driveways really cheap. He did all the work himself, earning enough to eat, to live, to buy abandoned tools in junkyards. Before long, he had his own dump truck, the asphalt furnace, the old steamroller. He needed a helper who was not afraid of labor. The unemployed men of the town were no good, he thought. They were weak from lack of work, sorrowful and self-piteous. The mama was gone, but they still wanted to suck her tit. They felt cheated when there was no milk for them. It would take too long to get even the best of them in shape to keep up with him. In the prison, though, there were men who had been breaking stones for years. To one of these, steeled in useless work, fixing streets might seem worthwhile. For a few weeks, he went every morning to the prison, examining from a distance the great gate and waiting for men to come out.

At first, there was no one. Then, one morning, there were four. Standing a head taller than any of them was a muscular giant whose name was Thomas Benson. Werner felt the man's legs and arms as if he were buying a horse or a mule. Satisfied and pleased, he looked the man in the eyes and saw the gentle blue calm of a placid animal. Whatever it was that had gotten him into custody, it was not in him now. Stock was not fool enough to believe that the man's sickness would never return. He was merely confident that when it did, he would be able to handle it better than any government.

"What kind of work did you do before?" he asked.

"Pick and shovel."

"And inside?"

"Hammer and rocks."

"What did you do wrong that they put you there?"

Benson smiled. "I hurt a fella real bad, but don't ask me why. It's too personal, if you understand my meaning. I won't do it again if I can help it."

"If you want a job, you got one with me," Stock said. "There's no cash right now, but you live in my house, eat my food. I give you smokes, if you want them and you drink the same wine I drink. If you want the strong booze, you got to get it yourself. I don't drink the strong booze myself. When some money starts to come in, I'll treat you right. That's the deal. What do you say? Yes or no?."

At that moment, Charlie Cohen was getting into the open car. The motor roared. The gangster looked briefly back at the prison, smiling bitterly and waving a perfunctory goodbye to the men on the steps in front of the gate. He leaned back and the car took off, leaving a wake of yellow dust hanging in the air. Benson watched the automobile disappear down the road. Might as well kiss it goodbye, he thought. That's the closest I'll ever get to the boys in the big

time—standing here in front of the joint with no place to go.

"Yes or no?" the squat German was asking him. The man looked like a condensed bull, a thousand pounds of muscle stuffed into a 5'5" body. It was not going to be easy to keep up with him. Still, it was a flop and eats. Where else did he have to go?

"Sure, partner," Benson answered with an enthusiasm that caught his own mood by surprise. "I am your man." He was embarrassed to feel himself believing that this was a new start, that there was more here than flop and eats, but as they walked toward the old truck on which the legend of Stock's new company was carefully emblazoned in yellow paint, he felt like dancing. He was out. He was in the open. He had a job. The sky was so blue, the light so yellow, the ground so fresh that he felt dizzy and faint. Everything was new and crisp and freshly formed. He was overcome by his own innocence and he leaned against the door of the truck and wept for a long time. When he was finished, Werner handed him a clean bandana. He wiped his eyes, blew his nose and got into the truck. He fell asleep instantly, purged of all emotion. He woke up as they stopped at the yellow bungalow, realizing with sudden force that seemed all out of proportion to the insight that he had not looked back at the prison gate. It was a satisfying moment. It was right not to have looked back. He was pleased with himself for recognizing the rightness.

*T*homas Benson courted a 17-year-old local girl who came out of the old Dutch line. She was a strange young woman, silent and solemn. The people in Evergreen said she had too much Indian in her to be quite right in the head, but she was beautiful and strong. She had been to college down in Elmira for a while, then come back home in the middle of the term. She would tell no one why, staring coldly at anyone who pried too hard and shutting the inquiry off without a word. Her name was Clove, Emma Clove. It suited her. She was shut tight against the local world, a brooding person with private thoughts. She had watched Benson and Werner lay a roadway in front of her father's house one week in the middle of summer and invited them in every day for iced tea. Her mother had died a long time ago, when she was eight. An only child, she looked out for herself and her father, a meticulous cabinet maker who did rough carpentry when necessary. She had spent a great deal of time alone in the house, hunting through drawers and chests for souvenirs of her dead mother. The most significant momento was on the walls of the parlor, a frieze of woods and flowers her mother had painted around the top of the room, softly colored vistas too beautifully crafted for this back-water hamlet. As she grew older, she began to see the frieze as a symbol of her own wasted genius. She saw herself imprisoned in these mountains, imprisoned by choice. She had hated college. Now she hated isolation. She read books and magazines and, sometimes, sunbathed naked out in the high pastures behind the little house.

Emma Clove was not interested in the boys of Evergreen. In some way or other she was related to every one of them. They aroused no excitingly incestuous thoughts, no sexuality of any kind, just a feeling of vaguely unpleasant neutrality. They were male mirrors of her own self. There was no mystery in them. For a while, the sun was her only lover. She lay out on an old blanket in the meadow and felt her body ripen. Swimming in liquid heat, she would turn on her belly and put her hands between her legs and satisfy herself. On some days, she would sleep and wake several times in a cycle of self-arousal and exhaustion. For a long time after she had watched the two men working on the road, she had used one or the other of them in her fantasy. When winter came and the sun was gone, she would wake into cold dawn and wish that she were not alone.

At Christmas, Thomas Benson came to her house carrying a box of candy Werner had gotten for him in Buffalo. Her father brought out a bottle of home-made apple brandy and the three of them drank and ate and talked into the night. The old man went up to bed and left them alone. They lounged in front of the fire. Benson reached for her, kissing her on the mouth and putting his hand underneath her skirt. She unbuttoned her blouse and gave him her breast, but when he began to open his fly, she drew away.

"Are you afraid?" he asked.

"No, I'm not afraid," she answered, rising from the floor and standing over him, her bosom glistening and damp, the small nipples peeping in and out of the open blouse as she breathed.

"What is it then?"

"I want to go upstairs—to bed. I want you to come with me." He gathered his clothing and followed her to the bedroom. They stripped naked in the lamplight and quickly cuddled under the covers, shrinking away from the icy sheets. He felt between her legs and found her wet. Benson massaged her sexual key between his fingers until her thighs were jerking spasmodically with that violent snapping movement that is impossible to fake. He spread her legs with his knees and moved to press his heavy erection home. Again, she pulled away.

After a silence she said, "I want you to do something for me. Kiss me the way you touched me."

"I have never done that," Benson said.

"Does the idea offend you?"

"I have never done it before, that's all, Emma." He hesitated a moment, then pulled the covers back and brought his lips up against her curly pubic hair. Like a diver about to descend into the depths, he held his breath and plunged on down as her thighs rose to meet him. Her cunt smelled sweet and tasted slightly salty. She clutched a pillow to her face and smothered her moans. Benson felt himself fill with power as she responded. He kept at her mercilessly, feeling the climactic shudders against his mouth and tongue. He came up on top of her again. She guided his throbbing prick into her open cunt with her hand. Benson pulled the pillow from her face. Emma turned her mouth away momentarily, then smiled and kissed him with open lips and soft, wet tongue. Balanced on the edge of a hot knife, he pumped her steadily. At the last moment she was crying, "God! Ahhh! God!"—over and over again as he delivered his load in a spasm of thrusts and fell forward helplessly spent.

"Stay here and sleep," Emma whispered. He dropped into a timeless void. When he awoke the following morning, she was standing over him fully dressed with that calm witch gaze in her eyes. The room was filled with sunlight. It poured through her red hair and ruddy skin. A halo of energy surrounded her. She was transparent light all the way through.

"I've spoken to my father," she said.

"What did you say?"

"I told him that you would be living here from now on."

"That's all?"

"My father and I understand each other very well."

Benson rose out of the bed and pulled her to him by the haunches, throwing her skirt up and licking her freshly-washed moist and fragrant cunt until she was unable to stand. He dragged her big body on to the bed and laid her forward on her belly. He fucked her rapidly from behind, feeling the cheeks of her ass press up against him each time he drove forward. They both came

worth worrying about. Anything you think you got to worry about, you tell me. I'll fix ya. Emma! Bring us that fucking bacon! Gimmee my eggs before I whip your ass." The voice was affectionate and sardonic, pleased with the effect.

In the years to come, Benson would find himself loving the old man almost more than he loved Emma. Now he was simply astonished. He had never heard anything like this before in his life. He came to understand the two of them slowly, believing eventually that he was dealing with a higher kind of intelligence. They were like

These are the acts of love — french toast, coffee, cleaning a houseful of hairbrushes mopping floors, barbecued chicken, skinning a deer, picking up dog shit. Not the miracles of the loaves and wine, but the daily devotions.

quickly and lay trembling together until the cold room brought them back to life. Her skirt was wet and wrinkled. She took it off and walked around the room in her blouse, her bottom and thighs flushing white and pink in hot patches, her bright red pubic hair glowing in front of her like an electrical cloud.

Despite her assurances, Thomas Benson was jittery coming down for breakfast. The old man was sitting at the kitchen table dipping a chunk of bread in his coffee. He motioned Benson to a seat. Emma fried bacon in a cast iron skillet. She looked over at the two men and smiled. William Clove chewed the coffee - soaked bread lustily, then drank the contents of the china cup. There was coffee in the saucer. He drank that too, holding the plate up to his mouth and leaning back. A few drops ran down his chin onto his neck. He wiped himself methodically with a linen dish towel, threw the cloth on the table and smiled at Benson.

"Worried about what the old man will think, eh?" he said. Benson kept quiet. "Well, don't you worry about nothing. We don't worry about nothing at all. We been on this piece of land for two hundred fifty years and we never found ought that was

people from another planet, a god and goddess who disdained mortal ethics as childish superstition. Their conversations were Biblical. Emma and her father were beyond judgment. Thomas Benson felt peace and pleasure flowing through him.

When Emma Clove's belly was big several months later, the old man brought a preacher out to the house on a Sunday and married his two children as Werner Stock and his wife Ruta, a slow, muscular, red-faced blonde looked on. They ate a picnic lunch out in the back yard under the ancient elms and drank the potent apple brandy. Even the preacher and his anxious wife grew giddy and hot, blushing and moistening. Werner leaned his head face down in Ruta's lap and ran his hands up and down her bare leg. She giggled affectionately.

"Come on, Tom, let's go up into the high pasture," Emma said. He followed her up, carrying a blanket and wondering what the preacher and his wife were going to say when they got back to Evergreen. He was drunk. Weaving wave patterns of light skimmed the high grass. Out of sight of the house, Emma stepped out of her dress and lay back on the blanket, her knees raised and her thighs twitching. In the brilliant sunlight, her big belly and heavy, swollen breasts were covered with fine violet lines. He touched the little knob at the top of her cunt and watched the lips moisten and open, a bright pink flower of delicate flesh petals.

At the end, he came so violently, he was afraid he might be spurting blood. He fell back on the hillside meadow and felt wave after wave of an agony beyond pleasure, beyond pain. The universe was pulsing out of his burning prick. Emma reached forward to bring him back to her, but he was senseless in his ecstasy, unable to coordinate his movements though he could see that she was on the verge of coming again. With an impatient cry of frustration, she let him go and viciously drove her fingers into her cunt and then smiled in total release as she brought herself off. They slept.

At the end of Indian summer, the boy was born. She named him Noble. It was their only child. He grew up with Thomas Benson's massive form and Emma's mystical intelligence. The old man taught him the craft of tools. At 15, he watched his father and Werner dig a grave in the high pasture and lower the old man to eternal rest in the earth of his ancestral home. In the years to come, he would return to the mountain homestead to bury each of them one by one.

The old man's death did not diminish the powerful currents of love that seemed to surround the Clove family home like a magnetic whirlpool. There was unconquerable life here. As he reached maturity, Noble Benson struggled to break free, leaving, finally, for New York. He got a job as a darkroom laboratory assistant at night and went to college during the day.

When Thomas Benson died after a massive coronary, Noble was 19 years old. He drove home through autumn mountains and picture post card visions of flaming trees. The coffin lay in the front parlor. Tom had made it himself, Emma told her son. She was nearly 40, but she looked barely thirty.

"I like having him here in the front parlor under my mother's paintings," she said. "The fashion these days is funeral parlors. That's cheap." Emma spoke quietly, polishing the pale wood with the oil of her hand. "Don't let other people cater your emotions for you. They give you hand-me-down rituals. Did you ever listen to the way they talk? The sentences come off condolence cards. Cheap condolence cards with embossed lilies and 'raised' printing. They embarrass me."

Her voice was growing stronger now, filled with the witch mystery he loved to hear, the aura of sure power that raised his skin to an electrical crawl.

"We will never settle for anything less than pure emotion," his mother said. "I am not afraid of grief. I am not ashamed to cry. I am not embarrassed by death."

They walked out into the pine grove that shielded the house from the road. She flicked a drop of sticky resin from the oozing bark of a tree, rubbing it in her fingers and bringing it up to her face so she could smell the tang. Noble bent and kissed her hands, pressing them against her lips with his mouth. The pine scent mixed with the clean, soapy smell of his mother's skin.

Emma opened the top of her print dress and pressed her cheek against her bosom. Her bare breasts were still as firm and smooth as if she were a young woman. Moved by an instinct more powerful than reason, he took her nipple in his mouth and sucked it soberly like a baby until it grew erect against his tongue. She sighed heavily and began to sob, leaning her head against the tree. Emma raised his face to hers and kissed him on the lips with an open mouth tasting of tears. He pulled away, weeping. She sat down in the pine needles and put up her hand to draw him down. Surrendering at last, Noble Benson put his face in his mother's lap and cried for a long time, at last falling asleep in total exhaustion.

Later, Emma and Noble sat silently holding hands in the sunset-filled parlor where motes of dust settled one by one on the polished oak of the casket Thomas Benson had made for himself before death. In this house even death was beautiful and grand. Would he ever be able to find such honesty outside? Until this day, he had not even known what he had been looking for. Now that he did know, Noble Benson felt strong and heavy, as if filled with thick steel springs coiled in tense readiness for his final release from the Evergreen home.

City in the sand

constructed out of the tombstones
of forgotten lives = place of cere-
monies and sacrifices repeated again
and again without meaning = recorded
laughter, canned happiness, dry eyes.

Supermarket of loneliness offering
mail-order cures for every affliction of
the soul = museum of prosthetic art;
rack after rack of artificial additions
promising to replace whatever you
have lost = computer of time-payment
balances in the dead storage compartments
of yesterday's memory, garbage and
rotten fruit are neatly cataloged in
concrete filing boxes, bronze tablets,
granite monuments, cheap varnish,
wax saints, strawberry satin, glass
coffins, celluloid eyes, rayon hair,
cardboard point-of-purchase display
cartons in which polyethylene dolls
sleep beneath lithographed name plates.
wandering ghosts of all ages float through
picture palace throne rooms, marble
urns, freshly-laundered tapestries of
unicorns and dragons and knights in
chain mail fighting suits, hotel
lobbies with cabbage-roses on the car-
pet, drapes and chairs, stained-glass
temples lighted by massed banks of
votive candles, automatic antique ticket-
tape machines selling tourist passes
to the show and tell projection screens

photographs, holograms, moving pictures, color portraits, sidewalk
sketches, printed magazines and
posters, bumper stickers, woodcuts,
collotypes, brass rubbings, greeting
cards, ceramic plates, enamel miniatures, pastels pen-and-inks, water
colors, oil paintings, silk scarves,
blackboards covered with chalk
drawings and equations vanishing in
the whispering sweep of a felt
eraser dipped in the water of change

questions from the audience, study
plans and college anthologies, shiny
book jackets, back pages giving credit
to the designer of the alphabet, front-
page dedications, titles, copyrights,
names and addresses of publishers,
chapter-headings, ornaments, typo-
graphical errors, illustrations, charts,
graphs, quotation marks, footnotes,
a table of contents, an index, page
numbers, periods, commas, apostrophes,
colons, semi-colons, dashes, amper-
sands and dollar-signs, summaries
and problems, calendars.

answers from the author, learned men,
professors, politicians, scientists, movie
stars, ushers, reverend doctors, hired
experts and the inquiring photographer
who has just come back from a wide-
ranging series of frank encounters
with the man in the street and the
woman of the house who confirm

what everyone already knows and is
afraid to say.

the children are gone and the lost=
and=found is empty and no one is
at home and there is nobody left
who can be expected to come out
and play.

city of mirrors reflecting shadows
of the light that was, echoes of
rustling static, tired breeze aimlessly
rearranging formless scatterings of
dust on blank panes of seamless
space...collapsing, melting, drifting,
drying, disappearing...
void, empty, motionless, silent, dark
zero=perfect... almost nothingness,
almost final rest, almost ending...

almost = but not quite = pin=point
bright spot gleaming growing pounding
roaring rolling river ocean universe
of boiling *Dawn Wave* arriving right
on time for a new and glorious fresh

beginning...

laughter, sunshine, white beach, blue
sky, cold sea, hot flesh, wet kiss, fall
down, green moss, out of breath, moan
and cry, spurting seed = spinning ball,

tree of light; screaming woman, agony
of love, blood, knife, choke, howl.

breast; nipple, milk, mama, papa,
hand, mouth, feel, taste, see, smell, hear
sleep, wake, feed, piss, shit; grow,
give, get; laugh, cry = speak a word,
begin to die, begin to live, begin to
fly = hello, get fucked, farewell, learn
love, ring bell, watch your kids
show and tell = see the darkness fill
your eye, wonder how to say goodbye,
wonder how to think about your creation
your city of sand, city of mirrors, sea of
light; sea of life. follow the piper,
pick up the pipe, play your own
love song, make a new tune =
cities of children sail through the
sky = how can you catch them if
you won't even try?

lovers and children dance in the
surf = the city you built is
awash in the tide = seashells and
seaweed have swept it away =
all that remains is the sand on
the beach = and the houses and
tombstones are powdered and gone,
time to forget them, time to move
on, time to surrender, time to dissolve,
time to start swimming, time to evolve,
time to quit stalling, time for the
surf, time to go home and start over
again.

Babylon, city of the desert, city
of music, where have your children gone? Remember when the beach
dance halls were filled with girls
with short skirts and bare, glistening
limbs wet with sweat; their long
hair shivering in the hot, staccato
light of the strobe — musicians
arching in ecstasy and pounding
the boards of the stage with their
flamenco boots — the crowd of boys
and girls tossing in waves of arms
and heads moving up and down in
time with a beat that flowed back
and forth from the band to the
dancers — voices chanting, sobbing —
a smell of perfume and flesh
and rut enveloping the young, moist
bodies in a mist of heavy desire.
Remember the fires on the beach
and the guitars and the old, slow
songs — the cold, damp sand — the
itching line where the bathing
suit cord had been — the salty
taste of the sea on sunburnt skin —
the hard, erect nipples — the tickle
of curly hair against the exploring
hand — the hard cock taut and stiff;
a tight pain bunched down at the
base; a thin, slick wetness at the tender
head — the thighs locking closed, then

loosening as the fingers search and find the hot little button — the lips of the cunt opening like an anemone, feeling the tough folds deep inside, everything wet and slippery — the last resistance, spreading her legs with his knees, his cock knocking clumsily against the open mouth of her cunt — her hand reaching down like in a yes-touch at last to guide him in. Remember how hot that first contact was — and how short — her body snapping and trembling, face thrown back, contorted, eyes open but unseeing, white teeth, wet mouth, line of saliva running down the cheek and throat, the muscles of her belly rigid and her toes curled — his buttocks clenching in shivering spasms as the scalding jets of pleasure-pain rasp through his leaping, jerking prick.

Swimming in the icy cold night sea naked — drying by the fire — cuddling together in one sleeping — wanting to do it again, but falling asleep instead.

Waking at dawn to see two naked girls riding matching bay horses bareback through the surf, screaming and laughing. Making love slowly and gently, taking a long time to come. The long walk back up the

beach, arm-in-arm, sticky and
itchy and sandy. Sneaking into
the house, showering, eating,
sleeping, meeting again in the
afternoon, doing it in a bed while
everyone else has gone down to
the water.

Remember that passion, citizens
of Babylon? You were those
children once. Now you sit in
crystal breakfast rooms and
listen to the percolater bubble.
You keep careful accounts and
pay your bills on time and read
best-sellers. You smoke a little pot
at night and play the Beatles
faithfully and watch the Stones
become businessmen and you keep
a loaded pistol in your bedroom
drawer. And you wait, and you
wonder, and you don't talk
about politics or religion, but you
notice that Marianne Faithful
~~has wrinkles~~ does not get older —
and neither do you
All of Babylon is yours now — topless
and bottomless bars, peep shows,
beaveramas, porno stores. There are
places where people dance naked in
public, theaters where you can see
naked couples fucking on stage.

On all the beaches bathing suits
are as old-fashioned as long underwear — and about as popular.
Or so you hear. You don't go to the
beach anymore. You are too busy
in Babylon. Besides, you don't think
you'd really feel comfortable without
a bathing suit.

And there is nothing great to see
there anyway. There are no
children on the beach laughing
and shrieking, no children any
where in Babylon. The children
all grew up and became citizens
and adults — but bore no babies
of their own. You have no answers
or explanations for this. It was
just something that happened
that no one wants to talk about.
Maybe it was the birth control
pills or the smog or the LSD
or the amphetamine or the
barbiturates or the tranquilizers.
It doesn't matter. You are the
last citizens of Babylon, sterile
capital of a sterile planet. No one
gets old — but people disappear —
and no one is born. That's the
way it is. And you wonder how to
say goodbye.   — 15 mg Desoxyn

Midnight
in Babylon

Call up the vision gardens and order me a newer planet to live and work on. This old earth is too bilboed and shackled, too chained, too sacked and sandbagged, too beat, too narrow, too filthy, too vile and poisonous, and too near death for me to dwell or to grow on. — Woody Guthrie, February 6, 1947

Winter is the rainy season in Los Angeles. In a city that has nothing going for it except sunshine, rain is a miserable trip, especially when the sun is screened down through a dirty gray swamp of smog for weeks at a time. People die in Southern California when it rains. They kill themselves on the freeways, which are glazed with a slippery scum of water and oil. This place is desert most of the year. They never really get the chance to learn how to handle skids. The roads are usually dry. The first rain is harvest time for death.

In Los Angeles they commit suicide during the long rains when they cannot get out to the beach, or the golf course, or the ball park. Television is not the universal antidote for the poisons of loneliness. And loneliness is the great disease of Los Angeles. Too many of its citizens are refugees and wanderers who ran away from the old tangles of family roots and class lines. They wanted to be individuals. They wanted to be free. Now, riding around in their cars, they are free to go wherever the freeway leads.

Each of them, in a personal cell of rubber and glass and plastic and steel, is the master of a rolling universe that can be as totally comfortable and self-sustaining as an egg — and just as fragile. And just as separate. The only real communication is contact. When you live in an egg, contact is the most dangerous game. The habit of the highway becomes the habit of life. Friendships are quick passages on a crowded road. Love is a terrifying accident.

But there are nights when you see a bigger picture. The freeway loops out into space. The signs are blank and meaningless. Everything is as clear and sharp and brilliant as if seen in a vacuum. This is the smooth, fast current of the high energy distribution stream. This is The Road. If you can be on this raceway, there is no reason to go anywhere else. This moment has been your destination all along.

When the heavy rain comes, this river is too turbulent for ordinary traffic. Home is a prison of endless time filled with meaningless objects counted and recounted over and over again. It is library of mirrors. It is not long before there is nothing new to reflect. Sleeping pills erase the clock. Almost everyone in Los Angeles has sleeping pills. Everyone knows how many it takes to make a final zero. In the rainy season,

november tenth = rain

where is your
golden lotus now?

57: the
Gentle

alone in a room with a bottle of nothingless, life is a game of solitaire easier to end than continue.

It was not yet winter and it was not yet raining, but it would be before the week was over. I had an assignment to interview James Taylor, a 22-year-old kid all the smart people had decided was going to be the next whirlwind of money. He was opening at Doug Weston's Troubadour, a folkie joint on Santa Monica Boulevard near Doheny just about where West Hollywood meets Beverly Hills.

It was the right time of year for James Taylor, the way heavy winter is the right time of year for Bob Dylan and summer is the right time for the Beatles. He is the voice of the borderline, of late autumn. I did not want to go see him. I was hung up in West Hollywood with a bottle of sleeping pills.

West Hollywood. It is one of those perfectly American hells where everyone who wants to make it in big-time show-and-tell goes to pay dues. The casualties are counted day and night at Hollywood Receiving, an emergency room without a hospital. Some of those who survive go back to Sunset Strip and try again at killing themselves. Others wind up punching supermarket cash registers unto enternity.

Right near by, there is Beverly Hills. That's where the superstars live. It is a different kind of hell with different dues, but it is hell. Or maybe it is only Purgatory. Beverly Hills is where you make your payments for admission to Big Sur. When it rains in Big Sur you stand among the big trees and listen to the song that Sibelius heard. You can let yourself get wet there. It is a clean rain. You need that rain when you get out of the mirror factory.

Mirrors are big business in Babylon. This city in the desert is a department store of loneliness offering mail-order prosthetics for every affliction of the soul—recorded laughter, canned happiness, celluloid orgasms said to be better than the real thing and much more sanitary. Out of the sands surrounding Los Angeles, they make mirrors for the artificial magnification of whatever you may have that is small and ought to be big.

Is your life too small? Fill it with friends. They come supplied on tape, film, record. They are almost real. They are reflections of the superstar, the image of yourself that you would like to see, the voice that you would like to hear. They give you thoughts to think, lines to speak, show you what to wear. They know what you want.

Here is Bob Dylan talking about his fans in a motel outside of Seattle while waiting to leave for a concert which ten thousand persons have paid to hear. Dylan is halfway through his tour. Hawaii and Australia lie ahead. He has been taking a lot of speed to keep going. He looks terrible, exhausted, wired. Sometimes he makes no sense at all, but at the moment, crossed leg chugging up and down, he is painfully lucid:

"They want me to be their friend. They want to take me home with them. They can't, so they buy my records instead. Where's that at, a piece of plastic? They sit around like lamps waiting for me to turn them on."

Dylan's Big Sur is Woodstock. James Taylor is building a house in Martha's Vineyard, an island in the Atlantic Ocean off Massachusetts. The superstars who find no island make the front pages the hard way: Marilyn Monroe, James Dean, Brian Jones, Jimi Hendrix, Janis Joplin. Listen to Janis Joplin talking on the telephone. It is the Christmas season, 1969. Playboy has assigned John Bowers to write an article about her. She is staying at the Chelsea Hotel in New York:

"Who is John Bowers?" asks Janis. "Do you really know him? Why does Playboy want to interview me? What do they want to know? I know that I'm not special. They act like I'm magic. I don't feel like magic. I don't understand what's happening to me. You can explain it to me. You're a writer. You know what they want. Why are they doing this to me?"

When the news of her death arrived, I felt nothing at all, but I remembered that John Bowers had done a cover story on Sharon Tate for the Saturday Evening Post.

And, of course, while it is midnight and we are in Babylon, there is the memory of that other superstar, Bobby Kennedy. In Oxnard, California, while campaigning for Pat Brown in 1966, he was in a car that was surrounded by shrieking people who began rocking it back and forth for fun. During the California presidential primary in 1968, he was riding in an open car to a rally at a college in the San Fernando Valley. Someone threw a dead flashbulb at him. It hit him in the mouth, chipping a tooth. He fell to the floor of the car holding his hands to his face. His hands were covered with raw red scabs from the friction of so many hands grabbing at him. Jack Newfield, his biographer, says that it is not true that Bobby went into a men's room and vomited after the incident.

The day of the primary I went to see Newfield at the Ambassador Hotel. I was an hour late. First it had been impossible to get a cab. Then the cab I did get broke down halfway to the hotel. Jack took me up to the candidate's suite. It was an awful apartment with pastel walls and cheap old white plastic furniture. The telephone men were pulling out the phones. Some young speechwriters were standing around.

Newfield and I had lunch in the hotel dining room. He signed for the check. We went into the press room. "Do you want to call anyone?" Jack asked. "Just dial any number you want." We called Dan Wolfe, editor of The Village Voice, in New York.

"How does it look, Julie?" Wolfe asked me.

"Not very good," I answered.

"That's funny. Jack says it looks great."

I made another call to a friend's wife in Chicago, and then another to the friend. Then Jack and the speechwriters took me home, stopping first at Head East on Sunset Strip to buy themselves hippie costumes. That night, I did not go to campaign headquarters for the victory party because I do not like crowds. A telephone call woke me from sleep. Bobby Kennedy had been shot. I went back to sleep without turning on the television.

In the morning, Newfield called.

"How does it feel to live in Dallas?" he asked. The same as it does to live in Jerusalem, I thought. Bobby Kennedy had paid his dues almost in full. There was a massive campaign debt left over. I have never felt quite comfortable about being part of that debt.

A month or so before the murder I had written a piece for the Voice in which I talked about running for President as a highly structured suicide attempt, electioneering for crucifixion. I concluded the article: "Only Bobby Kennedy can understand exactly what he is getting into. He is the only one I can vote for, because he is the only one whose insanity I can respect." The Voice rejected the story.

I recall it only as evidence that it was no special act of intelligence to judge the danger involved in Bobby Kennedy's campaign. I had met JFK during the 1960 campaign while I was doing publicity for Citizens for Kennedy in Nassau County, Long Island. I had chatted with RFK during the Pat Brown tour. "Are all Village Voice reporters beatniks?" he asked Newfield later on. That was the sum of my special knowledge.

When the manuscript of Newfield's biography of Bobby Kennedy was finished, he sent me a copy to read and, possibly, review. I read it, looked for my name, which seemed to be the only one missing, and wrote Jack a horribly depressed letter explaining that I just couldn't review the book because I was still too disgusted with the whole theme.

After the book was published, I met Phil Ochs one night by chance at the Troubador bar. We've known each other for a long time. While I was doing my first story on rock and roll in 1965 and hanging around the fringes of the Hullabaloo and Shindig scenes in Los Angeles, Phil was playing Ash Grove and fucking his first Hollywood groupies.

The following year, I was in Babylon again waiting for Bob Dylan to give me a royal audience for a story I was doing on him for the Saturday Evening Post. That story was to be my downfall. Ochs was playing at the Golden Bear in Huntington Beach. We spent a day together bullshitting about Dylan, with whom Phil had once been friendly, but was no longer, apparently because he had told Bob not to release "Crawl in Through My Window," which he thought a very bad record.

Dylan's road manager, Victor Maymudis, was living up on a hill in the Los Feliz district in Tom Law's castle, which was one of the earliest and classiest of the high-level crash pads masquerading as communes. It was an open house, with excellent dope and good food and lots of entertaining freaks. We went up to look for Maymudis in the hope that I might connect with Dylan.

We opened the unlocked door and walked in. There was Dylan sitting at the dining room table drinking apple cider with Lisa Law and other people, all of whom began screaming. Dylan screamed the loudest and with a Scorpionic venom although he is a Gemini. He directed the abuse at me, but I had the feeling that it was all for Phil.

The other people at the table must have felt the same way. Although they all had known Ochs for years, they pretended he was invisible.

Phil disappeared. Dylan calmed down and we had a semi-rational discussion about the interview. I agreed to give Bob a written set of questions, found Ochs pacing around outside on the terrace and put him in the car and split. He had his shirt open and was scratching like a hound with cosmic fleas, covered from head to toe with hives the size of quarters. "I think he's clinically insane," he said.

One of the questions on the list I gave Dylan was, "You are always complaining about the way the press treats you. Do you think that there is anything you might be doing to cause them to dislike you?" He called back as sweet as milk and invited me to come to Hawaii with him.

"Who was that with you the other day?" he asked. "I couldn't see so good." I told him. "He's terrible," Dylan said. "He's a terrible person. He should be sued for defamation of character for calling himself a songwriter."

After my article appeared, while I was glorying in the grandeur of Bob Dylan's reflected glow, actually being asked for autographs and giving them, I received a message by way of Sandy Konikoff, Dylan's drummer on the mainland section of the tour. Sandy was now with the Gentle Soul, a group being managed by Billy James, Bob's first press agent at Columbia.

The Gentle Soul consisted of Sandy, Pamela Poland and some other people I can't remember. For a while, they were living in Billy's garage. That was a standard thing with Billy's acts, living in the garage while they waited for the big time to fall down upon them. Billy was, and is, married to the former Judy Marichal, who produced *In White America,* and then came out to Hollywood in an ancient Jaguar convertible which fell apart on arrival. She became so adept at cooking for hordes of people that eventually she and Billy and Bobby Klein, a photographer, conned some money from a bunch of people and opened The Black Rabbit Inn, on Melrose, in Los Angeles. It is the best restaurant in Babylon. Now they are raising more money to open a hotel at Big Sur. On the back wall of The Black Rabbit there is a photograph of a beautiful blonde girl in a velvet dress

sunday
nov 29
1970

water
colors
raining =
hard
winter
coming on
among the
palms
of Babylon

freaking out in the woods. That's my wife, Chrissie.

The Gentle Soul was a Columbia act, produced by Terry Melcher. I met him at the Columbia Records convention at the Dunes Hotel, Las Vegas, in July 1966, just at the time the Dylan article came out. There was a paper bag full of extremely superior grass. I had just begun to get into dope and this was the best I had ever smoked. I remember being in a room with Simon and Garfunkle, David Anderle, Terry and Billy, stoned into a state of pure telepathy, doing imitations of Dylan.

Then I was down in Billy's room on the first floor lying on the bed refusing to go to the Discotheque Go Go event. He convinced me to come with him. As we approached the casino he said, "The important thing is to remember not to laugh." I fell to the floor in choking hysterics and crawled, literally, on all fours back through the corridor into the room.

The next day, Terry got bored and fled. A grass famine hit the hotel. People were hitting on Mexican waiters for joints. Paul Simon wandered through the casino complaining: "I don't mind that there aren't any girls," he said. "I can always jerk off. But I can't think up a joint." David Swaney, a Columbia press agent, managed to score one joint from a Famous Italian Singer. He shared it with me. Anderle and James accused me of being a prostitute who would get high with anyone.

Billy dialed room service and asked if could send up some grass. They told him to try the Sands.

Back in Los Angeles, Billy talked me into doing a story for the Saturday Evening Post on the Gentle Soul. It was going to be all about how a rock single is made. I had my lead already written in my mind: it was about guitars hanging in pawn shops, each one a broken dream. The Soul rehearsed and rehearsed and rehearsed.

Terry moved them into a house in the hills above Sunset Strip and paid all their expenses. He was producing Paul Revere and the Raiders, a group which was making him all kinds of money. He did not seem to be extremely impressed by the Raiders' musical talents.

The Soul took a lot of acid and began walking around telling each other how much they were learning. They couldn't cut their record because "We're just so far ahead of ourselves all the time." Pamela put them all on a meditation trip. It was a required attendance course, like Phys. Ed. One night I was sitting in Sandy's bedroom getting high with him and a chick he had been balling all day. They were lying in bed naked together. Pamela walked in.

"Sandy," Pamela said, in her best Sunday School voice, "we missed you at meditation today. What were you doing?"

The Gentle Soul never did cut that record in time for me to write my article. I got into the Beach Boys instead. The combined expense account for the two stories, covering a period of more than six months may have been one of the factors that sank the Post. I finally started writing the story on the Beach Boys. I had been warned that if I didn't get it in in time for deadline I would never write again for the Post. I took quarts of Desbutols and rammed my way through the piece within hours of the cut-off. There was no time to mail it, so I took it over to Western Union and filed it as a telegram.

No one at the Saturday Evening Post had ever seen a telegram that long. It came out of the teletype like toilet paper, raving on and on about these teenage idols. No one at the Post except the entertainment editor, Melvin B. Shestack, had ever heard of the Beach Boys. The managing editor, Otto Friedrich, had never heard of rock and roll records. He had never heard of the assignment, either. It was rejected. So was my next expense account.

I was forced to give up free-lance writing and take a job as editor of Cheetah magazine. This was being promoted by a couple of public relations types who had been the publishers of Signature, the Diners Club magazine. The only reason they hired me was because no one else would work for them. They wanted to publish TeenSet. I gave them a cross between the Los Angeles Free Press and the Psychedelic Review. There was not one page in the first issue that did not have a dope reference.

The publishers fired me the day before the first issue appeared. This may have had something to do with a heart attack that one of them suffered just before the magazine went to press. It was not a very bad heart attack, and although it is true that I once wished — before witnesses — that such an attack might occur so that I could do my work without being bothered, it is not true that I called the victim in his sick-bed to tell him I was hoping he would die.

What I actually said was, "Well, are you going to live or are you going to die?"

"Why do you want to know?" he asked.

"So I can decide whether or not to move into your office." I thought this was extremely funny. And still do.

Cheetah folded after eight issues. Fortunately for the Diners Club men, they latched on to a property that was more in their line, Weight Watchers magazine. This publication is said to be very successful.

They now claim that the reason Cheetah failed was that kids' minds change so fast it's hard to keep up with what they're thinking. That's probably true in their case, neither of them being speedy thinkers.

Not all the stupidity was theirs. A lot of it was mine. Maybe most of it. Going to work for them in the first place was not a brilliant move, but I was broke. It was stupid to be broke, but everyone makes mistakes. The really stupid thing was hiring a catatonic managing editor, an art director who was blind in one eye and had never smoked grass, and an editorial assistant who had fits in the office. I did all that.

Anyway, it was a season of great misery that lasted a long time, and I believe that it began with Sandy Konikoff's message. "Hey, Jules," he said, looking about furtively to make sure that no one was spying on us, "Hey, Jules, I heard from Bob. He's really hot about the story. He hates it. He says he's going to have you wasted."

I laughed.

*S*ince then, many bad things have befallen me, not the least of which was slipping and falling and breaking my hip in front of my mother's apartment. Phil Ochs was attacked by those terrible hives merely for criticizing a Dylan record. I don't know what Dylan disliked about that article I wrote, except, maybe, that I pictured him as a crazy, whining little boy, which is what he looked like to me, but I have no doubt that I have been living under his curse. What else could account for my misery?

You want to be careful about your relationship with superstars, for they are powerful people, and life does not consist only of science. There are thoughts that have fists.

In the Troubador bar, Ochs, looking fatter than usual and heavily dissipated, asked me what I thought of Newfield's book about RFK. I told him that I couldn't really comment about the book's value as a work of art or history, because I was so unhappy about the way in which it was created. Bobby Kennedy died because Jack Newfield wanted to write a book about him. He died because Jerome Kretchmer was tired of being an Assemblyman and wanted to get a leg up on a powerful horse.

It is viciously unfair of me to single out these two of my friends for so metaphysical an accusation. They happen to be the only ones whose names I know and whose actions I am close enough to judge. There were many others. They talked Robert F. Kennedy into running for President. They did it for the best of reasons. The country needed him. But they needed him more than the country did. Through him they could exercise power.

A man is responsible for his own acts. Bobby Kennedy made the decision himself. But if his friends had thought of *him* and not the country there was only one kind of advice they could have given him. If they had been thinking of his agony instead of their own ambitions there was only one kind of advice they would have given him. He was a superstar, the heaviest of the superstars, and superstars can't go out in public.

Never mind the assassin. It was the people he had to fear. They wanted to eat him alive. It was as if the Beatles, at the height of the mania, had walked through Yankee Stadium shaking hands. It might have turned out beautifully. The kids might have been polite and sweet and respectful. Or they might have torn them flesh from bone.

Anyone who has been in a crowd of people excited by lust should understand the danger. The people are a beast. When they collect in great numbers they become high. They are not used to being high. They do strange things. At the end of a Beach Boys concert in Indianapolis kids started tearing the seats up and throwing them at the stage. For fun. While the Beach Boys were still playing.

It is possible that the only reason Woodstock was peaceful is that it rained so hard.

That was a miracle. It is hard to arrange for miracles. There was no miracle at Altamont. There were no surprises either. *Gimme Shelter* would not be making quite so much money as it is without the sacrificial victim. It would be making a lot more money if Mick Jagger had been killed on camera.

Ochs thought my opinion was in very bad taste. He is not a superstar. He was once part of a superstar's circle. He was jealous. It is nothing to be ashamed of. Everyone is jealous of superstars, particularly the smaller people in their circles. Every superstar has a circle. The circles intersect, like spheres of influence. It is possible to become very rich where those circles intersect.

Once the circle is in existence it is difficult for new people to penetrate. Part of this has to do with the jealousy, and the money. The more important reason is that this is the way the superstar wants it. It is his protection from the energy wasters and the threats and the various uglinesses that are drawn to the center.

*T*he circle around James Taylor this night before the rain was hard and hostile. No one was swaggering, which is the worst vibration that whirls through the outer circles, but everyone was uptight. But people at the Troubador are always uptight.

Doug Weston knows what he is doing. The Troubador has somehow managed to make money out of folkies, an audience suffering from hardening of the bank account. Or maybe he is very lucky. There is nothing very special about the place. It is the standard large dingy room complete with regulation bare brick wall, plain wooden benches, and a complete set of schizoid beatnik waitresses.

This is where the Hollywood intellectuals hang out. Not all of the audience is intellectual. Most of them are college kids trying to look intellectual so that they won't have to be embarrassed about jerking off. The real intellectuals here are the ones who can read the menu without moving their lips.

The super-intellectuals are found in the bar. There is a Monday night super-intellectual tradition at the Troubador. That's when the new talent tries out. The super-intellectuals are kids who write for the underground press. Having written one article for Open City is still a decent ticket of admission to this caste, even though the paper has been dead a long time. These young writers all consider themselves superior to the new talent. They are wrong. There is no way to become a superstar by writing. You must be a performer.

It is more important to be a superstar than to be a super-intellectual. Superstars make more money. They also have groupies. Writers do not have groupies. Very famous writers sometimes are taken on by celebrity fuckers, but celebrity fuckers are not as good as groupies. They are usually older, and not as pretty, and not nearly so fanatic in their desire to please. I have heard that Erich Segal, the author of *Love Story,* has groupies, but I do not believe it, although it is possible.

To the young writers, the only performers who really count are the ones who write their own material. These are, if enormously successful, intellectual superstars. The Beach Boys, though they write their own material, are not considered intellectual superstars. I have never really understood why not. Their songs are just as good as Simon & Garfunkel's, maybe better. It is one of those peculiarities of fashion, like the prejudice against Norman Rockwell or Andrew Wyeth.

James Taylor, I had been told, is an intellectual superstar. If so, he would be one of the few I have met. In my own system, I count only Bob Dylan in this class, but I am probably showing my age there. I know one person who has been both an intellectual and a star, but not at the same time. This is Tom Nolan, who is now a really gifted writer. When he was a kid he played the juvenile lead in *Buckskin,* a Western TV series that was the second most popular show in America. You may never have heard of it, but at one time there were Tommy Nolan comic books. I once asked him how he felt about the comic books when he first saw them. "I thought it was only right," he said.

Taylor had once been on Apple. Now he was on Warner Bros.-Reprise. The publicity office had supplied me with a fat pile of press clippings, most of them reviews of his latest album, *Sweet Baby James.* Everyone liked the record. Someone did not like a song called "Steamroller." Corb

Dear Jules:

Let me tell you about James Taylor. You asked why I don't want to interview him. I'll tell you why. For the same reason you don't want to interview him. He is the Dick Haymes of Rock. Next year there'll be another James Taylor to interview. And the year after that, there'll be the Tommy Leonetti of Rock and the Julius La Rosa of Rock and the Guy Mitchell of Rock. James Taylor, indeed. If you do see him, tell him to take cold hip baths....they'll help...

The James Taylor

2 jiggers sloe gin
i dash garlic salt
3 lemon peels (ground)
1 clove of nutmeg

Pour all ingredients in
a mixer, mix. Yummy.

James Taylor
        23 E. 45th St.
        pants pressed

James Taylor
        100 proof
        Kentucky Sippin' Whiskey

James Taylor
        (name on the dining car
        on the Empire State Express)

Freelance Writers Digest

Donahue, writing in the Los Angeles Free Press, said James Taylor had a "laid back" style.

Alfred G. Aronowitz, pop columnist for the New York Post, gave him a whole column. That seemed significant. Aronowitz is the best writer in the world on the music scene. Dylan was once asked if there was anyone he thought might be able to save the world. "Alfred G. Aronowitz," he answered. Here are some of the things he had to say about James Taylor:

The songs that James sings are his own, born out of the torture that twice sent him into mental institutions. . . . speaks for his generation with the kind of cold authority that seems destined to elect him one of the spokesman of his time . . . son of the dean of the University of North Carolina Medical School . . . . 17 and in boarding school the first time he committed himself. "I was suicidal," he says. "It was the only place I could go." . . . second time after recording his first album. "It seemed like a good idea at the time."

Is James Taylor going to be the next public phenomenon. It's a little early in the cycle for such an event, but that's the league James has applied for. May the Lord have mercy on him.

Reading back over the column, I found something that my eye had skipped over:

Who is James Taylor, this young thin giant with long dark hair and a wispy beard who walks through the crowds that come to adore him with a half-smile on his lips and distant visions in his eyes like a Jesus in an era when we already have too many, and at the same time one too few?

Oh, of course, I thought, that heavy. Another one. No wonder Aronowitz asks the Lord to have mercy on him. I was developing less and less interest in meeting

James Taylor. Mental institutions. My mother was in one for a long time, a really good one. Her brother has been in one most of his life, a state hospital. I used to visit him with her. Those visits were the most painful hours of my life. Everything is entertainment in America. Here was someone singing songs about being in a mental hospital. There is a kind of escalation that goes on in the show-and-tell business. Once it was enough for Tony Perkins to specialize in psychotic roles. Now it is necessary to be actually psychotic.

"Jules is an absolute egomaniac."

But a job is a job. I had taken advances and expenses, including a ticket to Martha's Vineyard where I would get to see the young superstar in his island of privacy. I had been back and forth to the Troubadour a couple of times during the day, seen Taylor from a distance, had a hostile conversation with Peter Asher, his manager, (formerly of Peter & Gordon). Peter's skin had cleared up nicely since the last time I saw him, and he and Betsy Doster, former New York press agent for the Stones, were married now.

It was time for the second show of the first night and the traditional superstar crowds were lined up in the streets. There was a big white sound truck from Wally Heider's studio and a big white Rolls Royce with a television antenna. Naturally, there was a fuck-up at the box office and a hassle about getting in, a long period of waiting in the bar. Hello, Marilyn Wilson, wife of Brian.

A person from Warner Bros. arrived with the explanation that the reason everyone was so uptight was that there had been a bomb scare. Was that Doug Weston's karma or James Taylor? Finally, I was seated at a table, with my beautiful bride, and my friend, Girard Landry. There was another long wait. Landry went to the men's room and came back with big news. James Taylor had been coming out as he was going in. They had had a wonderful conversation.

Burning slowly, I thought of nasty things to write about James Taylor. Why were they just letting me sit here? I called one of the schizoid beatnik waitresses over. Didn't they know that I was important? In a very petulant voice, I demanded that the ranking Warner Bros. executive be brought to my table immediately. Why? Because I am an important writer with an important publication doing an important story on James Taylor. Well, why don't you just go up to the dressing room?

In the dressing room, which was definately a fire-trap and made me feel very nervous and claustrophobic, there was James Taylor, who looked a lot leaner and sharper than the photograph on his album; his drummer; Betsy Doster, a bit chubbier than I remembered her and speaking with an English accent, to which she is undoubtedly entitled after four years in London; Peter Asher; and one of the most beautiful women I have ever seen in my life. She turned out to be Joni Mitchell, James Taylor's current old lady.

It was just like old times with me and Betsy Doster. I first met her in 1965 while I was doing a massive article for Cavalier on the literary and philosophical and religious significance of rock and roll. It turned out to be a great article and it was accompanied by a piece on groupies written by Betsy, the result of a rather rapid crush on her that I developed at first sight, being always a sucker for a pretty face, and willing to do anything to make points. Actually, she wrote a good piece, but some timid person at Cavalier cut out the best parts for fear of libel.

There was an aluminum-foil package of joints on the table. "People are always giving me dope," Taylor said. A joint was lighted and passed around, but he let it go by without taking a hit. Joni strummed his guitar. She was wearing a grey woolen knitted long dress and a hand-knitted scarf. She had made the scarf herself. "I spend a lot of time on planes," she said. "It's a good time to knit." She had written a book of poems and Random House wanted to publish it in her own handwriting. She wondered if they would have wanted to do it if she were not Joni Mitchell. She had not yet made up her mind to do or not to do.

Under the dope package was a stack of telegrams. One of them was from

Taylor's publisher. It said something like, "Best of luck on opening night to one hell of a swell guy." Another said, "If one more person asks me what James Taylor is really like, I shall spit up. Good luck tonight. I wish I were there, but you sold out. I knew someday you'd sell out. John Stewart."

A girl came in and asked James—it was always James, never Jim—for his birthday so she could have his horoscope cast. March 12th, 1948, Boston, 5:06 PM. Another girl popped in and asked for advice about selling her poems. Someone took her phone number.

The drummer brought out a small vial that looked like a miniature sweet cream bottle and contained cocaine. He horned the white powder from a tiny silver spoon. The room became crystal sharp. Joni was even more beautiful and desirable than she had been before, her eyes crisp and glistening as she stroked the guitar.

"There'll never be another hysteria like there was in my day," said Peter Asher, already an elder statesman.

The door opened and a phalanx of young girls charged forward. The lead girl had an expensive 35mm camera. "Just one moment, James," she said, her tone very professional and commanding, "Let me take your picture." She might have been someone from a fan magazine. She was tolerated while she fumbled with the camera, suddenly less sure of herself as Taylor sat patiently posing for her. She snapped off a few shots, then fell apart. "Gee thanks," she said. "I'm really getting into this photography thing." She was just a fan, wasting his time. The concentrated hostility of everyone in the room blew her and her friends out the door.

Someone came up with a message. A Chris Cunningham was downstairs and wanted to see James Taylor. He was permitted to come up, a heavily spaced young man with a super stoned black kid about his own age. They stood there staring at Taylor, disoriented, not knowing quite what to say now that they were in the imperial presence. Taylor said nothing.

"Say, man," Cunningham said, his speech loaded and slurred, "I just thought I'd come by and say hello for old times' sake. You know what I mean man. Just to say hello. I'm getting it together now. Me and my brother here we're living up in Laurel Canyon. You ever get up that way, we'd like you to come by and say hello. You know, for old times' sake. No big thing. No hassle or anything.

"No big thing, man," his friend echoed.

"Sure," Taylor said.

"No big thing," his black friend repeated. Cunningham carefully gave Taylor his address and phone number. The two visitors left.

"He was in the hospital with me," James Taylor explained. "He never did seem to have his shit together." It was time for him to go on stage. He picked up the guitar and ran his fingers lightly over the stings and frowned. "Joni, did you retune my guitar?" She blushed, made a small "O" and put her hand to her mouth. Taylor began retuning the guitar, but there wasn't enough time.

2:45 a.m. I have never claimed to be a wonderful person.

Throughout the set, he continued to fidget with it. The uptightness that had filled the place all evening began to melt as he talked and played. By the end of the performance, he had even reached me. But I still did not really like him. During the next few days I went over to the Troubadour and sat in the dressing room with him trying to find some level of conversation at which we could have a dialog. One night, I brought my trip book with me. It is my proudest work, filled with my own drawings (which are pretty good for someone who can't draw) and my calligraphy (which is getting better).

Joni sat looking at the book, interested, enjoying it. I was back in kindergarten at last. The attention was focused on me instead of on this sour, hostile, closed

well, fuck me,
I'll never smile again.

Alexander
Taylor

Joni
Mitchell

A: What
fun it's
going to
be in
Martha's
Vineyard
standing
around
in the
cold.

Q: Why can't
I ever have
a bummer
that's fun?

I do not
love
Los Angeles
very
much — if
at all.

kid. Taylor sulked and pouted. Joni handed me back my book and stretched out her foot to touch his. He smiled reluctantly.

The following day, James was working up in Laurel Canyon, filming fill-ins for the movie he had just about completed. It was called *Two Lane Blacktop* and it starred James Taylor as the driver of a high performance drag racer hustling across country with a standard-issue weird hippie chick in the back seat and Dennis Wilson of the Beach Boys as his mechanic. The script is by Rudy Wurlitzer, who wrote *Nog*, a novel that resembles those Krazy Kat landscapes. Billy James was the musical director for the movie and he gave me a copy of the script to read.

It's one of those things where no one has any names and everything is very deliberately precise and heavy and nothing necessarily connects with anything else. The plot is slender: *The Hustler* with cars instead of pool. The Driver and The Mechanic and The Girl (a hitchhiker) are racing a guy in a GTO across country for pink slips, winner takes both cars.

Now this is where the circles really begin to close. I worked in the same office with Rudy Wurlitzer's girl friend for a couple of years. They lived together off and on for at least three years and were about to get married. Melvin B. Shestack and his wife made a dinner for her one evening about a week before the wedding was to take place. I brought a guy along, a writer. She and the guy went off together.

She left Rudy, moved in with the guy and his wife and two children. By the time the whole thing was finished, she was married to a third party and Rudy Wurlitzer was like a writing machine, his career finally beginning to take off. Shestack claims that I am responsible for Wurlitzer's success. If I hadn't brought the extra guy along that night, he would have never been traumatized enough to get down to serious work he says.

In the script, there is a conversation between a garage mechanic and a boy about James Taylor's car that goes something like this: "Is it a 396?" "454." "You build the headers?" and so on. When I came to this, I thought, really, now, no one talks that way. Wurlitzer has been reading too many old copies of Car & Driver.

The fill-ins were being shot on a dirt road called Elusive Drive. The name was just too symbolic to be real. It was right up near the house where Chris Cunningham was staying. I hadn't looked him up and I didn't know whether to feel guilty for not doing my job, or self-righteous for not stooping that low. Girard Landry and I drove up there to the site at the appointed time, had a terrible time finding it, and finally got down to where the director, Monte Hellman, was supervising the shooting.

Landry, who was once a drag racer, flashed on the cars.

"Is it a 396?" he asked, and then the conversation from the script was replayed verbatim, and extended with arcane technical details that were beyond my ability to remember. Joni was there too and I showed her the new entries in my book:

The new royalty—rock stars—are they as important as they think they are?

No one is that important.

Doing an interview with a superstar is an exercise in humility and patience.

I have never claimed to be a wonderful person.

Laid back—Van Morrison, Neil Young, Harvey Mandel.

What fun it's going to be in Martha's Vineyard, standing around in the cold.

Why can't I ever have a bummer that's fun?

Well, fuck me, I'll never smile again.

James Taylor came over and we talked about the story I was trying to do on him. He said no one had ever done anything that seemed right. I said, "No one of any literary significance has ever done a full-length portrait of you." Joni choked back a laugh. "My stories are works of art," I continued, "they are not journalism but history."

I talked with Monte Hellman for a while, asking him if Rudy Wurlitzer had known a lot about cars. "He just got a lot of copies of Car & Driver," Monte said, "and did a lot of research." I told Monte about Dennis Wilson. Dennis Wilson was the Beach Boy who was always fucking up. His main trip was to fall down. Once, we were all up at Brian's palace breathing nitrous oxide out of Redi-Wip cans. Brian had just spent a thousand dollars to have his windows stained gray. The stain was still wet. Dennis breathed nitrous oxide and fell down, smearing one of the windows beyond repair.

It was Dennis, you will remember, who brought Charles Manson into the Beach Boys' life. Dennis was insane about racing cars. He went to see *Grand Prix* and became insane about making movies about racing cars. He bought a Bolex, which he handed to Brian to shoot from the front seat of the Ferrari while Dennis drove at speeds upwards of 140 mph through Benedict Canyon Boulevard.

The car hit an oily spot, skidded, crunched into a telephone pole. "All the while," Brian reported, "Dennis was shouting at me, 'Keep shooting! Keep shooting!' When we got out of the car I couldn't believe that we were alive. The front wheel was completely smashed off and was rolling down the hill and this torn piece of axle was just hanging there. Dennis looked at me and pleaded, 'Now don't get mad, Brian. I know you're going to get mad at me. Please don't be mad at me, Brian.'"

A pool of yellowish light illuminated the white building of Los Angeles down in the basin. It was a dead light, the edge taken off it by smog, ugly and without flavor.

"Look at that light," Monte Hellman said. "Isn't it just beautiful? It's really great." He was not being sarcastic. I decided that I was not going to have to see *Two Lane Blacktop*.

On the way back, I asked Landry what he and Joni had been talking about.

"You," he said. "She said, 'Jules is an absolute egomaniac!' and I said, 'Yes, but he's so honest about it.' She's really a great chick."

"What do you think, would those cars make it cross country?"

"Never," Landry answered. "They're made for a quarter mile. They have to tow them to the track."

"Even if they had an expert mechanic along with them?"

"Never."

From Los Angeles, I went on to New York. When I got there I spent some time listening to Taylor's albums. The music was extremely pretty, but thin, just like the emotions. It did not seem to me that James Taylor had seen fire and rain. He might some day, and when he did he had the technical equipment, training and talent to do something really remarkable.

I wondered, too, about that mental institution. What kind of place do you suppose it is that the son of the dean of a medical school goes to? There was one verse that seemed especially significant to me:

> *Just knocking around the zoo on a*
> *Thursday afternoon*
> *There's bars on all the windows and*
> *they're counting up the spoons*
> *And if I'm feeling edgy there's a chick*
> *who's paid to be my slave*
> *But she'll hit me with a needle if she*
> *thinks I'm trying to misbehave.*

Do you see what I see? It sounds like a sado-masochistic fantasy. Even in the mental hospital, James Taylor is still the aristocrat, still in control. The female attendant is paid to be his slave. And she'll hit him with a needle. I wondered what Bob Dylan would have thought of all this. And Janis Joplin. And John Lennon. And RFK.

I reluctantly made my reservations for Martha's Vineyard. It was beginning to snow in New York. I called James Taylor's brother Alexander and told him when I would be up to see James. Then I went to my trip book and began to write:

> *The city is on snow watch today. Everyone knows the signs—a white sky pearling into a damp gray, the air moist and sweet and still and not too cold. Scattered sprays of fine sleet tickled the streets for a while. Now as twilight thickens and condenses into darkness, the office buildings—great illuminated ice trays—sharpen into brilliant focus under the opal glass dome of cloudy night.*

> *Sliding through crystal curtains of snow trees and ice ferns, bunches of transparent needles, each one separate and distinct and furred with its own frozen mist of crushed velvet frost.*

> *Coming down. Vapor to liquid to solid.*

> *Oh, I was airy once and flew about from cloud to cloud, but now my thickness has begun to set. From heaven into heaviness I fall, and what was light turns into night and what was quick slows into rest.*

> *The sleep of snow is dark and slow. The heat of day is far away. Embrace the cold, the growing old, and stretch and yawn and wait for dawn.*

> *Muffled horns*
> *soft drums*
> *mellow music*
> *and soothing vibes.*

Documents of Transit, certificates of existence and awards of merit are not valid without the official seal of the Recording Angel.

Songs of melancholy softness fading into the winter dream. Mirrors covered with sheets and dust. Empty rooms, tired footsteps that drag and end. A sigh, a sob, a whispering flutter of sagging breath.

Silence, except for the pen of the Recording Angel scratching a receipt for another soul given into safe deposit in the cold storage chambers of eternity.

The noise in this city is a guarantee of life eternal. If death is sleep and sleep requires silence, where there is no silence there can be no sleep. Yet people do die here, cemetaries full of them. Exhausted by the mill, they lie beneath its floor in sodden coma, kept from falling into final rest by the accum-ulative groans and cries of the machinery that ground them down.

I am not sure at all that I want to interview Paul McCartney.

James Taylor is a burden.

I stopped writing.

My wife was in Palm Beach, Florida, in her fifth month of pregnancy. The price of a ticket to Palm Beach is exactly the same as a ticket to Martha's Vineyard and return. I decided not to go see James Taylor. In the morning, I called Alex.

"Oh, James split," he said. I wondered if James Taylor had thought about how I might have felt, arriving in Martha's Vineyard and finding him gone.

Chrissie believes that the baby,
was born at 10:20 rather than
10:25, which would make her
Leo Rising.

waiting for
the
slow
yellow
summer
evening
light
to thicken
and
condense
into
liquid
darkness

separated by walls of olden manufacture from the clear radiance of the
early stars. Faera[1] = from the
old language = faierie, a class of
supernatural beings, having human
form and possessing magic powers.

The word is ultimately derived from the Latin *fata*, fate.

Faera[2] = everything we mean by *fair*: clear, unblemished, just, pleasing in appearance; archaic: a beloved women; comes to us from Old English *faeger*

August 3, 1971

Lagunitas = The house is filled with plants, garden blooming. Russell has gone to live in a Christian house. "I am going to let Jesus make all the decisions from now on," he is reported to have said.

Moving into a big beat.

The Refugees

The blonde girl nursing the baby is my wife, the former Virginia Christine Jolly Teter of San Marino, California. Her mother wanted her to be either a social climber or a movie star. Here she is—a refugee. She is hoping to graduate to pioneer. She is social climbing as planned, but the direction seems to be healthier.

Chrissie doesn't like that picture. She is young. She is only beginning to learn that despair can have a clarifying beauty. She believes that she is alone, an individual, private and complete. That's what they teach you in San Marino, a town dedicated to America's national religion: selfishness.

Martha Mitchell makes a lot of sense to the people of San Marino. They admire greed and worship big cars, cashmere sweaters and New York-cut steaks. Even their servants are white. Rich refugees are always worried about becoming poor refugees. San Marino is filled with rich refugees. No matter how carefully they may pretend to be Californians, they know that they are merely Americans, at best.

It is not enough to be an American. America is a place filled with niggers. Not just black niggers, but all the other kinds: wops, spicks, kikes, hippies. The San Marino definition is a broad-spectrum device. It curves back into anxiety. Purity of breed is rare. It might be the that most of the people of San Marino are themselves niggers—uppity niggers, of course, but niggers.

America is the country of refugees, the worst kind of niggers of all. This is a story about the worst kind of refugee of all—not the one who came here from another place, but the one who was born here yet cannot call it home.

1 know exactly what you are thinking. Another depressing examination of scabs picked and repicked. Despair is so romantic. Nigger is such a dirty word. Why can't we have some entertainment— dancing girls, dirty movies, a lot of laughs? I feel the same way myself, but since I became a refugee I got very serious. Notice the slightly European accent. I feel heavy. Worldly. Cynical. Amused. Also nervous.

Refugees are always nervous or melancholy. They do not tell happy stories. Their gaiety is infrequent and frantic. This is an international style. Maybe there is a school

somewhere in Geneva where all the refugees from overseas learn the rules of behavior. The American refugee style appears
to be based on the European. The inflec-
tion is different but the attitude is the
same. Here are some voices from both
genres:

"When I was a little boy, Hitler invaded
Hungary. My father took me to the parade.
I was thrilled. I loved the SS. I prayed to
God to let me grow up to be a German
soldier. We were Jewish. I wound up in a
concentration camp. I shared a narrow
coffin of a bunk with another boy my own
age.

"One day I stole half a stale roll. I knew
that I should share it with my buddy, but
I ate it secretly myself. The following morning, I tried to wake him for work detail. He
was dead." *Hunter College in the Bronx,
1957.*

"I am 23 years old. I have had more than
a hundred men. My tubes are chronically
inflamed from having had the clap so many
times. I have recently become pathological-
ly photosensitive. See these blisters? They

are from the sun.

"Altamont was the heaviest day of my
life. I was sitting in the back on one spot
all day, too wasted to move. The Stones
came on stage and the arc lights crackled
on. We tripped forward toward the music.
The energy at the front was insane. I
thought the world was coming to an end.
Jagger was the Devil manifesting himself
on earth. We were sucked into the vortex
of screaming faces crying, 'No more! No
more!'" *The Chinese House, Lagunitas,
California, 1971.*

my wife and I used to live in
Brooklyn Heights, N.Y., just across the
water from Wall Street, in a fine old Vic-
torian brownstone townhouse whose back
windows looked out onto a garden over-
grown with high grass. It was a fragile
island of elegance floating on the lip of a
cataract of rushing violence.

One night we both dreamed of soldiers
with machine guns spraying bullets into our
windows. At the end of a hot, humid day

not long later, we ran down into the subway as an almost tropical thunder shower crashed around us. The subway was still filled with the foul breath and sweat of the rush hour, but the station was empty.

Three trains arrived simultaneously in a pounding screech that bounced hideously against concrete platforms and glistening tile walls. In our car there was a greasy girl dressed in fluorescent rayon satin reading The Daily News. The front page headline was, "Con Ed Predicts Brown-Outs for Summer."

Deep in the East River tunnel where a thousand riders were trapped for eight hours during the great black-out, the train slowed and stopped, lights flickering and dimming. Let me tell you, the next minutes were long. I vowed never to go into the subway again. I mean, I *vowed*. I was really worried. There was no nobility left in my nature at all. I was going to howl and cry.

The train hiccuped into motion, passing the lights of a construction or maintenance crew. When we got home I was as sticky as warm adhesive tape. Chrissie insisted on kissing me on the neck, brushing her long hair against my exposed nerve endings. The horn from the harbor was thick and sullen, with an edge of unpleasant playfulness.

I checked my watch against the telephone. There was four minutes difference. Was the watch slow? Or was the telephone fast? Maybe the power that controlled time was speeding up the treadmill.

We fled to the air-conditioned apartment of a friend, a stock market lawyer who had managed to save $20,000. "The situation in the United States resembles Russia in 1905," he said, "but the next twelve years will go faster. Everyone will be forced to take a position. My plan is to make as much money as possible in the next two or three years, then get out. My analyst says I'm the sanest person in the country. Of course, he's a radical."

There was a booklet on Swiss banks on the coffee table. "Don't put your money in a Swiss bank," I advised, feeding his paranoia jovially. "Convert it into those platinum medals the private mints are manufacturing. When everything falls down, each of those coins will buy you a one hundred pound bag of rice."

We left for California the following week. We have been on the road ever since, living in communes, with friends, in motels and hotels of every class from $6-a-night clapboard cottages with yellowing sheets and old gas heaters to a $90-a-day suite in a grand hotel, looking for an existence that makes sense. But there is no existence that makes sense. There never is for the refugee. There is only the next destination.

*n*otes from my journal mark the moments of the voyage. Here is a passage that begins in purple—really—ink:

Alone in the woods, walking to the end of a dirt road, finding that it does not lead to the deeper forest but to picnic areas with campers and public toilets. Men climb Everest for the silence, not the adventure. We need more zero time.

A girl spent many hours of arduous practice learning to play the piano, assaulting the ears of her friends, teachers, family and neighbors. At last, when her skill was almost perfect, she went to live with a man who loved music. Although he was poor, he managed to provide her with a piano. Now she refuses to play it for him or for anyone in his house, performing only when alone, only for herself.

Another girl had a miraculously astonishing gift for drawing the human form. Surrounded by handsome people, she glides invisibly from scene to scene leaving behind only a trail of crumpled papers, unmade beds and dirty dishes.

A writer friendly with these sad ladies earned his living imprisoned in a cubby hole with an electric typewriter, dreaming of pine and eucalyptus and wild bay. Awakening from his dream to find himself living in a world of crystallized vomit, he drifts along rapping endlessly about the meaninglessness of life.

Pale violet thoughts at twilight. A small birdvoice. The spring where salmon spawn. The last flutter of cool night settling among the dark trees.

Heaven has many flavors; one day, many moods; and from heaven to heaven there are many hells.

Orange candlelight in the living room. Philosophical discussions between men and women about miracles and other evening subjects. Mindy Thal got a D in bookkeeping at Hollywood High because she was intimidated by Jewish girls with big bosoms.

Deepest night, darkest sky. The stars—

what can be said about these glorious stars glistening through the feathered groves of holy trees. Almost quiet at last. Waiting not for dawn, but sleep.

Awakening to the last puffs of fog retreating over the seaward hills, blue sky and strong sun coming up out of the other side of the valley. The simple but demanding morning personal tasks: shaving, bacon, tea, eggs. Birds and insects calling messages from other worlds.

A woman with five children living in a brown shingled house surrounded by trees and wire cages. Most of them are empty. There is a great aviary built around a stand of tall, thin redwoods; a white peacock, a white peahen, a brown peahen; in the center of the cage, a white egg lying on the moist, dark ground. Scorpio woman with peacocks and children, her sepia pen and wash drawings—heavy flashes rendered in rapid, delicate line; a bedspread of summer flowers in the white studio; a place to be at noon when the steaming sun hangs outside her shadowed cave of ferns; a place to be at midnight when she is a naked white goddess in the black womb of trees and the brilliantly baroque peacock spreads his luminous fan.

Golden princess washing slender feet in a white basin. Everything she does is beautiful. Jealous even of the soap in her hand.

High school crushes that lasted months as you tenderly groped from night to night on living room couches while babysitting with the lights out, long, wet kisses leading nowhere at all. Putting up with the girl you got while hungering for the one you wanted; enjoying that pleasantly poetic melancholy among books and Vivaldi; and now, so many lovers later, remembering incense and organ music, roaming through the traces and scars.

Nothing left but telephone numbers that will never answer again, a head full of waiting room time-fillers; destination unknown, travelling orders smeared by fate, lost in the space that separates the last fading dream from the next full color production.

Question marks lead to a city in a cliff, a peek behind the scenes, a stage-loft filled with dusty props, empty rows of worn plush seats. Authors, actors, actresses, directors, producers, clowns, grips, ticket sellers, audiences, beggars—they are all silent now.

Only the demons of the forest keep eternal time. No record-keeping metro-nome counts them down to final winter. The people of the life are writing scripts about freedom of the will. Hard-driving Time, riding a sea of flesh and faces, is flogging souls through predetermined dances.

Watch the wild water where the wind whips the waves home. Turbulent sea, fog breaking over the coastal hills like the arm of the ocean, low-blown trees swept back hard, the land molten and flowing. Walking down the road, finding the path, surrendering, falling, floating, drowning. Painful final rushes before the end:

Earth tones and small white flowers appear and disappear in the country of Kali.

There are no crimes against humanity; only crimes against one's self.

Taste the soil of your birth. Do not ask the land for more than it can give. Oh stream where salmon spawn you are ever fresh in Springtime.

Wail on night wind.

Let's all try our best, because all we've got is what we are.

*T*hat's the way it has been on the road, beyond structure, beyond habit, always moving among strangers, one dissolve after another, individual memories and meetings bursting into light and fading, no story line, no plot, no connections. It seemed as if the whole nation was roaming. Caravans laced from temporary camp to temporary camp. Young girls with babies on their backs walked the highways.

"Where are you going?" we asked them when we stopped to pick them up.

"Just tripping," was the inevitable reply. Anywhere we were going was good enough for them.

When I was a boy in summer camp, one of my counselors was a young refugee. For a while he had lived in Israel, where he was picked up by the British intelligence service, who accused him of working for the Jewish underground. They asked him for names. He didn't know any names. They beat the soles of his feet with a leather strap. He screamed names and addresses as fast as he could invent them. Some days later, an officer came to his cell.

"Why did you make up this foolishness?" the officer asked, genuinely disappointed and puzzled. "Don't you realize all the useless trouble you have put us to?"

"Your men were beating the soles of my feet with a leather strap," the refugee said.

"Impossible," the officer retorted coldly. "That is clearly against regulations." He released the man the following morning, noting in the official dossier that he was most probably a psychopathic liar. Not long afterward, the refugee did, in fact, enter a mental institution. He was convinced that

ple are moving, looking perhaps for some high authority to surrender to, but finding none. Everywhere there are casualties.

Who is it, really, that we are looking for? What is it that we want? What place will we find peace?

"Whatever's right," the kids say. We'll know when it feels right. But will it ever feel right? Or must we come to believe that

Faera 17 June 1971

his head was made of glass, that he must lie carefully in bed without moving to keep from breaking it.

"Do you want to know how a war ends?" he asked us one night by the campfire. "I remember the day World War II ended. I was in Bavaria, on my way home to Frankfurt, a long way from the prison camp in which the American soldiers had found me. The roads were filled with mobs of refugees. Quite suddenly we were joined by German soldiers who wandered along with us, looking for Americans to surrender their weapons to.

"'The war is over,' they told us. Then an American supply convoy came up the road. The German soldiers stood in the highway and handed up their rifles and pistols and ammunition to the men in the trucks. 'Go that way,' an American officer told them. And they did. And so did we. But there was nothing there except more people like us wandering. That was how the war ended."

America is at war, not merely in Southeast Asia, but at home. There is a war against poverty, a war against drugs, a war against pollution of the environment. At times it seems as if there is a war of the old against the young. At times it seems as if we are at war against ourselves. These are long wars. There are many casualties, more than we can count. Everywhere, peo-

our heads are made of glass before we can allow ourselves to find a safe pillow to rest against? When all these wars are over will we still be wandering?

Maybe as you read this, you find it too personal to be quite true. You are accustomed to journalistic conventions in which the reporter interviews the man in the street and the experts in the offices and builds a mosaic of quotations and opinions and statistics. I am not interested in any of that. I am trying to make you feel what I have felt, not lecture you about the sociology of change.

I am trying to make you see the snapshots I have seen, supplying the voice-over for photographs that speak more clearly perhaps when captioned with these random narratives. I began by telling you about a photograph of a blonde girl nursing a baby. She is only one of many. Here are the voices of others:

Nursing Mother: "I was born in Kentucky. I came to California with a man who turned out to be hooked on speed. I left him and found Bill, an alcoholic. I have two children. We live in a trailer without water, electricity or heat, parked on the property of a commune which lets us stay in return for Bill's hauling the garbage to the dump in his old pick-up truck. Bill has been drunk for a week. The garbage is piling up. New people are moving into the commune. Will they let us stay?"

Bearded Man with Wife and Two Children: "We used to live in San Francisco. We supported ourselves by baking ten loaves of bread a day and selling them from door to door. Our rent was $200 a month. Now we are on the road. We don't know where we are going, but at least we don't have to pay rent."

Bob Baker: "I am 63 years young, a millwright by trade. I can install the most complicated equipment you can imagine—pour the concrete for the bases, run the electrical lines, the air lines, the water lines, set it up and make it run. If something goes wrong I can figure out what has to be done to make it go right. If it needs a new part, I can make that part. I have been coming up here to Oregon for ten years on my vacation. Each year, just before I would leave to go back to Ventura or Torrance or wherever we were living, I would tell my friends up here, 'I'll be back in two or three months to stay.' Well, I'm here to stay now. I am here to stay."

Ole Bacon: "I am 48. In 1961, I was a salesman in Long Beach, California. The pumps were going up and down all along the beach. Night life was Vivian Laird's and

gave me a dirty look and said, 'Daddy, we can't hear.'

"I walked into the kitchen where my wife was cooking dinner and I said, 'There is something wrong. The only reason for our existence is for our progeny. We're not getting through.' We decided then to make a move.

"We planned for about six months to take a vacation and look for a different way of life. We bought a second-hand station wagon. We went down to Sears and Roebucks and bought the tent, the fishing tackle, the cookstove and the licenses.

"We drove four hundred miles and came to a place up in Northern California in Sonora County. We pitched our tent and, oh, we were so happy. We were right on the Trinity River. We cooked our dinner on the camp stove and went to bed. The next morning we got up to go fishing and I looked around. There were fifty tents on each side of me.

"Then we decided that what we needed was a place in the wilderness. We bought 160 acres of trees in the mountains above Azalea. We built a cabin there with our own hands and I lived there for two years until we ran out of money. Also a gap was developing in the children's education.

= we are not radicaly but super conservatives trying to recover that old simplicity we read about in myths and fairy tales = seeking childhood in forests of tangled history.

the Cooper Room. We had the Wilton Hotel, Pierrepont Landing, the Pike. The only interesting thing to me there was my family, my wife and children.

"I came home one evening tired after having lost a deal, a little sad about everything. There were my two little children watching television. I said, 'Hi! Kids!' They

"What did we accomplish? After doing what we did there—surviving on our own, building our own home, hunting for our food—we have no fear of meeting whatever comes along in life.

"Something happens when you go to the mountain. You begin to understand that you are the master of your own fate, that

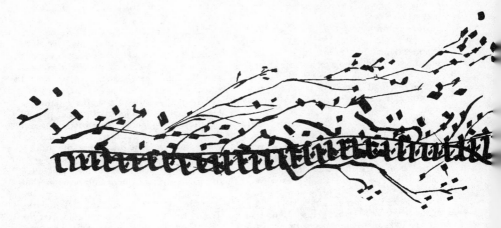

whether or not you survive is up to you. There is that first time you get lost hunting. You follow a deer in the snow and you get all turned and cold and tired and you know that you can't go on. And you cry and you pray and you promise to change your ways. And you get up and walk and somehow you find your way home."

I wonder sometimes if the police read Kafka. To become a refugee is to become afraid of the police. You must have the proper papers: a driver's license, automobile registration, credit cards. I used to have all those pieces of paper. I no longer do. I am winging it most of the time. I manufacture documents as I need them. That's what it is to be a writer. I am in the business of creating proof of identity. I lost the ones they gave me and now I must make my own.

Have you ever tried to cash a check without any identification other than a picture of yourself in a magazine? Have you ever tried to cash a check without any identification at all? I have become expert at little miracles like this. I have become something of a confidence man. It is a fragile talent.

It would be easier for me if I cut my hair more often, but the only barber I trust is in Los Angeles. I would rather face a highway patrolman with my hair as long as Charles Manson's than submit to the kind of prison chop you get in small town barber shops. Sometimes paranoia outweighs vanity. I have such a haircut now. This is the way it happened:

As you may guess from reading those notes from my journal, there was, for a while, a place that made some sense. Chrissie and I fought and separated. We longed for each other. We came together again. We fell in love again. For most of my life I had considered life a game that was trying to trick me into having a child. I surrendered to the trick. She conceived.

Toward the end of her pregnancy, we travelled to Oregon with friends to look for a house, then returned to California to the place that had made sense to have the baby. Although we mistrusted hospitals, it seemed wisest to have the birth take place in a conventional delivery room with a conventional obstetrician and conventional nurses.

Chrissie had been born in China in 1948. Her mother squatted on a wooden stool and screamed her out while midwives shouted instructions in a language she had never been able to learn. She developed dysentery and her milk dried up. She believes that Chrissie is still searching for her breast.

This is what we wanted to do right, to make a good baby. Chrissie wanted to nurse. The hospital gave the baby formula. Babies started on formula often prefer it to their own mother's milk. It is sweet as candy and easy to suck. When they brought my wife her baby, it refused to take the breast. They gave Chrissie a bottle of formula. She would not feed it to her little girl.

"You're starving that baby to death," a nurse told her, putting the formula bottle in Faera's mouth as Chrissie lay chained by

guilt and confusion. Home from the hospital, she regained her own will and went to live in the house of a friend who was a registered nurse and herself pregnant almost to full term. Faera screamed for six hours. Then, furious with the anger of hunger, she sucked at last at her mother's nipple.

The hospital was America, a place of expedient solutions, an assembly line of life and death, an immaculate institution which seemed to have forgotten somehow that there was more to taking care of people than plastic and glass and stainless steel and chemicals. The hospital was civilization at the end of the line, turning back in on itself, sterilizing all who passed through it.

We knew there was no real escape from any of this, but we fled to the mountains of Oregon in the hope of finding a more dilute strain of the disease. We had planned to fly, but at the last minute it became necessary for logistical reasons for me to drive.

Our car was a Subaru which had been lent to me by the manufacturer in the hope that I might write about it favorably. Passing through Red Bluff, California, we stopped by the side of the freeway attracting the attention of a highway patrolman who noticed the dealer plates. For the next forty-five minutes I tried to explain to this officer how it was reasonable for a man without a driver's license or any other conventional form of identification to be operating a vehicle in which no registration certificate could be found, carrying as passengers a baby and a girl who claimed to be its mother and my wife, but who did not know the baby's date of birth, my date of birth or the date of our wedding anniversary.

It was not a beautiful moment. He let us go, but the fear followed me to Oregon. I got a haircut and applied for a driver's license. Now I was truly a refugee, for to be a refugee is to understand fully that you have no rights, that you must submit, that you are nothing at all as long as you depend totally upon others for your existence.

We have become friends with Ole Bacon and his wife Evelyn. If we want it, we can have their cabin. They're finished with it now. They've built a conventional house right on the Rogue River, on Highway 62, right next to a store.

"I don't know whether you are a religious man or not, but if you're not, when you live up there the way we did, something will happen to you," Ole Bacon said.

"I was told that about my place," one of his guests interjected, "that I'd find something there. 'What am I going to find?' I asked. 'Well, I can't tell you, but when you find it you'll know.'"

We aren't going to take Ole Bacon's cabin. There is something about the view that does not please us. It's not important enough to explain. We are moving on, looking for our own special vision. We can't tell you what that is exactly, but we know that when we find it, we'll know.

August 19, 1971

A dream = wandering through the administrative
offices of the George Washington Bridge, on the
Ft. Lee side of the river. The guards have shot
some kids trying to cross. "Is there going to
be a trial? Are they going to be punished?"
Worrying about my car, my book. The
book is brought to me. Knife holes have been
dug in the thick leather bindings. Crying
and weeping. A conference table... getting
mixed up here ... first there was a store room,
my favorite old china teapot, bowl, cup —
blue, coarse, chunky, heartbreakingly,

beautiful = are shown to me by a plain,
round, fairhaired (curly) woman. "My (me)
mother's." "mine too" (her) I cannot have them.
The conference room... mixed up again...
looking out a window at a herd of deer
"When I was in Oregon the deer came
into the yard and ate out of your

hand." The conference room. Men in business suits. One shows the book. Purple transparent glazes picturing faces. Much more advanced technique than mine. Pages are wet—soaked, as if by 'drowning.' A joint is passed. Take a hit, try to pass it. "Who are you men in business suits?" The one who showed the book says, "People who committed suicide ~~like~~ like you, you 500 years ago."

The Replacement

Meeting Campo was a total coincidence. If the airport had not been so heavily damaged, they would have missed each other. Ron would have arrived through one of the domestic terminals while Campo was leaving from the international building. Now there was only one terminal, a great prefabricated sheet metal hangar the engineers had put up as soon as the field was secure.

Ron Wolf had seen the videos of the destruction of the airport, but he was not ready for the reality. The blue bus took the passengers from the runway to the terminal along a pitted road that curled through sandbag revetments. A black attack bomber was snuggled in each revetment like a table in an upholstered booth. The terminal area was a giant trash dump filled with scorched rubble. Not one building had survived. Prisoners of war were working on the ruins, their uniforms sloppy and dirty. They were guarded by soldiers wearing freshly laundered combat denims. The men did not look up as the bus went by.

The driver stopped at the guard box in front of the passenger hangar. A sergeant armed with a .45-caliber submachine gun of foreign manufacture stepped aboard and examined the men and women in the bus with a long, jagged look, his eyes methodically scanning each face. He signalled thumbs-up and a captain came in. He wore a small-caliber machine pistol on a Sam Brown belt and carried an aluminum clipboard.

The two soldiers went down the aisle checking orders. Although most of the passengers were civilians, they were all wearing crisp new combat denims and shiny boots, and travelling under military orders. The entire nation was still nominally administered by the military government, but in most sections the work was done by civilians, and it was possible to believe that everything was normal, the way it had been before the fighting. At central headquarters in the loyal heartland of the continent, there were no uniforms. You could only tell the officers by the unfashionable cut of their suits, the enlisted men by their command-issue sneakers. Here on the treacherous coast, there was no pretense. The soldiers were out front.

Wolf handed over the xerostat packet of orders. The officer read them carefully:

*WOLF, RON. ID NO. 062-28-1667. NATIVE-BORN, STABLE. VIDEOCOM

TECHSERVER, G-14. RELEASED CEN-
TRAL HQS [REHAB-SEC] TO NON-
COMBAT STATUS COSTAL URBAN
ARMY GRP FOR SPEC DUTY CIVIL
INFO ED SERV. TRANS PRIORITY:
URGENT.

"Welcome to Coastal Urban, Mr. Wolf,"
the officer said respectfully. "I recognized
your face right away. We've missed you on
the tube. Will you be broadcasting here?
How do you like your new throat?"

"I'm replacing John Campo," Wolf
answered. "And the new throat is fine,
but it's still a little rough talking."

"I know exactly how you feel," the captain said. "Takes a while to get used to a
prosthetic. I'm still breaking mine in.
Amazing devices, aren't they? Look at
this." He peeled open the back of his wrist,
revealing a gleaming metal and novoplasm
structure. He twitched and flexed the unit,
then pressed the skin-like covering back
into place. It had the flexibility of silicone
putty, blending back into itself without a
wrinkle or a line.

"Amazing," Wolf said.

"Yes, it certainly is. Your voice sounds
really good, perfect, just the way it always
did. We all used to follow your coverage.
I was watching when you took that throat
wound. A magnificient performance.
Superb newscasting. I'm glad we're going
to be seeing you on the tube again." Writing slowly with the artificial hand, the
captain entered Wolf's ID number in his
notebook, detached one copy of the orders,
clipped it to his board, and returned the
rest.

In the terminal, Wolf walked briskly to
the ground transportation desk, acknow-
ledging the smiles of recognition with a
nod or a casual salute. He could have gone
to the head of the line, but he waited his
turn, refusing to exercise the special privi-
leges that went with his status. He considered himself an enemy of the brass, an
advocate of equality, a champion of the
enlisted men and women.

The place was filled with young people
in denim uniforms. They were working,
waiting, walking, sleeping on the floor.
Sweethearts snuggled in each others' arms.
One group sat in a circle around two boys
playing guitars and singing. Over the loud
buzz, he heard someone calling his name.
Without turning, he knew who it was.
There was only one voice that big in the
world. Wolf blushed with pleasure and
turned to greet John Campo, who was
striding toward him through the crowd,
smiling at fans, stopping to give autographs.

"Talk to me, Ron, baby," he boomed.
"Let's hear those golden tones, the rotund
undulants of the boy with the stainless
steel throat."

"And now, directly from the red light
district of Fire Zone Bubbles," Wolf orated
in the soothing vibrato he had made famous
on the tube, "here is Combat Correspon-
dent John Campo."

"Beautiful! That's *spectacular*. They
really gave it back to you, didn't they?"

"A little weak, Johnny, but it looks as if
it's going to be all right."

"Any pain?"

"Not much anymore."

"Let me look down your throat," Campo
demanded. "I've got to see it. You're a
walking miracle of modern science."

"There's nothing to look at. It's all inter-
nal." Wolf was now at the head of the line.
He handed his packet of orders to the girl.
She was pretty, with a freckled face, brown
hair, gray eyes. Her denims were pressed
and starched. She was about seven months
pregnant. Her mouth moved stiffly when
she spoke.

"Your...car...and...driver...are...
at...the...non...com...bat...ant...
gate," she said, forcing the words through
clumsy lips. "Wel...come...to...Coas
...tal...Ur...ban...Mis...ter...Wol
...f," the girl continued painfully. An
almost natural smile twitched on and off.

"Hold that car for him sweetheart,"
Campo told the girl. "Me and my friend
have to go chatterbox." Wolf allowed himself to be led away. "Unbelievable luck
catching you like this," Campo said. "My
flight has been delayed over and over again.
I was so pissed off I thought I was going to
have a major shit-fit in public. You know
how I hate to wait, Ron. And then there
you were."

They walked through a low corridor
with 25-watt bulbs strung down the center
of an arched steel roof. Campo knocked at
an unmarked door. A crack opened and
an eye looked out, visibly widening as it
recognized the newsmen. Inside, there was
a dimly-lighted large room furnished with
old-fashioned leather chairs and couches.
A couple was sleeping on one couch,

Deja Vu — not merely the feeling of having been here before, but also of living simultaneous existences, faint ghost images of other persons in this body, slightly out of phase memories like echoes of what others have seen through my eyes, perceiving in the stream of consciousness cross-currents like the voices you often hear on the telephone when circuits cross.

stockinged feet sticking out from under a command-issue blanket. Other young people were lounging on the floors and chairs, passing a brass pipe.

"Nepalese hash," one of them said, offering the pipe to Campo. He drew deeply, coughed, shook his head and extended the pipe to Wolf, who motioned it away. "Killer hash, boy," Campo said. "You can't get this back in the Central."

"The stainless steel throat doesn't tolerate smoke," Wolf explained.

"Now, that is a tragedy," Campo said. "What do you use to turn yourself on? Pills?"

"Command-issue, as a matter of fact," Wolf answered. "The poppers are better though." He pulled a small medicine box out of his pocket, and took out a fabric-covered glass ampulet. He broke it between his fingers under his nose and sniffed. "Here, try one." He handed Campo a popper.

"The old ways are the best ways," Campo said, "but anything for a new thrill. Does it do the job?" He broke the thin glass and inhaled the vapor. For a moment, he was still. Then he smiled broadly. "Un-be-liev-a-ble!" he breathed. "Command-issue synthetic killer weed poppers! The Revolution is a success at last."

Wolf did not reply. Campo did not miss the significance of the silence. "Still doubting, pal?" he asked. "You're an Old Believer, aren't you? Ron Wolf, the old-fashioned revolutionist, has been backing the loser so long he doesn't know how to

feel when it wins. You'd better get used to it, baby. We've won."

"Have we?" Ron asked.

"What are you talking about, man? It's all mopping up from now on. The good guys won."

"The good guys?" Ron said quietly. They were sitting off in their own corner, their faces barely visible in the pale light of the tube. "We don't have to talk about good guys and bad guys, do we, John? I've been living in the Central. You've been up here on the line. It's two different revolutions. But let's not talk politics to each other. It makes the stainless steel throat sore. Tell me where you're going."

"I'm going into the front, all the way, the way you did. This isn't the line here. You know that. They don't make you up for the camera up on the line. The Central is already here, Ron."

"Then you know what I'm talkin' about." Ron was tired and loaded; his speech beginning to slur slightly.

"I know what you're talking about," Campo said softly. "But what is there to do about it? You get out. You get into the heat. I'm so dragged and bored, man, I'm ready for anything. All I am here is an announcer. They put it in my hand and I read it. I've been doing that for eighteen months. Five days a week. I do the same things over and over. I say the same words at the same time every morning. I can tell exactly what time it is by the layer of make-up they're putting on me."

"So you're going to be a hero," Wolf

said, a sarcastic edge in his fading voice.

"Why not? You were a hero, weren't you? I mean, you were great, you know. You were really great. I mean that, Ron. I'm not putting you on. I always watched you. We all did. It was thrilling, man. The soldiers couldn't say it. But you could. You were *real*." Iridescent bubble patterns were floating across the face of the tube, a soft haze of abstract music flowing with them.

"Right. And now I've got a real stainless steel throat," Wolf said. "That was really thrilling."

"Please, Ron, baby, pal, don't be bitter with me, man. I'm not trying to tell you that you didn't get hurt. Everyone who watched the tube that day knows how you got hurt. I really believe that everything changed for a whole bunch of people after that. Your voice. When it hit. The pain. You really told them how it hurt. It was so weird. That incredibly beautiful voice. The blood churning out of your mouth. And you just stayed there on camera telling them what it was like."

"Some day I'll tell you what the operations were like," Wolf whispered. "Do you think you want to hear about that? No, you don't want to hear about that, Johnny. I think about those things a lot now, what I can tell and what I can't. Let me tell you something." He leaned forward and put his mouth against his friend's ear. "The . . . revolution . . . is . . . just . . . another . . . *government*."

Campo moved away from him, in his eyes a little bit of fear, a little bit of disgust. "You've been back in the Central too long, pal, " he said. "They make you think like that. That's why I'm getting out of here. It's closing in again. Hey, look at that." There was a digital clock and a flight progress display on the tube. "There's my number. Time to fly."

The two men walked back to the passenger hangar slowly. At the flight gate, they shook hands, embraced, kissed.

"I'll be watching you, Johnny," Wolf said. "Tell it like it is."

"You know me, Ron," Campo answered and was gone into the blue bus.

On the way into the city, Wolf leaned back into the plush cushions in the dark back seat of the command limousine, turning his face away from the rubble of buildings and homes, the rusted barbed wire, the abandoned, burnt-out tanks and trucks.

The sky was a darkening purple when they got to the first cluster of new apartment buildings. In many of the windows he could see the glow of tubes, almost make out the forms of the viewers sitting before them, lips glistening and expectant.

It was all beginning again. They were replacing the ruins the way they had replaced his throat. They could replace his body, his brain. They could make a total prosthetic and it would work. There was no way out. It was going to go on forever. He had wanted to tell Campo that, but what was the point? There wasn't anything that the Central couldn't remake or replace. They had abolished death. But they couldn't abolish pain.

The car was off the highway now, heading through clean streets, heading, ultimately, toward the studio and the camera and the front, heading for the morning when he would know the time by the layer of make-up that was going on his face, heading toward the bullets and the churning blood.

Acknowledgments

The handwriting and drawings were selected by the art director from some 700 pages in three journals accumulated since early 1969.

I find the material from the journals to be the most successful and satisfying elements of this book. They appear here exactly as they were created without the intervention of the rewriter, the copy editor or the retoucher.

Jules Siegel
Guadalajara, Jalisco,
Mexico
February 18, 1972

Much of the writing in this book originally appeared in considerably different form in various magazines. Wherever possible, I have restored the text. In some cases, either through my own negligence or that of the magazines' filing departments, the manuscripts have been lost, as noted.

"Family Secrets" was completed in December, 1969, and published in New American Review No. 10.

"Deja Vu" was written in September, 1963, and published in Esquire, November, 1970, and in *The Best American Short Stories of 1970.*

"Another Dawn" was written in September, 1963, and originally titled "My Mother Bore Me." Heavily edited, it was published by Cavalier, September, 1964. The manuscript is lost and I have not attempted to reconstruct it.

"The Big Beat" was published by Cavalier, April, 1965. The original is missing.

"Bob Dylan" was written in April, 1966, and published under the title "What Have We Here?" in the Saturday Evening Post, July 30, 1966. It was rewritten twice and drastically edited. The manuscripts are gone.

"The Subcontractor" was written during the summer of 1966 and rewritten in 1970.

"Goodbye Surfing, Hello God!" was written as an assignment for the Saturday Evening Post, which rejected it, was then purchased by New York, which folded for a time, and was finally published in the first issue of Cheetah, October, 1967.

"The Man Who Believed in Christmas Trees" was written during the spring of 1968 and appeared in New American Review No. 5.

"Conversations With Eminent Americans" was taped at various times during 1968 and 1969. The tape with the Smothers Brothers was for a Playboy interview that was purchased but never published. The conversations with Paul Gorman and Jack Newfield, John Sinclair (founder of the White Panther party and manager of the MC5 rock band) and Abbie Hoffman were undertaken as part of the research for a Playboy article called "Revolution" which appeared in April, 1969.

"The Black Panthers" was written for the New York Times Sunday Magazine, which rejected it, in July, 1969.

"Anger" was written early in 1970.

"West of Eden" was written for Playboy at the end of 1968 and appeared November, 1970.

"The Evergreen Home" is a fragment of a novel in progress commissioned by New American Library. It was written during the winter of 1970.

"Midnight in Babylon" was written in January, 1971, for Rolling Stone. It was published in issue No. 76.

"The Refugees" was written for West, the magazine of the Los Angeles Times, in August, 1971, and rejected.

"The Replacement" was written early in 1970.

—J.S.

Alan Rinzler is giving me a hard time.

Designed by Sandra Payne.
Production: Jon Goodchild, Tom
Hardy, Vickie Jackson, Carol Raskin,
Brec Brown